AF394670

By the same author

The Corinthian War, 395–387 BC
Pen & Sword Military

Themistocles: The Powerbroker of Athens
Pen & Sword Military

The Battle of Leuctra
371 BC

The Battle of Leuctra
371 BC

The Collapse of Sparta's Empire and the Rise of the Theban Hegemony

Jeffrey A. Smith

Pen & Sword
MILITARY

First published in Great Britain in 2026 by
Pen & Sword Military
An imprint of Pen & Sword Books Limited
Yorkshire – Philadelphia

Copyright © Jeffrey A. Smith 2026

ISBN 978 1 03611 818 1

Typeset by Mac Style
Printed in the UK by CPI Group (UK) Ltd, Croydon, CR0 4YY.

The Publisher's authorised representative in the EU for product
safety is Authorised Rep Compliance Ltd., Ground Floor,
71 Lower Baggot Street, Dublin D02 P593, Ireland.
www.arccompliance.com

For a complete list of Pen & Sword titles please contact:

PEN & SWORD BOOKS LIMITED
47 Church Street, Barnsley, South Yorkshire, S70 2AS, England
E-mail: enquiries@pen-and-sword.co.uk
Website: www.pen-and-sword.co.uk
or
PEN AND SWORD BOOKS
1950 Lawrence Road, Havertown, PA 19083, USA
E-mail: uspen-and-sword@casematepublishers.com
Website: www.penandswordbooks.com

To my family.
I love you.

*   *   *

With gratitude to Phil Sidnell and the team at Pen & Sword.
Many thanks also to Gabriel Moss for his cartography.

Contents

Chronology

c. 550   The formation of the Boeotian Confederacy

404   End of the Peloponnesian War and Sparta's crushing defeat of Athens

399   Agesilaus ascends to the Spartan throne

396   Agesilaus' invasion of Asia Minor and the incident at Aulis

395   Outbreak of the Corinthian War

387   The King's Peace and the end of the Corinthian War

385   Epaminondas saves Pelopidas at the Siege of Mantinea

382   The Spartans conquer and occupy Thebes under the command of Phoebidas

379   Thebes rebels under the leadership of Pelopidas and overthrows Sparta's occupation. The Boeotian War begins

378   Formation of the Sacred Band of Thebes. The Spartan commander Sphodrias leads an abortive attack on Athens, pushing Athens to join forces with Thebes. Athens founds the Second Athenian League

376   The Spartan fleet lose to the Athenians at the battle of Naxos

375   Pelopidas and the Thebans defeat a larger Spartan force at the battle of Tegyra

374   A peace conference in Sparta fails to conclude the war

373   The siege of Corcyra

371   The battle of Leuctra and the advent of the Theban Hegemony

370   Epaminondas and the Thebans invade the Peloponnese with the goal of conquering Sparta. Three subsequent invasions occur, lasting until the year 362

364   The death of Pelopidas

362   The battle of Mantinea and the death of Epaminondas

338   The battle of Chaeronea and the end of the Sacred Band of Thebes

335   Alexander the Great destroys Thebes

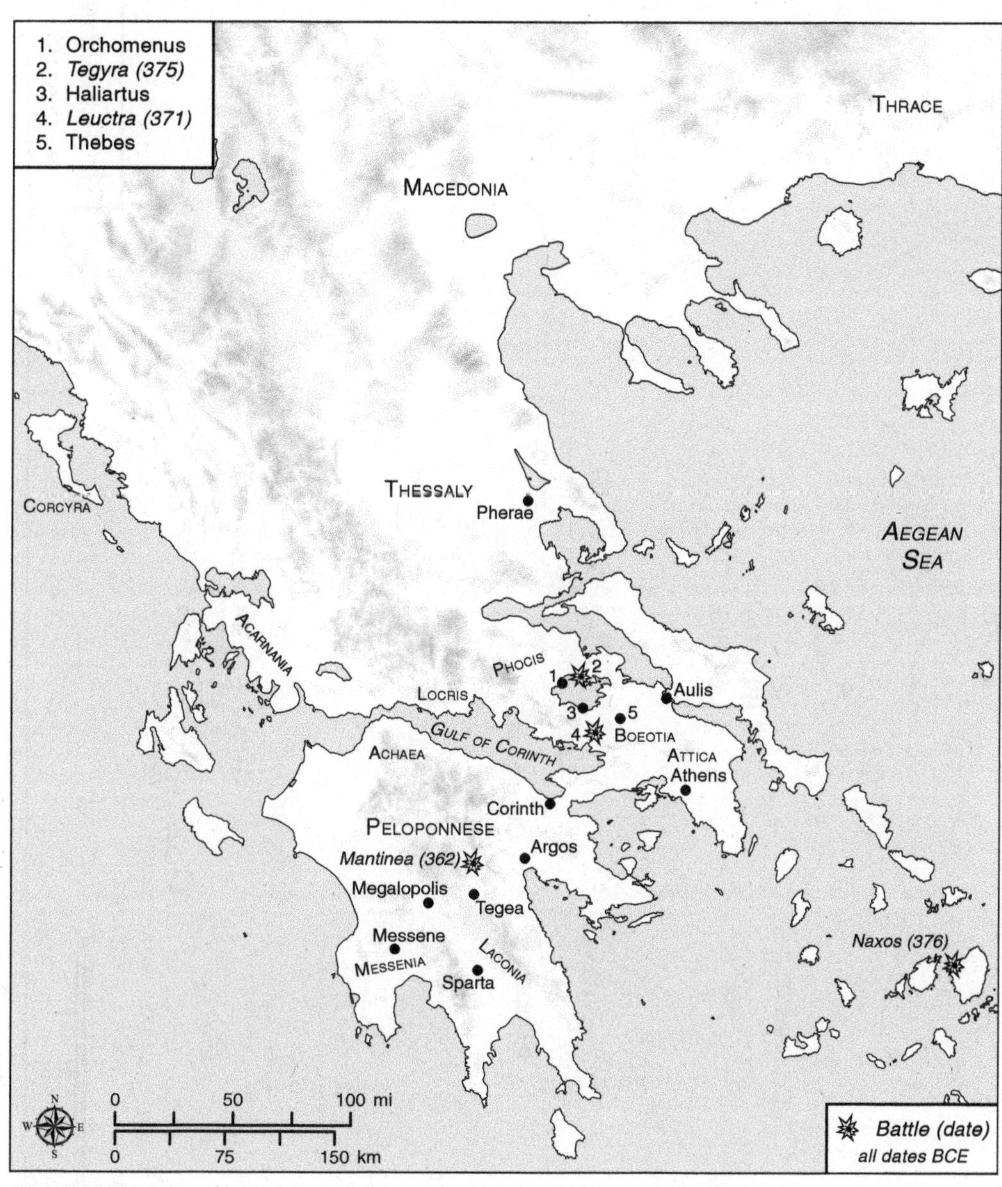

Greece in 371 BC.

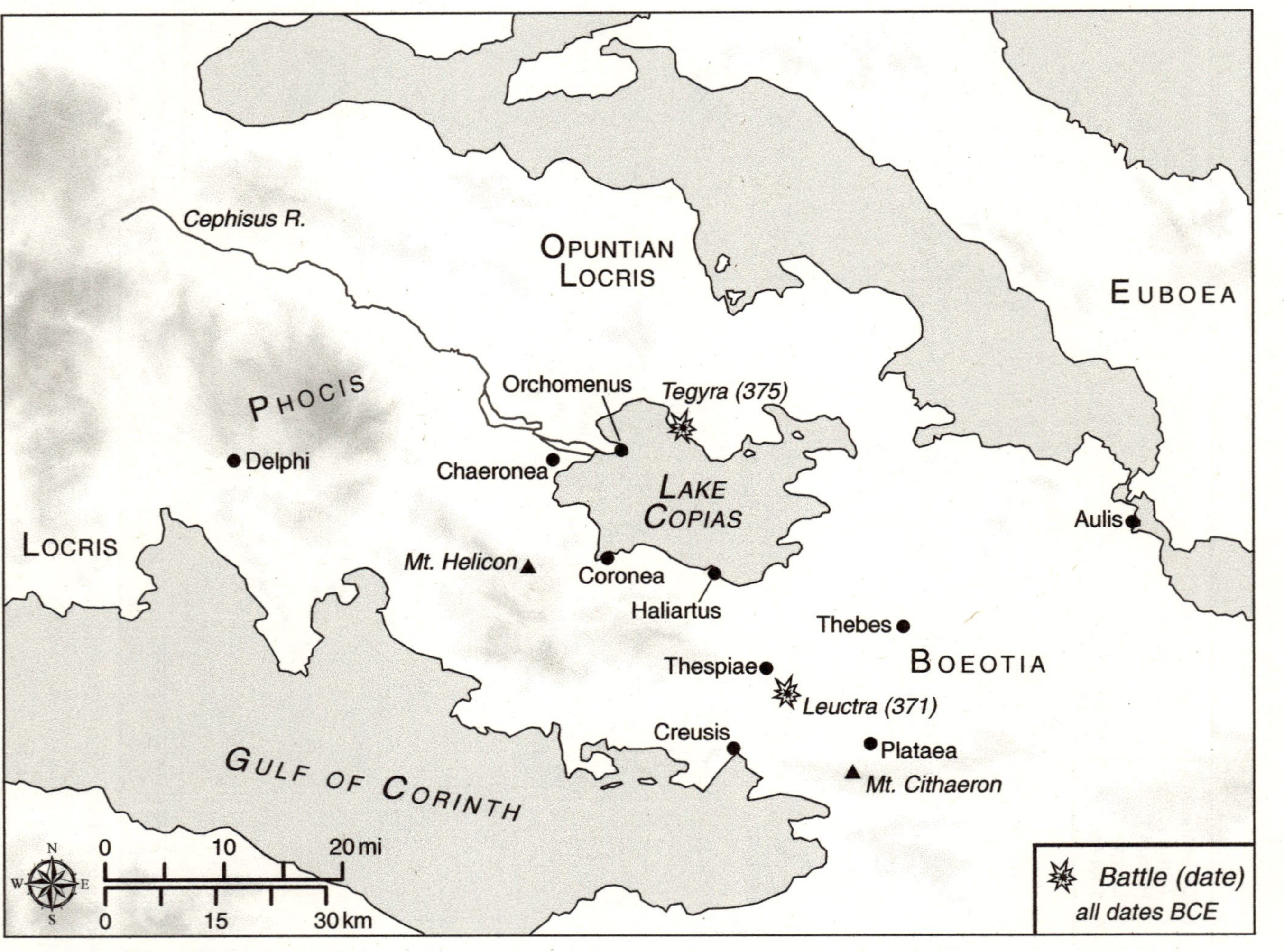

Central Greece in 371 BC.

List of Characters

Agesilaus II The greatest Spartan king, Agesilaus overcame a leg handicap to become a successful conqueror and brilliant commander. His disability kept him out of campaigning late in the Boeotian War, so he did not take part in the battle of Leuctra.

Agesipolis A king of Sparta in the Agiad line, he became king as a young boy during the Corinthian War. As monarch, he served alongside Agesilaus until his death during the First Olynthian War in 380.

Antalcidas A Spartan diplomat with deep ties to Persia. He brokered the King's Peace of 387 which concluded the Corinthian War and pledged autonomy for all the city-states in Greece.

Artaxerxes II The Persian King of Kings during the early fourth century BC.

Chabrias An Athenian general and politician, he helped establish the Second Athenian League and won the battle of Naxos during the Boeotian War.

Charon A Theban aristocrat and supporter of the Theban coup in 379.

Cleombrotus I An Agiad king of Sparta, he ascended to the throne after the untimely death of his brother Agesipolis. Known for his frequent avoidance of direct combat, he commanded the Spartan forces at the battle of Leuctra in 371, where he was killed by Pelopidas.

Conon A great Athenian naval commander and hero of the Corinthian War. His son Timotheus followed in his footsteps and led many Athenian fleets into battle for the Second Athenian League.

Diodorus Siculus A first-century AD Roman historian of Greek heritage, his name means 'Diodorus of Sicily'. He wrote a comprehensive history of the Greco-Roman world that compiled and quoted many sources now lost to us.

Epaminondas The greatest general of Thebes and victorious commander at the battle of Leuctra in 371. Epaminondas helped overthrow Spartan rule in Thebes and then built the Theban Hegemony. Renowned for his wisdom and virtue, Epaminondas led Thebes from 382 until his death in 362.

Gorgidas A Theban general and politician. He took part in the liberation of Thebes in 379 and was the founder and first commander of the Sacred Band of Thebes.

Iphicrates A brilliant, disciplined Athenian general who revitalized Greek infantry warfare with his innovations. He led Athenian forces during the Boeotian War and the Second Athenian League's expansion.

Ismenias The leader of the democratic (or federalist) faction in Thebes' *stasis*. He was killed when the Spartans conquered the city in 382.

Jason of Pherae A Thessalian tyrant who unified Thessaly and threatened to build his own empire in the north of Greece. He arrived late to the battle of Leuctra and brokered a brief peace treaty.

Leontiades The leader of the pro-Spartan oligarchs in Thebes. He invited the Spartans to conquer the city in 382.

Lysander The visionary leader of Sparta who defeated Athens at the end of the Peloponnesian War. He wished to create a Spartan empire that modernized the state, and founded colonies and set up ambassadors across Greece. He died at the start of the Corinthian War, when the leadership of Sparta was ceded to Agesilaus.

Melon A Theban general and statesman who played an integral role in the Theban revolution of 379.

Pelopidas Great statesman and general of Thebes. Along with his colleague Epaminondas, he was directly responsible for liberating Thebes, toppling the Spartan empire, and creating the Theban Hegemony. He led the Sacred Band of Thebes and turned it into the best fighting force in Greece.

Phoebidas A Spartan general who conquered Thebes in 382, without the permission of the Spartan ephors or the government. Sparta happily kept hold of Thebes, but the unwarranted seizure of the city rattled Greece.

Plutarch A second-century AD Roman historian of Greek heritage. He wrote a famous set of biographies called *Parallel Lives* that chronicled the great figures of Greece and Rome. His lives of Pelopidas and Agesilaus are especially helpful for the battle of Leuctra, though sadly his account of Epaminondas is lost.

Sphodrias A Spartan commander who was manipulated by the Thebans into marching on Athens in an abortive attempt to conquer the city, without the permission of the Spartan ephors. The event so enraged the Athenians that they joined forces with Thebes in the Boeotian War.

Timotheus An Athenian statesman and general. The son of the great admiral Conon, Timotheus was instrumental in expanding the reach of the Second Athenian League.

Xenophon An Athenian historian and former student of Socrates who penned many books covering philosophy, biography, husbandry, and history. His *Hellenica* was a continuation of Thucydides' *History of the Peloponnesian War* and contains the most detailed account of the early fourth century in Greece. His close relationship with the Spartans influenced much of his work, but his writings are invaluable for the historical narrative of the era.

Introduction

In 371, on the eve of the battle that decided the future of Greece, a ghost appeared to the Theban general Pelopidas. Unlike Hamlet's father, this spectre came bearing good news – at least for Thebes. The ghost's name was Scedasus and he had been a poor farmer in the plains, near a Theban village named Leuctra in central Greece. Before his death, two Spartan travellers had asked to stay the night at his home, on their journey to the religious centre of Delphi, and he had offered them food, wine and lodging. As any noble Greek would, he prized the virtue of *xenia* – hospitality and guest-friendship.

But during the meal Scedasus was dismayed by the men's open lust for his two young daughters and he sent them on their way as soon as he could. Several days later, coming back from making religious sacrifices at the Oracle of Delphi, the two Spartans returned to Scedasus' farm. Tragically, they raped and murdered Scedasus' daughters.[1] Hellbent on justice, Scedasus determined to travel to Sparta, some 250 kilometres away, to demand retribution from the Spartan *ephors* (elected oligarchs). On the way, he commiserated with a man from Attica whose son had been kidnapped and murdered by a corrupt Spartan governor. Many Greeks had similar stories of Spartans' abuse and mistreatment of them.

Scedasus, more determined than ever, made his way to Sparta – but found he was pleading his case to deaf ears. Desperately, he visited every legislative power in Sparta: the kings, the ephors, the councils, and finally the citizens. All rejected him. Heartbroken, Scedasus returned home to Leuctra and built a tomb for his beloved daughters. Then, in despair, he appealed to the Furies, the goddesses of vengeance, to issue divine justice where earthly justice had so clearly failed.

The response did not come immediately. But on the fields of Leuctra, the day after the Theban general saw the ghost of Scedasus in 371, justice came in spades for Sparta. Their mighty empire was broken by the Thebans. The Spartan military machine – long the gold standard of military power in Greece and once viewed as unbeatable – came to a grinding, disastrous halt. Sparta never again returned to imperial power.

Leuctra, 371

The evening of 5 July 371 BC, however, had not started well for the Theban general Pelopidas. He had been wracked with anxiety over the bad omens portending a potential loss for his nascent rebellion against Spartan rule, and sleep was fleeting. He feared the Spartan war machine would steamroll over his upstart Thebans the next day and that all Greece would be under the yoke of the fearsome burgundy lambda painted on the Spartans' shields. This was, after all, what had happened to so many other Greek city-states that had tried to throw off the Spartan yoke. Athens, Argos, Corinth, Elis, and even the Achaemenid Persian empire had all learned this lesson the hard way. At any moment over the last few centuries Sparta's power might be waxing or waning, but its position at the apex of Greek politics seemed suffocatingly static.

Then the ghost of Scedasus appeared to Pelopidas bearing good tidings: the Spartans were returning to Leuctra to pay the price for the murder of Scedasus' daughters. Scedasus told Pelopidas of his tragic loss at the hands of the Spartans, but also of their looming retribution, saying he should 'be of good courage, for the Lacedaemonians were coming to Leuctra to pay the penalty to him [Scedasus] and his daughters.'[2] For lesser men than Pelopidas, this would have been cheerful news.

Pelopidas was not much for superstition and apparitions, however. The grizzled commander of the Sacred Band of Thebes, the elite strike force unit of the Theban army, needed cold, hard evidence. He had cut his teeth on tough times, as an exile from Thebes after the Spartans seized his hometown, and then from his home-in-ostracism in Athens he had designed and successfully executed a coup to take back Thebes from the Spartans. He had led the rebellion of Boeotians (the region of central Greece where Thebes was located) against Sparta's tyranny for nearly a decade and everything now hinged on whether or not he believed this ghostly prophecy – more evidence was required. This was especially true as he had recently learned he also needed to convince the federal council of Boeotia, the *boeotarchs*, because a plurality of their members were voting to withdraw from Leuctra before the battle could even begin.

And so, with a prayer and much anxiety, Pelopidas despatched his scouts to search out the tomb that Scedasus had supposedly built for his beloved daughters, who over the years had become known as the 'Leuctrides' or the 'maidens of Leuctra,' and to interrogate the locals about the ghost's claims. His scouts returned quickly with the best of news: it was all true. There was indeed a tomb to the Leuctrides and the citizens of Leuctra all attested to the story. And, shockingly, there was even a Spartan prophecy that backed it up.

Diodorus Siculus, a Sicilian-Greek historian writing of the time of Julius Caesar, even named a Spartan-born member of the Theban army who could describe the prophecy. The Spartan exile Leandrias described to Pelopidas 'an ancient saying amongst the Spartans, that they would lose the supremacy when they should be defeated at Leuctra at the hands of the Thebans.'[3] Fortune and fate were with the Thebans. Pelopidas and his fellow statesman-general of Thebes, the great commander Epaminondas, were able to convince the other boeotarchs, and the battle was won soon after.

For half a millennium, Sparta reigned over Greece as the dominant military power. None could match their prowess in a pitched land battle. Even the famous Athenian empire had built her military strength primarily on the seas and was no match for Spartan might on the battlefield. For Athens and the rest of Greece, diplomatic alliances and naval power had been the only redoubts against Spartan supremacy.

Then, on a hot summer day in 371, on the plains outside the small village of Leuctra, the indomitable Spartans were at long last vanquished. The Spartans' vice-like grip on Greece ended and Thebes supplanted Sparta as the major power in Greek military and diplomacy. Sparta's empire would never return: the imperial and military superpower faded, slowly but surely, into geopolitical irrelevance. Their helots, the slaves working the fields that fed the bellies of the hoplites, revolted. They had often done so before, but the weakened Sparta was no longer able to quell them. Sparta became just a regional power, then a defensive state with limited offensive capabilities in the Hellenistic era, a formality during the Roman Republic, then dwindled into a tourist destination during the Roman Empire until finally, by the medieval era, it was little more than an historically significant village. Thebes had been the cause of it all.

With the victory in 371, Thebes was no longer a second-tier city-state. Their historic role as an important but not elite player in Greek politics was a thing of the past, as they established a new order with the federal system of the Boeotian League reigning over Greece. The victory at Leuctra ushered in a new era, known as the Theban Hegemony.

Sparta's Painful Empire

Sparta's 500-year dominance over Greece might have evaporated in the summer heat, but it did not result in a sudden disappearance. By the dawn of the fourth century BC, the Spartan 'empire' – a misnomer in many ways – had reigned over Greece for three decades through the Peloponnesian League. The league was a loose coalition dominated by Spartan interests. City-states in the Peloponnese and beyond, such as Tegea, Elis, Corinth, and even Megara in Attica formed its core. Sparta held a council of representatives from each city, debating each issue and dutifully voting afterwards. Sparta even abstained from its own bureaucratic vote, as the Spartan citizens voted on its behalf. Then, after respectfully hearing the input of the council and each member of the league, Sparta's leaders did whatever they wanted.

The Peloponnesian League's origins lay in self-preservation. Sparta had stalled in its subjugation of the southern tip of the Peloponnese in Laconia and Messenia. Their aim was to add more territory to insulate themselves from another revolt by their helot slaves. At the end of the day, Sparta was a deeply agrarian *polis* (or city-state) that depended on the wheat harvest from their vast farmlands. That harvest depended on farmers, but Spartan citizens had long since evolved past mere farmwork, delegating this task to their helots. Spartan citizens were groomed for war and it was that martial power that kept the helots in line. Helots supplied food for the Spartan army, which became the first year-round standing army in Greece, while other Greek states had to schedule their military endeavours around the planting and harvest seasons. This simple yet brutal arrangement fuelled the Spartan military machine.

In the sixth century BC, during their first major expansion past their Laconian homeland, however, Sparta failed to defeat Tegea. A military power in its own right, Tegea was trapped between Spartan expansion in the south and the expansion of Argos in the north. Argos was a historical oppressor of the other Peloponnesian city-states so, hoping to find the lesser of two evils in the ascendant Sparta, Tegea, Corinth and others opted to form the military alliance dubbed the Peloponnesian League. Argos did not have the honour of being admitted to the League and would eventually become the only Peloponnesian *polis* never to do so.

In its operations, the Peloponnesian League was ostensibly an equal confederation of city-states and Sparta held no special power. But if this was ever truly the case on paper, its perception was quickly extinguished. With her highly trained hoplites and ability to raise an army at any time, Sparta held the largest stick and wielded it liberally. Their bullying leadership over the League, and eventually the rest of Greece, is described under the English terms of hegemony, supremacy, or ascendancy. The Greek word, however, is *symmachy*. A symmachy literally meant 'fighting together', referring to the melding of militaries between allies. Thucydides originally describes a symmachy as 'a defensive, not an offensive alliance'[4] in reference to an older alliance, though modern historians tend to describe it as a full offensive and defensive alliance against a common enemy. Even in contemporary Greek politics, the symmachy signifies a temporary coalition of rival political parties coming together to pass legislation or push back against a party seen as inimical to all.

Over the past century, the Peloponnesian League's symmachy had been Greece's shield against Athenian oppression. Athens' great naval empire, a symmachy of its own through the Delian League, was every bit as ruthless as it was wealthy – and it was exceedingly wealthy. After staving off the Persian invasions of 490 and 480, Athens and her newly minted navy became the new imperial oppressor. With an exponentially increasing number of ships and triremes compared to even the second-ranking Greek city-states, Athens instituted taxes and tributes that crippled any *polis* that didn't fall in line.

Despite their brutal dominance over the Peloponnesian League, Sparta quickly became the populist champion willing to stand up to Athenian tyranny. While traces of the Spartan-Athenian conflict were present even during the Persian Wars, a full-blown Greek civil war broke out within a few decades. The resulting Peloponnesian War razed Greece as all *poleis* took sides either with Athens' Delian League or Sparta's Peloponnesian League. As Greece burned, the twin titans of Athens and Sparta delivered knockout blows to each other. Athens, diminished by plague and financial ruin as her naval influence waned, was at last defeated by the unexpected emergence of a Spartan navy at Aegospotami in 404. That navy was funded by Persia, of all places, who had regained her interest in seizing Greece for the King of Kings.

By the end of the Peloponnesian War, the Athenians were so unpopular across Greece that the Peloponnesian League deliberated destroying Athens permanently. Xenophon, the philosopher-warrior of Athenian citizenship and Spartan loyalty, recounted how Thebes and Corinth – both staunch supporters of Sparta – advocated for the annihilation of Athens and her citizens. Xenophon notes that this was the sentiment in most of Greece. The Spartans, however, responded that they 'would never reduce to slavery a city which was itself an integral portion of Hellas, and had performed a great and noble service to Hellas in the most perilous of emergencies.'[5] While this was a great quote, it played poorly for the Spartans in the long run as Athenian power – despite some stipulations like the destruction of city fortifications and the surrendering of her already-destroyed fleet – would soon rebound.

Sparta was celebrated by most of the Greeks for bringing liberty and freedom, but instead of playing the role of liberator opted for taking Athens' place as oppressor. With the same fervour that they had rescued Greece, Sparta systemically took over the tools of Athenian imperial power. First, the Spartans accepted the fealty of Athens at the head of a new symmachy. Xenophon notes that Athens formally acknowledged 'the headship of Sparta in peace and war, leaving to her the choice of friends and foes, and following her lead by land and sea.'[6] While dismayed at the end of Athenian power, Thebes and Corinth accepted the terms. They perhaps assumed that with Sparta there would be a reasonably fair, if heavy handed, superpower in Greece and that Sparta would govern in a manner similar to the way the Peloponnesian League had operated.

But Sparta's new leadership in Greece was less like their management of the Peloponnesian League and more akin to how they treated their helots.

As more and more Greeks experienced what poor Scedasus, the father of the Leuctride maidens, had endured, popular opinion turned against Sparta.

The breadth of their cruelty was almost impressive: they massacred allies, replaced the leaders of city-states across Greece with puppets, dismantled democracy and anything close to Athenian-style administration, raised taxes and levies, demanded troops to invade distant Persia, and allowed their soldiery to misbehave with impunity. Disgusted by such behaviour, most of the Greek states decided to put aside their own differences and join forces in a new league aimed at toppling Sparta. Thebes and Corinth, who just nine years earlier had pushed for the destruction of Athens, now allied with Athens against Sparta. And it was not just their short-term memory that seems to have been deficient. The new anti-Spartan alliance also joined with Persia, who had tried to destroy Greece a century earlier. In 395 BC the Corinthian War began, refracturing Greece less than a decade after the civil war was supposed to have ended.

Even with the entirety of the eastern Mediterranean allied against them, Sparta prevailed. While they lost standing and the firmness of their grip, Sparta remained the dominant military and political force in Greece. Any straw poll, however, would have shown their deep unpopularity. Their empire had been hollowed out by population decline, a lack of hoplite reinforcements, and a shallow bench of diplomats. Despite these dim prospects, Sparta was yet more determined than ever to refocus her efforts on an obeisant Greece, no matter the cost.

Thebes in the Early Fourth Century

Where were our protagonists, Thebes, during all the misadventures of fifth-century Greece? They were keeping themselves busy with regional politics in central Greece, especially in their budding rivalry with Athens. Thebes had allied first with Persia in the great Persian Wars, which proved a catastrophic strategic error. After the Athenians and Spartans pulled off an astonishing victory against far-superior Persian forces, Thebes became a pariah to the rest of the independent Greek city-states. In the ensuing Peloponnesian War, Thebes was demoted to a secondary role, while the rest of Greece fought fiercely for their chosen patron in Athens or Sparta. When Athens' mighty naval empire was replaced with the iron-fisted hegemony of Sparta following the Peloponnesian War, Thebes slowly re-entered the diplomatic scene and joined the alliance of Athens, Argos, and Persia in revolting against Spartan rule. During this war, the Corinthian War, Sparta was weakened but victorious, and Thebes' fate was sealed as a result. Though it had shown real confidence in resisting Spartan rule, Thebes ended the Corinthian War in a far worse position militarily and diplomatically.

Thebes' experience in the Peloponnesian and Corinthian Wars ultimately was one of frustratingly unfulfilled promise and potential. Thebes saw herself as the titan of central Greece and the head of Greece's most influential alliances in the Boeotian Confederacy. Yet while Athens and Sparta had managed to conquer Greece with their leagues, Thebes had barely managed to hold central Greece. The most painful element was Sparta's occupation of Thebes. At the conclusion of the Corinthian War, Thebes had managed to provoke Sparta in a quite personal fashion. The Spartan king Agesilaus, a very powerful leader who had nearly conquered Persia and was renowned as the most capable general in Greece, held a special hatred for Thebes. Thebes had offended Agesilaus in his attempts to reincarnate the Homeric king Agamemnon, spoiling his ritual sacrifices at Aulis before the invasion of Persia in the 490s.

Agesilaus made sure to squeeze every drop of liberty out of Thebes in his vengeance. First, Thebes was ejected from the Boeotian Confederacy and the league itself was dismantled. Sparta even refused to acknowledge Thebes' existence in formal treaties, not mentioning her by name but referring instead simply to the collective 'Boeotia' in the King's Peace of 387 that ended the Corinthian War. Lastly, and most embarrassingly, Sparta occupied Thebes and her sister *poleis*. A Spartan garrison was constructed in the Theban acropolis and, for the first time in living memory, Thebes was not a free city. She had managed to avoid occupation by previous oppressors, Thessaly, Persia, and Athens but now Sparta – her longtime ally – allowed Thebes no liberty. The deep hatred that Agesilaus held for Thebes became a reciprocal feeling. An entire generation of Thebans grew up despising their Spartan oppressors and yearning for a free and independent Thebes restored to former glory.

Unfortunately for Sparta, counted among this new generation were two men skilled equally in statecraft, military command, and willpower. They were

Pelopidas and Epaminondas, and they changed the course of Greek history. Though they came from different social classes and political parties, their shared passion for Theban liberty – and their hatred of all things Spartan – gave them a common goal and they quickly became the closest of friends. Pelopidas and Epaminondas would soon transform not only their hometown of Thebes but the entirety of Greece and the Mediterranean world. Their friendship became a legendary fulfilment of Thebes' historical and cultural promise. Expelling Sparta from Thebes, shattering her vaunted army on the battlefield and dethroning her empire was only the beginning. Pelopidas and Epaminondas eventually established Thebes' ascendancy over all Greece. At long last, Thebes' political position matched her cultural standing. This city of greatness – heroes like Heracles, poets like Pindar, kings like Oedipus, generals like Pelopidas and Epaminondas, founding fathers like Cadmus, historians like Plutarch, painters like Nicomachus, musicians like Pronomus, and philosophers like Crates – at long last found her place at the very top of the proverbial pyramid.

With this new role as hegemon of Greece came all the trappings of power and the challenge to hold it: they would eventually be ousted by the new ascendant power of the Macedonians. But during the fourth century, no Greek city-state shone as bright as Thebes. For all the admiration of Sparta and Athens in modern society, the contributions of the Thebans are criminally undervalued. Thebes gave the modern world everything from federalism to Stoicism. Of course, this is not to diminish the legacy of Sparta. The famous Spartan war machine had saved Greece many times over and her story is every bit as essential to today's world as that of Thebes, Athens, Rome, and others. But this is the story of the rise of Thebes and the consequent fall of Sparta. The transition sent reverberations across Greece and the Western world. And it all climaxed one hot summer's day on the fields outside of Leuctra.

Chapter 1

Seven-Gated Thebes: The City of Cadmus

The Mythological Origins of Thebes

Perhaps more than any other city-state, Thebes was at the heart of Greek mythology and literature. While the majority of surviving texts come from the Athenian tradition, Thebes was every bit the epicentre of Greek history, culture, humanities, and arts that Athens would ultimately become. Thebes held the title first.

Thebes was central to a great majority of Greek myths and literature – she was home to the great demigod Heracles (often now known as Hercules), to the Sphinx and her riddles, and to the mythological hero Cadmus. In the Greek popular mind, Thebes was as steeped in their heritage and identity as any city could be. One only needs to look at the mythology of the city and its origins. Thebes is said to owe its existence to a unique type of seed – the teeth of Ares' dragon – which, when scattered into the earth, grew an equally unique crop, of human warriors. The warriors sprang from the ground fully-grown and became the first aristocratic families of Thebes. In fact, our soon-to-be heroes of the Theban-Spartan Wars would claim heritage from these families and dragon's teeth.

But before we return to Epaminondas and the rebellion against Spartan tyranny, we must understand the legendary origins of the Thebans. Theban heritage can be traced back to a prince named Cadmus, heir to the Phoenician naval empire which ruled the eastern Mediterranean long before the Athenian navy held sway. Phoenicia, in modern day Lebanon, was then the home of mighty seafarers who made a fortune trading and colonizing across the Mediterranean. Phoenician colonies were created all around the known world and the colony of Carthage eventually grew to challenge the Roman Republic in the Punic Wars. Two components constituted the backbone of the Phoenician empire: their shipbuilding and their sea snails. Phoenician shipbuilders were the first to create a seaworthy keel and the battering ram, allowing them to trade as far as the Atlantic Ocean and giving them the prowess to defend it. The sea snails, however, were the true secret to their power. Found only on the beaches near Tyre in the heartland of Phoenicia, vast quantities of snails were subjected to a methodical extraction of their innards, with which talented craftsmen could create a highly desirable purple dye for clothing. For hundreds of years in the ancient world, this was the only way a nobleman or artisan could obtain the colour purple. It became a symbol of royalty and prestige, and no royal in the Mediterranean world could afford to be seen without it. Until the fall of the Byzantine Empire in 1453 AD, Tyrian purple was synonymous with Mediterranean royalty.

Fittingly, the Phoenicians also gave the world letters. The Phoenician writing system is the foundation for nearly all Western alphabets, from Arabic to Cyrillic to Greek and, eventually, English. With these Phoenician-inherited letters, the Greeks composed their rich tapestry of mythology that has captivated the world, including the adventure of Cadmus.

In the origin myth of Thebes, Prince Cadmus was on a mission to rescue his sister, Europa, who had been kidnapped by a formidable foe – Zeus. The king of the gods, as he was wont to do, had wanted the unfortunate Europa as one of his brides and whisked her away from her home in what is today Lebanon, to Greece. (The continent of Europe takes its name from her story, though that hardly serves as a consolation prize.) Cadmus searched far and wide for his sister but failed to find her. He had been ordered to return with his sister or not return at all, but after searching all through Asia Minor, the Greek islands and mainland, he had to admit defeat. He did however find himself a bride, Harmonia, and many of the Greek gods and goddesses even attended his wedding.

Cadmus eventually made his way to the Oracle of Delphi, where he was commanded to follow a cow until it stopped wandering. By divine decree, wherever the animal settled down, Cadmus was to found the city that would become Thebes. The cow wandered east for a long time, into the fertile valley of Boeotia, due north of Megara and south of the Euboean Gulf and Mount Parnassus. The farmland there, near the now dried-up Lake Copais, was famous for its wheat, while the rolling hills and defensible hilltops made a strong location for the great new city. Soon, though, Cadmus found himself harassed by a dragon that guarded the local water source and was loyal to Ares, god of war. In an act that solidified his role as a mythic hero, Cadmus slew the dragon. Shortly afterwards, the goddess Athena – always eager to score a point against a divine rival like Ares – advised Cadmus to scatter the dragon's teeth on the ground like a farmer sowing seed. He did so and up sprouted an equal number of fully-formed soldiers, the Spartoi as they would become known. The warriors immediately began to behave as Greek soldiers might and to fight amongst themselves. Cadmus tossed a stone among them, adding to the chaos, until eventually only five of them remained. These five Spartoi became the first citizens of the new city of Thebes.

Now that he had manual labourers, Cadmus set about constructing the great building that would be named after him – the Cadmea. Set on a mighty oval-shaped plateau over 700 yards long and overlooking the surrounding plains of Boeotia, the Cadmea became the beacon of Theban civilization. It fulfilled a similar function to the acropolis in Athens: temple to the patron god, refuge from invasion, marketplace, civic centre, and – when necessary – the spot where citizens would make their last stand. The Cadmea was the essential physical feature of Thebes and without it Thebes could not have existed. It housed all the major public and governmental buildings. Today, we know that beyond its mythological history the Cadmea was originally a Mycenaean citadel, established in the fourteenth century BC, and was likely a vital regional capital for the Bronze Age trading empire before the days of the Trojan War. Existing remains show traces of treasure rooms eight feet tall, that would have housed precious stones imported from across the Mediterranean and even from Afghanistan and beyond. It would have been wealth enough to make Midas jealous.

When the Cadmea finally fell at the hands of Alexander the Great and the Macedonians in 335, the identity of Thebes perished with it. A few centuries later, the geographer Strabo was hesitant even to refer to those living in the remains of the city as Thebans; he instead dubbed people living near the Cadmea, but not upon it, as 'Hypothebans'.[1] But in its heyday Cadmea was the physical representation of Thebes' empire and the health of its city-state. It would play a major role in the toppling of Spartan rule over Thebes and then become the nexus of Greek politics – surpassing the Athenian and Spartan acropolises during the Theban Hegemony. With its impressive mythology and fearsome warrior class, Thebes quickly grew into a dominant force in ancient Greece.

Boeotian Geography

To properly understand the rise of Thebes, an understanding of the geography of Boeotia is essential. Boeotia was a region of arable farmland, with access to trade by land and by sea, and rolling plains that grew wheat in great quantities. In short, it was an ideal situation for a flourishing civilization that relied on agriculture and commerce. Indeed, Boeotia took its name from the Greek word for cattle, *boûs*, perhaps in a nod to the mythological cow that Cadmus followed to find the site for Thebes. It is a relatively narrow strip of land just 30 miles across, if one travels from the shores of the Gulf of Corinth in the south and the Gulf of Euboea in the north, but it is the principal region of central Greece, constituting about 1,240 square miles between the cosmopolitan land of Attica, home to Athens and the gateway to the Peloponnesian Peninsula and Sparta further south, and Phocis and Opuntian Locris to the west, with the Pindus Mountains still further west.

In the classical world, Boeotia also had Lake Copais. The largest lake in Greece until it was drained in the nineteenth century, Copais was famed for its fish and eels. Like most of Boeotia (and Greece at large) it had an origin myth and was said to have been filled when Heracles re-routed a river. The lake gave great strategic and military advantages, with traders and armies following the roads forced to hug its shores. Fortified cities such as Orchomenus, Haliartus, Coronea, and Chaeronea dotted the shoreline, excelling in trade and warfare alike as their geography funnelled both to them in equal measure.

In a showing of just how essential Boeotia was to the course of Greek history, all these cities near Lake Copais, along with Leuctra and Plataea in the southeast, hosted decisive battles that reshaped Greece. Through the Persian Wars, the Peloponnesian Wars, the Corinthian War, the Theban-Spartan Wars, and during the conquests of Alexander the Great, Boeotia was the site of battles with deep consequences. Such a concentration of major conflicts is foreign to the other regions of Greece during the classical period. The main reason is that the primary land route for travel and trade (or invasion) into southern Greece ran directly through Boeotia and Thebes. Traders and invaders travelled south along the coast through Thessaly and, after taking the narrow pass at Thermopylae curving into central Greece, took a road following the Cephisus river through Phocis. This route led into Boeotia through Chaeronea, following the road south of Lake Copais and then directly to Thebes. From Thebes, travellers went straight to Athens or turned south into the Peloponnese, crossing the Isthmus of Corinth.

Sea trade for Thebes and the Boeotians came through the ports on the southern Boeotian coast along the Gulf of Corinth. Cities like Creusis and Ciphae were access points both for the Mediterranean Sea trade network and, perhaps more essentially, the city-state of Corinth across the Gulf, second only to Athens in maritime commerce. To the north, Anthedon – Thebes' 'primary' harbour' – or Delphinium, the port town of the contentious city-state of Oropus, that was sometimes Boeotian and sometimes Athenian, offered access to the Aegean Sea and its lively trading system. Delphinium was across the bay from Chalcis, a major *polis* on the island of Euboea which offered trading connections similar to those offered by Corinth to the south of Thebes. Whether Boeotian wheat was exported to the south or the north, sea trade was accessible enough to sustain healthy, if not prosperous, commerce and trade.

In the west of Boeotia was the sacred Mount Helicon, home to the Muses of Greek mythology who inspired literature, poetry, art, theatre, and sculpture. Homer's *Iliad* and *Odyssey* and Hesiod's *Theogony*, the pre-eminent Greek creation story, began only with the divine invocation of the muses. Helicon was also the home of springs sacred to the muses, as well as being the site of the narcissism of Narcissus himself and the fabled adventures of the winged horse Pegasus. It was perhaps the next most important mountain in Greece after Mount Olympus, a point of great pride possibly mixed with disappointment for the perennially second-place Boeotians.

Standing on the cliffs of Mount Helicon and facing east, one could see the cereal fields of Boeotia and, on a clear day, the city of Thebes herself. Thebes sits on a ridge 700 metres above the plains of Boeotia, in the centre of the valley and somewhat equidistant from the Mediterranean gulfs to north and south, the Pindus Mountains to the west, and Cithaeron Mountains in the east towards Athens. A quick glance at an elevation map of Greece shows Thebes on its own in the middle of a flat area of some thirty square miles, about twelve to fifteen miles from any major geographic landmark. With its temperate climate and ample water from the mountains for irrigation, the land was ideal for growing wheat, the great cash crop of Boeotia. Wheat was not only the primary crop of Boeotia but probably its greatest legacy as well. The Roman politician and historian Pliny the Elder rated Boeotian wheat as the best in the world, remarking that 'the wheat of Bœotia occupies the first rank, that of Sicily the second, and that of Africa the third.'[2] Even today, wheat from this area is one of the hardiest varieties and its genus is found across the Balkans and the Caucasus, being the primary variety grown in regions like the Black Sea. Even modern nomenclature often refers to Ukrainian wheat as 'Boeotian'. The variety grows well throughout the Mediterranean, but Boeotia was its ancestral home and it is inextricably linked to the Boeotian identity.

Greek colonization across the Mediterranean, and especially in the Black Sea, funnelled wheat back and forth from mainland Greece and her colonies, especially through the trade ports in Corinth and Athens which often dealt with Boeotian wheat. Boeotia, like any Mediterranean region, also grew olives and grapes (and subsequently produced olive oil and wine), but wheat and the namesake cattle were the main exports that, proverbially and literally, put food on the table.

At a rigorous pace, one could walk from the Theban Cadmea to the centre of Athens in just over twelve hours.[3] Such proximity to Athens was of paramount importance to Thebes both culturally and economically. While they shared a mutually beneficial trade relationship at times, the two city-states were bitter rivals. Writing in the fifth century, the Theban poet Pindar often refers to a popular Athenian epithet that encapsulated their perception of the Boeotians as uncivilized and unrefined – 'Boeotian pigs'. Aristotle helps us see the extent of this view in his *Rhetoric*, when he quotes the great Athenian statesman Pericles:

> [Pericles] likened the Boeotians to oak trees, which damage each other when they clash together – so too do the Boeotians harm themselves through their civil conflict.[4]

Much of the hostility stemmed from disputes over the city-states along the Boeotian–Attican border. Plataea, the site of the final battle of the Persian Wars and where the Athenians and Spartans finally stamped out the Persian invaders, was paramount. Other cities, especially Oropus on the northern coast, were contested by both Athenians and Thebans for generations.

Despite their economic links and shared literary and religious heritage, Athens and Thebes often allowed their diplomatic disagreements to erupt into armed conflict.[5] This alternating romance and rivalry would inform much of the cataclysmic events of the fifth and fourth century, including the Theban-Spartan Wars.

Thebes in Literature and Mythology

The magic number for Thebes, beyond a doubt, is seven. The city famously had seven gates in its walls. The geographer and historian Pausanias lists them in this order: the Electran Gate, the Proetidian Gate, the Neistan Gate, the Crenaean Gate, the Hypsistan Gate, the Ogygian Gate, and the Homoloid Gate. Each has a rich history in myth and culture. The Electran Gate was named after the sister of Cadmus, the Neistan after a string of the harp, which was invented by a Theban, while the Homoloid Gate was named after a local mountain where the Thebans once took refuge from invading Argives. The gates became linked with Thebes' very identity outside Boeotia. Homer repeatedly refers to the city as 'seven-gated Thebes',[6] in part to distinguish the city from the more famous Thebes in Egypt which was said to have 100 gates, but also marking its role as a major cosmopolitan centre worthy of such a Homeric epithet. The seven gates also proved crucial in the great war that established Thebes as a pre-eminent military power. In the Heroic Age of Greece, coinciding with the Bronze Age, the most famous war was, of course, the Trojan War. That great civil conflict would shape all Greek culture, reflecting the struggles and adventures recounted in Homer's epic poems, *The Iliad* and *The Odyssey*.

Thebes did not play a central role in these, but the second most pivotal war of the Heroic Age is known as the Theban Cycle. In this conflict, the throne of Thebes is up for grabs and seven generals from Argos must wage war to win it for their champion. The seven invaders became known as the Seven Against Thebes. After their failure, a decade later their sons staged a second invasion, which was successful. The poet Hesiod claimed that these two Theban wars were equal to the Trojan War in forming Greek cultural identity during the classical era.[7] A series of four epic poems was written to celebrate them, *The Theban Cycle*, but sadly it has been lost to time. However, multiple ancient authors including Pausanias and Callinus claim that the author of these poems is none other than Homer himself.

This a perfect example of how poor fortune cost Thebes its rightful role as a co-equal of classical Greek standard-bearers, alongside Athens and Sparta. Had Homer's epic poems about Thebes survived, even to the ancient and medieval worlds, the fame of Thebes would have soared to greater heights. The Theban Wars did, however, survive in one form – they were forever memorialized by the poet Aeschylus in his fifth-century play *Seven Against Thebes*. Originally part of a trilogy chronicling the wars, the first two plays have been lost. Even better known perhaps, Aeschylus' fellow dramatist Sophocles wrote a trilogy about the Theban king Oedipus and his family, the *Oedipus Cycle*. Of course, both Aeschylus and Sophocles painted a less than rosy portrait of Theban power and, in the usual Athenian fashion, they treat Thebes as little more than a setting with which to critique Athenian politics without directly angering the oligarchs. Thebes was, however, seen by the Romans as a great north star for Greek culture, and the Roman poet Statius wrote his own version of *The Theban Cycle* called *The Thebaid*. Though it failed to capture the attention of the ancients, it found a fresh new audience in the medieval world especially during Charlemagne's classical revival.

The number seven features in other curious ways for Thebes. A founding myth for the city-state, paralleling Cadmus' adventures, tells the story of Amphion and Zethus, two sons of Zeus who took refuge from the political situation in Sicyon on the Peloponnesian Peninsula and of their father's dastardly actions there. In the myth, they conquer Thebes and construct the seven gates themselves (they and their family members giving their names to several of the gates). Amphion, the more musically inclined of the two brothers, and his wife Niobe had seven sons and seven daughters.

While Niobe boasted too brazenly of her children to the goddess Leto, and many were murdered as a consequence, it is these seven favoured princes and seven princesses of Thebes that may explain the city's links with the number seven. Seven was a revered number for the ancient Greeks, perhaps due to the iconic Greek lyre which has seven strings. Thebes and its several connections to this important number was a point not lost to the classical audience, and bolstered the city's role as one of the great titans of the Greek world.

The Dancing Floor of Ares

The nature of the Boeotian people themselves, however, was not that of simple farmers labouring in the bucolic valleys of central Greece. Boeotians were fierce warriors and cunning diplomats, who developed one of the most complex political systems in the Mediterranean world.

Boeotia, and specifically Thebes, had a martial culture, like much of Greece. Splintered by the mountainous terrain into warring city-states with overlapping but individual identities cultivated both a sense of independence and conflict among them. When the conflict inevitably turned into warfare, Boeotia's geography and cultural significance meant that its rolling valleys were at the heart of the fighting. As we saw with the battles in Boeotian cities at Plataea, Haliartus, Coronea, Leuctra, and Chaeronea, the valley seemed to magnetically attract seismic battles of the Greek world. Recognizing this pattern, the ancient historian Plutarch – himself a Boeotian – dubbed Boeotia 'the dancing floor of Ares'.[8]

In the archaic and classical eras of Greece, major conflict first arrived in Boeotia in the sixth century BCE, in a border dispute with Athens over the city-state of Plataea. Plataea was on the fringe of Theban territory and would have preferred Athenian leadership. She had in fact appealed for aid to the Spartans, who were then the dominant military and diplomatic power in Greece, though they had not yet expanded north into central Greece. The Spartans, rather mischievously, refused to become involved and delivered a message to the desperate Plataeans: 'We dwell afar off, and such aid as ours would be found but cold comfort to you; for you might be enslaved many times over ere any of us heard of it. We counsel you to put yourselves in the protection of the Athenians, who are your neighbours, and can defend you right well.'[9] The Spartans counted on Thebes and Athens butting heads over their claim to Plataea, and they were correct. Perhaps because of this, when Athens became the target of multiple invasions by the formidable Persian Empire, Thebes saw a chance to get the upper hand on their neighbours in Attica.

So it was that Thebes sided with Persia during the Persian invasion, motivated more by ambition and a hatred of Athens than love for Persia. Though allied to Persia, Thebes still sent 400 hoplites to the Battle of Thermopylae, only to surrender to Xerxes the Great before the famous last stand of the Spartans. This seems to indicate the presence of at least a handful of malcontents in Thebes who had hoped to join the pan-Hellenic resistance to Persia. The historian Herodotus, nevertheless, repeatedly asserts that the other Greek city-states mistrusted Thebes because they were the largest Persian ally in mainland Greece during the invasions.[10]

After the Persian Wars, Thebes was punished by Athens and her mighty new naval empire. The Athenians expelled Thebes from its leadership of Boeotia, neutering its position in the alliance of city-states known as the Boeotian Confederacy. This act was supposed to have made Athens sworn enemies of Thebes for life, though Thebes' eventual siding with Athens against Sparta in the Corinthian War proved that such sentiments can change.

In the Peloponnesian War, the Thebans tried to leverage their hatred of Athens into territorial gain. The dispute over Plataea was revisited but Plataea remained resistant to Theban rule – she had for over a century now rejected Thebes as the *de facto* leader of central Greece and still leaned towards Athens. Unwilling to give up their claim to Plataea, control of which would bolster their defences against the rising tide of Athenian power, Thebes invaded again in 431. This invasion took place at the height of Athenian-Spartan tension, immediately prior to the breakout of the Peloponnesian War, so the Thebans knew it was like throwing a match into tinder. In fact, they were counting on it. Thebes now briefly took the city of Plataea and massacred many of the residents, but it was unable to hold the city in the long term. The move, however, had succeeded in their secondary goal of igniting the war between Athens and Sparta. The Peloponnesian War soon engulfed the entire Aegean world. Sadly for the Thebans, it was their first and final success in the Peloponnesian War – thereafter they supported Sparta and took a back seat. While Thebes did expand her influence across Boeotia, she remained relegated to the second tier of Greek politics.

In the ensuing Corinthian War (395–387 BC), after rebelling against Spartan leadership, Thebes was initially a major player in the opposition to Spartan supremacy. Key battles such as Haliartus and Coronea took place on Theban home territory, with mixed results. But a fractured position atop the Boeotian Confederacy and the slow bleeding of the anti-Spartan alliance led Thebes to withdraw from the war in its closing years. By 386, Thebes and her allies in Boeotia were in tatters. Sparta and its king Agesilaus had a particular hatred for the Thebans after a perceived insult. Prior to the Corinthian War, Agesilaus had been hellbent on an invasion of Persia – long a Greek ambition following the Persian invasions of Greece. It had seemed a far-off dream with little substance behind it, until 396 when he called together a fleet and army to sail across the Aegean Sea and into Asia Minor, where they would eventually march to Persia.

Aulis was chosen for its Homeric connections. It was the site where Agamemnon and the Greek army had sailed away from the mainland of Greece to attack the beaches of Troy, thus beginning the Trojan War. It was also the site where Agamemnon, driven mad by the adverse weather delaying his departure, offered his own daughter Iphigenia as a human sacrifice to the gods. Aulis, however, was a Boeotian city, claimed by Thebes. Thebes refused to tolerate the symbolism of Agesilaus the Spartan at Aulis, as the new Agamemnon, and sent emissaries who scattered the offerings and enraged Agesilaus. He carried on a vendetta against Thebes until his dying day.

Accordingly, when Agesilaus and the Spartans won the Corinthian War against Athens, Thebes, Argos, and other Greek city-states in 386, Thebes received specially harsh treatment. Exacting just a portion of his vengeance, Agesilaus dismantled the Boeotian Confederacy, obliterated Thebes' role as the chief Boeotian city, and occupied Thebes itself, building a Spartan fortress atop the Cadmea. As we will soon see, these vindictive measures would motivate Thebes to return the favour. But until 379, Thebes was not even able to maintain her historic second-tier status and was subjugated to a much lower position.

Federalism and the Government of Boeotia

Their alliance with Persia in the latter's invasions had cost the Thebans greatly during the fifth century, as they watched Athens and Sparta forge their empires. Over the next decades, Thebes and others who had *medized* were seen as traitors to Greece. The geographer Pausanias, however, places precisely zero blame on the Thebans for their allegiance to Persia and the myriad of diplomatic and military tensions that followed. Instead, Pausanias blames a temporary lapse in the 'ancestral form' of Theban polity:

> The Theban people are in no way responsible for this choice, as at that time an oligarchy was in power at Thebes and not their ancestral form of government. In the same way, if it had been while Peisistratus or his sons still held Athens under a despotism that the foreigner had invaded Greece, the Athenians too would certainly have been accused of favouring Persia.[11]

That 'ancestral form' of government is known today as federalism. While their cousins in Athens are famous for founding democracy, the Boeotians were equally innovative in forging a new governmental system used across the world today.

Like most of Greece, the residents of the Boeotian plains were in constant competition with each other over resources and land, and this led to martial conflict as well as the formation of independent city-states. The city-states occasionally banded together in a shared alliance and common political league, dubbed a *koinon*. There were many such examples of these 'leagues' in Greece, named after the region – so the Aeolian League, the Ionian League, the Delian League, and so forth. When the *koinon* took on a militaristic objective, either for self-defence or expansion, it became something else: a symmachy. This centralized alliance was primarily a military treaty between states that included both offensive and defensive military cooperation. Sparta's Peloponnesian League was the shining example of a symmachy, as the various city-states of the peninsula unified under Spartan leadership to expand their influence and protect themselves from Athenian invasion. The Greek term symmachy remained prominent through the history of the Balkan peninsula, describing various treaties in the medieval and Ottoman eras and even into twentieth century, where NATO is described as a symmachy within Greece. The notion of the symmachy predated the *koinon*, and the latter soon became the umbrella term for any type of city-state alliances in the fifth and fourth centuries in Greece.

Boeotia's political alliance held many common features of both the *koinon* (the official term used in Boeotian documents) and the symmachy. The alliance would eventually be named the Boeotian Confederacy or the Boeotian League by modern historians. Founded around 520 BC, it was originally a standard-fare *koinon* and united the Boeotian city-states in an ostensibly equal power dynamic, though in reality Thebes dominated the league. The likely origins of the Boeotian Confederacy were in a self-defence symmachy rooted in the Boeotians' ancient homeland of Thessaly. The Thessalians made an annual tradition of invading their southerly neighbours, and Boeotia needed mutual protection. The shared cultural, linguistic, and religious heritage among the Boeotians unified them against the invaders, and with their pooled resources came a shared tradition of athletic games and religious festivals that strengthened the league. As the most populous city-state with the strongest military, Thebes took an unofficial lead in coordinating the league. This early, unofficial Boeotian Confederacy was even headquartered in Thebes on the Cadmea, though all citizens of Boeotian city-states were able to participate equally in the assembly meetings.

The catalyst for putting the Boeotian Confederacy on a formal footing came in 520, when the Boeotian city of Plataea defected to Athens. As we previously saw, this defection led to a brief military conflict and a long diplomatic tension between Thebes and Athens – a situation strongly encouraged by Sparta and her imperial interests. Thebes was enraged at the loss of Plataea. It was a wound that wouldn't heal, and even had salt rubbed into it in 499 when Plataea helped Athens to victory at the Battle of Marathon, and again in 479 when Plataea was the site of the final victory of Persia.

By the end of the fifth century, however, the Boeotian Confederacy began to tilt its favour more officially towards Thebes – who refused to allow the other Boeotian cities to seek foreign masters as Plataea had. Thebes tightened her grip on the Boeotian Confederacy and seized Plataean representation in the voting assembly, which helped transform the Boeotian *koinon* into its unique federal system. Boeotia's federal model developed a style of representation that paralleled Athenian democracy or Sparta's mixed constitution in several ways, but included its own innovations that diffused power across multiple city-states. Unlike the Athenian model in Attica which eventually functioned as one large city-state, Boeotia placed great emphasis on the power of each individual city-state as a member of the greater league.

Each city-state was a member of a district that annually elected its own political magistrate who, in collaboration with the other districts, also commanded the Boeotian military and directed foreign policy. This leader was known as a *boeotarch*, and achieving this position formed the apex of a Boeotian political career. At the formation of the league, there were eleven districts each with a boeotarch. The council of boeotarchs functioned as the oligarchic leaders of Boeotia, ostensibly representing the interests of each city-state equally. Their executive role primarily oversaw military and diplomatic matters, with little evidence of formal judicial or legislative involvement. As politics are wont to do, however, the most influential boeotarchs extended their reach into all aspects of power regardless of the law.

In 395, an anonymous author we now call the Oxyrhynchus Historian dedicated several paragraphs to the Boeotian constitution as it looked then. Though merely a small digression in his larger history of Greece, it would become our only surviving description of the Boeotian government and is therefore a precious resource for understanding Thebes and the rise of the Boeotian Confederacy. By 395, Thebes held four boeotarchs. The first two came from Thebes proper and two more from Theban annexation of the boeotarch position from Plataea and 'the other places previously linked to them in one political entity but at that time subject to Thebes.'[12] After Thebes, the cities of Orchomenus, Hysiae, and Tanagra each held their own boeotarch positions. The city-state of Thespiae shared two boeotarchs with Eutresis and Thisbe. The final two boeotarch positions were shared among Haliartus, Lebadea, and Coronea for the first and Acraephnium, Copae, and Chaeronea for the second. Clearly, securing one single boeotarch position was a coveted prize – and one that Thebes hoarded for herself.

In addition to their one boeotarch, each of the eleven Boeotian divisions annually had to contribute 1,000 hoplites, 1,000 cavalry, and 60 councillors, who were comparable to those of the Athenian Council of 500. The councillors ran daily affairs for their city-state and contributed to the larger Boeotian assembly which combined the 60 councillors from each of the eleven districts for a total of 660. This council met atop the Cadmea in Thebes, where they oversaw each city-state's payment of taxes, tribute to the shared treasury, appointment of judges and juries, and international affairs.[13] This larger body of councillors was further divided into four sub-councils that met across Boeotia, not just in Thebes. Each of these four sub-councils, comprising 165 men each, was tasked with localizing the bureaucratic functions including items like taxation, local elections, and public works. Like most Greek city-states, these senatorial positions were limited to those with wealth. The Boeotian Confederacy, like Athens, had a popular assembly open to all male citizens.

Most popular assemblies in Greek city-states operated either like Sparta's, where the public vote was seen as a formality and rarely a true tally of public opinion, or – less commonly – like the Athenian assembly, where the public vote determined the fate of the *polis* and its politicians. The Boeotian assembly, the *damos*, split the difference. The *damos* primarily ratified laws that were already destined to pass, but they held unique powers of impeachment and veto. In instances of corruption, the *damos* could remove bureaucrats from office or recall judges. If public opinion demanded it, the popular voting assembly could also overrule, or even impeach, a boeotarch. While doing so, the *damos* famously counted the heads of citizens in the voting process. As the historian Hans Beck notes:

> Boeotian foreign relations were widely subject to vote of the *damos*. The assembly also held annual elections for the magistracies of the confederacy. In cases of abuse of office, incompetence or maladministration, the assembly could remove the concerned magistrate from office and hand them over to federal courts… these rights of impeachment greatly enhanced the political powers of the *damos*, especially since they also applied to the boeotarchs.[14]

The Boeotian Confederacy therefore struck a fine balance between regional identity in Boeotia and fidelity to the *polis*. In Athens, the tribal identity – once heavily influential and redesigned by the 'father of democracy' Cleisthenes to equalize social classes – had lost its lustre amidst confusing alliances. Athens' ten tribes were intermixed across the city centre, the hills, and the coastal regions in a deliberate attempt to dilute the influence of the wealthy. It was a noble aim, but clever statesmen like Themistocles and Pericles quickly found the proper levers to pull to exploit the model.

The Boeotian Confederacy on the other hand, aimed to be true to its name, with the individual states holding greater autonomy on local issues beneath

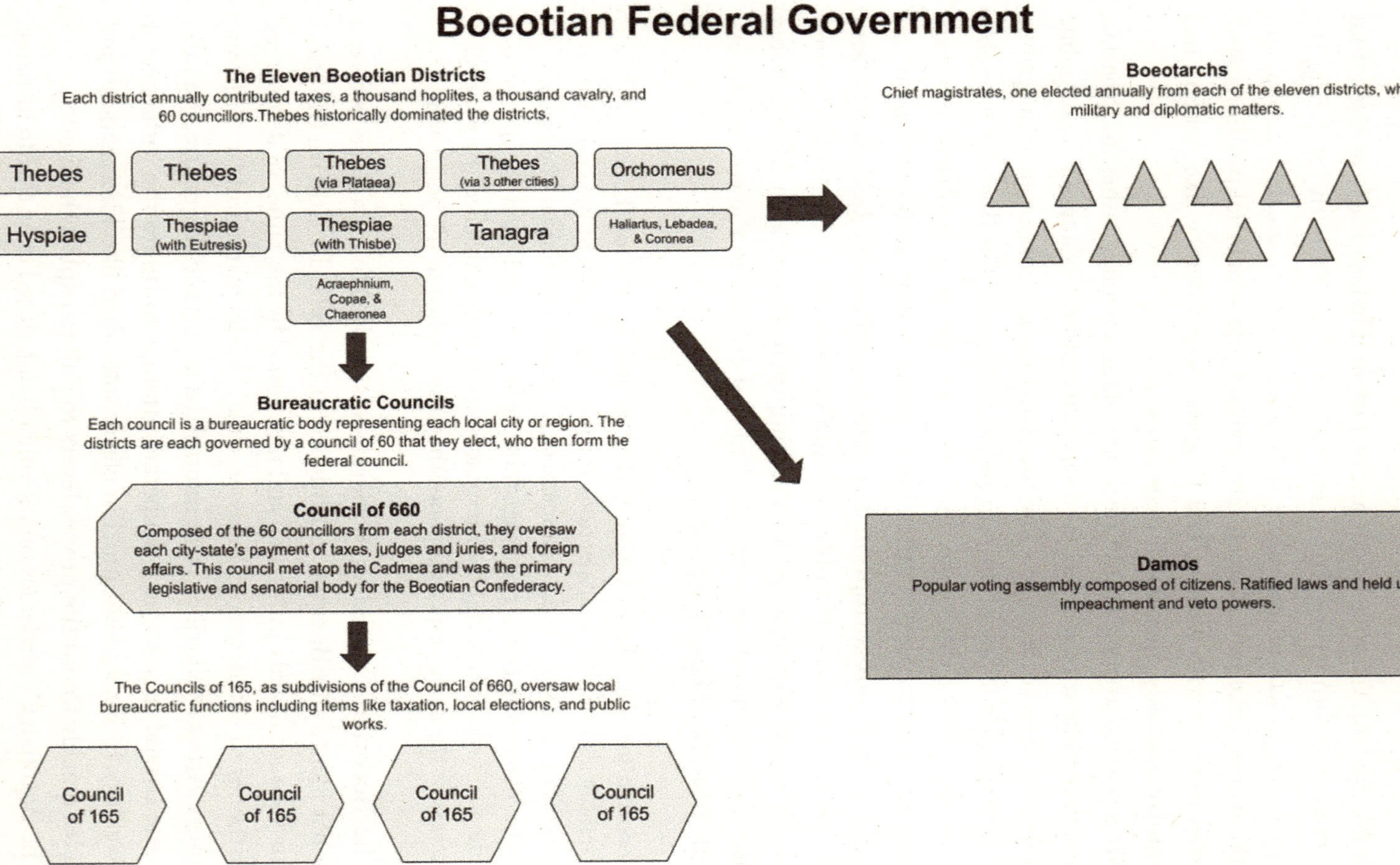

Figure 1.1. Boeotian Federal Government.

the broader political union. In the sixth century, the Boeotian Confederacy's power was held primarily at the city-state level and coordinated through the shared system of the councils, the *damos*, and boeotarchs. The larger states, especially Thebes, certainly exerted influence over their dependent cities, even sending 'councillors and officials to the federal government on behalf of their *syntelic* cities'.[15] But Thebes soon decided that her greater share of power in Boeotia should not be shackled by this confederal system. Soon after Plataea's defection to Athens, Thebes realized the threat of Athenian power in central Greece and grew more imperial in her own diplomacy, both within the Boeotian Confederacy and outside it. The federal structure nevertheless did serve as a check on the growth of Theban power, first in Boeotia and later across Greece. Beck notes that 'when Boeotia was at the height of its power, Thebes' foreign policy was not determined by ideological concepts, but was subject to power politics.'[16] If their powers were combined, the other city-states in the Confederacy could outman and outmanoeuvre Thebes, but only with a coordinated and organized effort, which rarely occurred.

From time to time, however, states like Orchomenus and Thespiae succeeded in stifling Theban power play and holding Thebes in check. After some rounds of this political jockeying, in 457 the Thebans fully realized the extent of other Boeotians' distrust of them. This led them to make a deal with the devil and offer themselves to Sparta, in exchange for alliance against the Boeotians and Athens. Diodorus Siculus describes how things stood as the First Peloponnesian War began:

> Since all the Boeotians held the Thebans in disdain and no longer paid any attention to them, the Thebans asked the Lacedaemonians to aid them in winning for their city the hegemony over all Boeotia; and they promised that in return for this favour they would make war by themselves upon the Athenians, so that it would no longer be necessary for the Spartans to lead troops beyond the border of the Peloponnesus.[17]

This move backfired, leading to Athenian control over Boeotia for a decade, but the Boeotians outside Thebes seemed to remember the protection and perhaps the anonymity that Thebes could provide for central Greece.

Thebes therefore never truly left the Boeotian Confederacy, and likely never dominated it in the ruthless way Athens did the Delian League or Sparta did the Peloponnesian League – at least at first. They did, however, clearly direct the Boeotian federal system. We can use simple arithmetic to determine the extent of Theban dominance in the Boeotian Confederacy – since Thebes controlled four of the eleven districts, they also populated four of the eleven boeotarch positions and 240 of the 660 senatorial positions, giving them a permanent grip on about a third of Boeotian councillors and leaders.

As we have seen, each of the districts also submitted 1,000 hoplites and 1,000 cavalry, so historians logically tabulate the size of the Boeotian military at 11,000 hoplites and 11,000 cavalry. This was, however, likely to have been the bare minimum. States that could give more to the cause often would, if for no other reason than to better bend military affairs in their interest. Population estimates for the Boeotian region in the fifth century range between 165,000 and 250,000,[18] making them roughly equal to Athens. Of that total, however, Thebes had an outsized influence, with up to 50,000 citizens. Thebes committed an increasing number of soldiers to the Confederacy's combined military, and soon became the dominant political and military force in both unofficial and official capacities. Specific numbers have been lost to time, but it is clear from sources that Thebes came to lead all diplomatic and militaristic matters for Boeotia. Eventually, elite military units such as the Sacred Band of Thebes contributed not only to a statistical imbalance in favour of Thebes, but also a qualitative one. By the dawn of the fourth century, Thebes was unequivocally directing the Boeotian Confederacy. Though a true confederacy in its founding, championing the individual rights of its city-states, as Thebes began to directly challenge Athens and then Sparta for Greek power, the Boeotian Confederacy became more of a federal polity, with a centralized government overseeing the state. City-state autonomy still existed and was championed at select times, but delegated powers moved clearly towards the federal government and away from the states. When the Corinthian War broke out in 395, Thebes represented all matters of Boeotian diplomacy and not only spoke for Boeotia at large, but negotiated directly with the other Greek city-states and bypassed the formalities of the Confederacy.

Eventually, the Boeotian Confederacy was simply subsumed by Thebes. By the time of the battle of Leuctra in 371, Thebes governed not only Boeotia directly but also the former Spartan empire and much of the former Athenian empire. It was no longer a confederacy or a federal state, but a hegemony. The Theban hegemony would last from 371 until at least their loss at Mantinea in 362, perhaps even until 346 when the conquering Macedonians arrived. The Boeotian federal system had become the nexus for Theban control over Greece for decades. But before they could assert their dominance over the rest of Greece, they first had to topple their Spartan overlords.

Chapter 2

The Legacy of the King's Peace

The Corinthian War and Sparta's Reasserted Empire

From 395 to 387, the Corinthian War ravaged Greece. Despite a valiant effort from an astonishing alliance of former enemies in Athens, Persia, Thebes, Argos, and Corinth, the mighty Spartan empire emerged victorious yet again. And Sparta set the terms.

Sparta's victory over the rest of the eastern Mediterranean in 387 was determined by a treaty known as the King's Peace. The namesake king was none other than the King of Kings, the Achaemenid Persian emperor Artaxerxes II, the great-grandson of Xerxes I, whose failed invasion of Greece in the Persian Wars had catapulted Athens and Sparta to new imperial heights. The King's Peace was brokered by a Spartan diplomat named Antalcidas, who played such an integral role that the treaty is alternatively named the Peace of Antalcidas.

Antalcidas had a knack for finding himself at the centre of major events during the Corinthian War, and charting his story is strikingly similar to charting the course of the entire conflict. The son of a Spartan ephor, Antalcidas served as a diplomat to the Persians in Spartan-held territory along the Aegean coast of Asia Minor at the outbreak of the war. These city-states were ethnically Greek and since the sixth century had held their allegiance to Persia, who preferred to organize local governments in the local tradition and therefore installed Greek-style tyrannies and oligarchies across Asia Minor. After the failed Persian invasions of Greece, however, they primarily became vassals to the Athenian empire.

With Athens toppled after the Peloponnesian War, Sparta's cunning admiral Lysander set his sights on establishing his own personal empire. Lysander had been the leader who finally conquered Athens, sailing into the harbour of Piraeus in 404 and disassembling the city walls brick by brick. It was a festive occasion, with Lysander and the Spartans 'with great enthusiasm [tearing] down the walls to the music of flute-girls, thinking that that day was the beginning of freedom for Greece.'[1] Lysander turned out to share Athens' imperial vision for an Aegean naval empire, with one important distinction: it should be Sparta – or more precisely Lysander – ruling that empire. Under the guise of liberating Athenian colonies across Greece, he set about installing his allies in government and reshaping those city-states into 'decarchies', that is with ten oligarchs directing policy.

A corollary of the decarchies was a new Spartan diplomatic position of *harmost*, a role that blended the work of emissary and dictator. The harmost's primary job was to dismantle Athenian-style democracy and replace it with a Spartan-friendly dictatorship administered by the decarchs. Between 404 and 395, Antalcidas was likely a member of these Lysandrean diplomatic models on the homefront in Sparta (and potentially abroad, though it is unknown whether he was officially posted in Asia Minor). He quickly forged a reputation for ruthless effectiveness. In this hiatus between the Peloponnesian and Corinthian Wars, Antalcidas developed a special skill for diplomacy in dealing with the complex model of Persian statecraft. Persian governance structure relied on local governors, the satraps, overseeing approximately twenty provinces across the Achaemenid Persian empire. In their tradition of allowing autonomy, these satraps were chosen from the local population and governed their home territory – contingent upon unflinching fidelity and obedience to Persia. Two Greek-speaking satraps shaped Persian policy over the Aegean coast of Asia Minor: Pharnabazus and Tiribazus. Antalcidas would befriend both.

Pharnabazus, the governor of Hellespontine Phrygia and a powerful voice in Artaxerxes II's ear, had an especially close relationship with the Spartans. Pharnabazus worked closely with Spartan delegates in the final phases of the Peloponnesian War and the years immediately following. He also befriended Lysander and likely conspired with him to assassinate the fascinatingly traitorous Athenian politician Alcibiades. Pharnabazus, though, had to reconcile the feuding factions within Sparta's newly expanded empire. While Lysander's imperial vision for Sparta was transforming her into an Athenian-style thalassocracy, his compatriot rivals felt differently. They envisioned a properly traditional land-based empire, fuelled by subjugation of rivals by means of the mighty Spartan hoplite army. On the one hand there were traditionalists, like the Agiad king Pausanias, who believed Sparta should simply settle for control of the Peloponnese and give up any broader empire-building schemes, but on the other, the prospect of inheriting Athens' Aegean empire was too intoxicating for the Spartan nobility to ignore.

The champion of this grand imperial vision was the Eurypontid king of Sparta, Agesilaus II. A thoroughbred of Spartan hoplites, with the pedigree of graduating from the Spartan *agoge* training camp that kings were normally exempt from, Agesilaus was singularly impressive both as a military commander and a statesman. He was famed for nobility and virtue, and philosophers such as Xenophon and Plutarch waxed eloquent about his pursuit of truth and goodness. A prime example of Spartan virtues, Agesilaus was lionized by many Greeks – even those under the boot of Sparta's tyranny. Agesilaus was respected across Greece and Persia for his fairness, magnanimity, and bravery. With his wisdom and eloquence, he brought in more diplomatic bounties for Sparta than by his military victories. Agesilaus soon became a foil to Lysander; where Lysander represented the oppressive nature of Sparta's empire, Agesilaus exemplified the best of Greek civic virtues.

To understand the gravitas of Agesilaus, we should look to the warrior-philosopher Xenophon of Athens. An Athenian aristocrat and student of Socrates himself, Xenophon soon felt disillusioned with the vicissitudes of Athenian democracy and became a mercenary. He was recruited into the army of the Persian prince Cyrus the Younger, who, acting on his friendship with Lysander, was assembling an army of Greek mercenaries to seize the Persian throne from his brother, the emperor Artaxerxes II. Xenophon joined the ill-fated campaign in 401 and after Cyrus the Younger fell in battle at Cunaxa, deep in Mesopotamian territory, the remainder of the 10,000 Greek mercenaries made an arduous retreat for thousands of miles, over 18 months, back to the Black Sea and then home to Greece. Harried by Persian troops throughout the long journey, many lost the strength and stamina to survive. None other than Xenophon took command, and he led them all the way back. The 4,000 who made it home were greatly lauded and counted among the most heroic Greeks of the day, the likes of Plato and Aristotle singing their praises. Of special note is that the Ten Thousand, as they came to be known, included 1,500 Boeotians and 1,000 Spartans. It would be the final time they fought as allies for centuries.

Xenophon won fame for his leadership during the march of the Ten Thousand but matched his reputation with humility. Instead of advancing his own interests, Xenophon proved himself a true soldier, becoming fiercely loyal to the new Spartan commander who had hired him: Agesilaus. He entered Agesilaus' service in 396 in Asia Minor, and went on to fight for him across the Aegean, finding that his worldview matched Sparta's better than his native Athens'.

Xenophon probably fought against Athens in the Corinthian War, which earned him a sentence of exile from his home city. Taking up residence in Corinth, he penned a series of impressive philosophical, political, and historical texts, including a biography of Cyrus the Great, a work on husbandry, and a Socratic dialogue on the trial of Socrates that rivals *The Apology* of his classmate Plato. But two works stand out: his treatise praising the government of Sparta and his life of Agesilaus. *Agesilaus* opens with lines that reveal the text will be more of a hagiography than a biography:

> To write the praises of Agesilaus in language equalling his virtue and renown is, I know, no easy task; yet must it be essayed; since it were but an ill requital of pre-eminence, that, on the ground of his perfection, a good man should forfeit the tribute even of imperfect praise.[2]

His reputation assured throughout Greece, Agesilaus set out to assert Sparta's manifest destiny in Asia in 396. The conquest of Persia had long been a Greek goal and was seen as a Panhellenic divine mission, one that had the potential to unify the warring city-states of Greece. Since the days of the Persian Wars, many Greeks had called for such retribution against the Persians and Sparta now saw the invasion as a chance to reinforce its empire. Lysander and Agesilaus, working in lockstep for once, arranged for an impressive Spartan army to sail from Greece and meet with a mercenary army in Sparta-controlled Asia Minor. From there, they would breach the Persian heartland. Though Lysander's imperial vision drove much of the planning, Agesilaus was explicitly seizing the mantle of 'the commander of all Greece'[3] – taking on the trappings of Agamemnon and the Homeric role of kingship. But it was not to be: Agesilaus was denied such glory and his first setback came with the flat refusal of Corinth, Athens, and Thebes to participate in the invasion.

Originally intended as a Panhellenic mission, the absence of these three great city-states reduced the invasion to a purely Spartan enterprise – a turn of events that enraged Agesilaus. Corinth and Athens pointed to the devastation of their cities and the poor omens, two points which Agesilaus could not refute. However, Thebes offered no real explanation: they simply refused to participate. Agesilaus rather desperately sent one of his own family, Aristomelidas, to Boeotia to persuade them, but to no avail.

Undaunted, Agesilaus gathered his great army at Aulis, in northern Boeotia on the coast. The location was personal for Agesilaus. It was here that Agamemnon had sacrificed his own daughter to the goddess Artemis, quelling the storms and allowing the Greek army to sail off to glory in the Trojan War. Styling himself as the new king of Greece, Agesilaus was like a reincarnated Agamemnon from *The Iliad*: a respected but ruthless leader who invaded Asia and eventually brought peace to the Greeks through brute force. The events at Aulis deserve more focused consideration, however, because their ramifications were to last through the entire fourth century in Greece.

The Boeotians' noncompliance with Agesilaus soon evolved into outright rebellion. Though on the border with Attica, Aulis was a thoroughly Boeotian city. Its name comes from the eponymous daughter of a mythological Boeotian king; a princess who was also one of a collective of goddesses sacred to the region, known as the Praxidike. Because Aulis features in *The Iliad*, its name is perhaps the best known mention of Boeotia in classical literature and accounts for its presence in the works of Hesiod, Euripides, Ovid, and Statius. The sacrifice of Agamemnon's daughter is often mentioned by the major Greek playwrights and philosophers, and is at the heart of Euripides' tragedy *Iphigenia in Aulis*. In addition to playing an important role in maritime trade, Aulis was thus inextricably linked to Boeotia's cultural identity – and perhaps to uncomfortable reflections, since it recalls one of the most infamous incidents in Greek mythological history.

For such cultural reasons and because of the obvious anti-Spartan sentiment, as Thebes reeled from their imperial oppression after the Peloponnesian War, the ambassadors sent from Thebes were icy. While Agesilaus prepared for one of the biggest moments of his career, the Thebans refused to even initiate conversation. They pulled down the animal sacrifices and ransacked the Spartan altar. No traditional Greek *xenia* – hospitality for guests – was to be found. Plutarch describes the incident in the most detail, though Pausanias, Xenophon, Diodorus Siculus, and other historians all emphasize its impact. Plutarch recounts the moment as follows:

> [Agesilaus] would honour the goddess with a sacrifice in which she could fitly take pleasure, being a goddess, and would not imitate the cruel insensibility of his predecessor. So he caused a hind to be wreathed with chaplets, and ordered his own seer to perform the sacrifice, instead of the one customarily appointed to this office by the Boeotians. Accordingly, when the Boeotian magistrates heard of this, they were moved to anger, and sent their officers, forbidding Agesilaus to sacrifice contrary to the laws and customs of the Boeotians. These officers not only delivered their message, but also snatched the thigh-pieces of the victim from the altar. Agesilaus therefore sailed away in great distress of mind; he was not only highly incensed at the Thebans, but also full of ill-boding on account of the omen. He was convinced that his undertakings would be incomplete, and that his expedition would have no fitting issue.[4]

Charles Hamilton aptly summarizes the legacy of the moment for Agesilaus: 'The incident at Aulis became for [Agesilaus] a public insult, an unjustified affront to his pride, which he never forgave nor forgot.'[5] Though he surely desired to take immediate revenge on Thebes, Agesilaus also knew the diplomatic crisis that would bring about. He instead opted to strategically delay his retaliation, hoping the riches and fame from the successful invasion of Persia would provide ample opportunity to punish Thebes for their insult. For now, Agesilaus was concentrating on the endless opportunities of a conquered Persia and an expansionist Spartan empire. His campaign got off to a dashing start, as he conquered cities along the coast and deposed Lysander as his primary intra-Spartan rival. In 395, Agesilaus wrongfooted the Spartans with a feint and marched on the regional capital of Sardis, capturing the city in a massive blow to Persian control of Asia Minor. It seemed, for a brief moment, that Agesilaus' audacious campaign might succeed.

But the Fates did not allow it. Instead, just weeks into the invasion that had begun so seductively well, a new threat emerged on Sparta's homefront, in the form of a nascent alliance between those Greek city-states who shared life under Sparta's boot. Athens, Corinth, Thebes, and Argos capitalized on Agesilaus' absence from mainland Greece to rebel against their overlords. The binding element for these unlikely allies was none other than Persia. Panicking at the invading Spartan force, the Persians turned to their oldest foreign policy: interventionism. They sent a cunning diplomat named Timocrates of Rhodes to lure as many dissatisfied Spartan vassals as possible into an alliance. Timocrates hardly needed to offer more than a chance to dethrone Sparta – he had brought fifty talents of gold as a bribe but the Athenians declined it, content simply with the chance of vengeance.[6] Thebes, Argos, and Corinth accepted the gold and eagerly combined forces. A new symmachy was born with the sole purpose of ending the Spartan empire.

What followed was the Corinthian War, a civil war that further devastated mainland Greece for eight years, from 395 to 387. Across the Peloponnese and central Greece, the anti-Spartan coalition fought the Spartan hoplites valiantly. At Haliartus in Boeotia in 395, the Thebans gained a shocking victory over the Spartans and even killed the great Lysander at the city walls. It was an astonishing coup for the underdogs and exactly what Persia had hoped for. Agesilaus was quickly recalled and ordered by the Spartan ephors to return to Greece.

The following summer however, outside the sacred city of Nemea in the Peloponnese, home to the Nemean Games which were second only to the Olympic Games in cultural prestige, the Spartans turned the tables and defeated the combined forces of Thebes, Argos, Athens, and Corinth. A few weeks later, on the waters outside the city of Cnidus on the Carian coast of Asia Minor, the Persians entered the fray, fighting against Agesilaus' brother-in-law who was leading the naval fleet. It was a catastrophe for Sparta. Not only did they lose their fleet, but they also managed to create a new Athenian hero. Conon, an exiled admiral whose failure in the Peloponnesian War had led him to medize and join the Persians, expertly commanded the Persian triremes at Cnidus, earning the respect of the anti-Spartan alliance and positioning him for a triumphant repatriation to Athens.

As the Corinthian War raged on, Agesilaus and his Spartans marched back to Greece overland, tracing the very same path Xerxes the Great took during the Persian Wars. When Agesilaus arrived back in Greece, he took out his full frustration on the Thebans, who suffered especially brutal losses in a devastating defeat for the allied forces. Agesilaus returned to Sparta, where he was sidelined for much of the rest of the war, though Sparta still held the advantage. Nevertheless, the conflict continued for seven more years. Athens spent much of that time rebuilding her navy, now under the leadership of Conon, and forging a new empire under their ruthlessly effective leader Thrasybulus, who had liberated Athens from Spartan captivity. Corinth succumbed to internal conflict, with pro-Spartan oligarchs feuding with pro-Athenian democrats, reducing the city to chaos. Thebes meanwhile, dismayed at the loss at Coronea, also saw a grand opportunity to close ranks on Boeotia and strengthen their grip on the Boeotian Confederacy. They were surely motivated by the fact that both Athens and Sparta had grown more powerful since 394, and were effectively withdrawing from the war to prepare for the next inevitable conflict.

Throughout all this, the Spartan diplomat Antalcidas had been at work masterfully brokering deals with Persia satraps, harmosts in Asia Minor, and *proxenoi* (citizens hosting their ambassadors) in Greek city-states. In 392, he spearheaded a series of peace negotiations in Asia Minor, where he cleverly aimed to convince Persia to withdraw their support for the crumbling anti-Spartan alliance.

There was a real chance to end the war in 392, either in Asia Minor or at the ensuing summit in Sparta which occurred several months later. Hubris, though, ruined the negotiations. Each member of the anti-Spartan league was unwilling to let go of their new acquisitions. Athens refused to part with her numerous conquests across the Aegean islands and her revived prospect of an Athenian naval empire. Argos refused to give up her interest in conquering Corinth, long a dream of the Argives and a tempting prospect while Corinth struggled in the grip of civil war. Thebes refused to lighten the burden on the Boeotian Confederacy and cede Boeotian land back to Sparta.[7] Antalcidas appeared to have failed at brokering the end of the war.

Antalcidas, though, had broken through to the Persian satrap Tiribazus. The governor of Lydia, Tiribazus was a new appointee to the role and eager to make his mark. And what better way to impress Artaxerxes II than by ending the troublesome war with the Greeks? Tiribazus took swift action. First, he gave Antalcidas and the Spartans a mountain of gold to furnish a new naval fleet, replacing the one they had lost at Cnidus. This was more to demoralize the Athenians and encourage them to sign the peace treaty, than to make any real investment in Spartan interests. Next, Tiribazus arrested the Athenian admiral, Conon. Though Conon soon escaped, he died shortly after. The spirit of the new Athenian empire perished with him, at least for a time. Instead of giving up the Corinthian War, Athens fought on – but she found fewer and fewer allies. Persia was now suing for peace and funding Sparta's navy. Thebes was concerned exclusively with Boeotian matters, absconding their role in the anti-Spartan alliance. Corinth's civil conflicts had boiled over, while Argos – long covetous of Corinth and eager to conquer a regional rival – concocted the creative solution of assimilating Corinth into their own *polis*. The specific mechanics of this union remain elusive to modern historians, but Argos and Corinth functionally combined governments and citizenship in 392. Argos claimed this right as the means of saving a Corinth overcome by pro-Spartan oligarchs, but the rest of Greece plainly saw through this veneer. No matter its integrity, the Argos-Corinth union ended both city-states' participation in the Corinthian War. Athens was left alone against Sparta.

The twilight battle of the Corinthian War occurred in 390, outside the port of Corinth. At the battle of Lechaeum, a new Athenian hero emerged in the innovative young commander Iphicrates. Iphicrates upended the traditional Greek approach to infantry, eschewing the heavy-armoured hoplite in favour of the *peltast*. This force of skirmishers were not overburdened by heavy shields or weaponry, but armed as lightly as possible down to their spears and boots – all in the name of speed. Iphicrates and his lightning-fast peltasts dismantled an entire Spartan regiment outside Lechaeum in short order. The confused Spartan survivors broke ranks and retreated. To make matters worse, this was one of Agesilaus' units – and he was only just recovering his status in Sparta.

Lechaeum was the final major conflict of the Corinthian War. It dragged on for two more years, but little of consequence happened beyond skirmishes and feints. Thebes remained reclusive, absorbed in their Boeotian affairs, while Argos focused on subsuming Corinth through joint citizenship. Athens tried to steadily expand her naval presence across the Aegean Sea and she did have some success, but overlooked her underbelly. While the Athenian fleet was off conquering Aegean islands, the Spartans launched a surprise attack from nearby Aegina and destroyed by fire the Athenian harbour at Piraeus. Despite it not being a pitched land battle, the burning of Piraeus was the largest conflict on land in the waning years of the Corinthian War.

The King's Peace and the Humiliation of Thebes

In 387, sensing that Sparta was not necessarily victorious but was surviving the best, Antalcidas revisited the failed peace talks of five years earlier. This time, he found success. Antalcidas set sail for Ephesus with the Spartan fleet that had been funded by the Persians and met with the satrap Tiribazus. Together, the two diplomats plotted the end of the Corinthian War. The first part of the treaty was to be Persia's abandonment of the anti-Spartan alliance. Tiribazus agreed to support Sparta's cause if the allies refused to end the war, which of course they did. Persia allowed Sparta unfettered access to its territories in Asia Minor, as a means to prohibit all Athenian naval activity. With Persian support and a fleet of eighty ships, Xenophon declared that 'Antalcidas ruled the seas.'[8] It was an ironic reversal of fortune from Agesilaus' invasion of Persia less than a decade earlier.

It was enough to bring Athens to the negotiating table, at last. All parties were sick of the war by this point, and eager for a conclusion to the huge drain on resources. Tiribazus held a summit in Persian territory, at which all major parties were represented, although Sparta and Persia were clearly in the suzerain position and declared their terms plainly:

The king, Artaxerxes, deems it just that the cities in Asia, with the islands of Clazomenae and Cyprus, should belong to himself; the rest of the Hellenic cities he thinks it just to leave independent, both small and great, with the exception of Lemnos, Imbros, and Scyros, which three are to belong to Athens as of yore. Should any of the parties concerned not accept this peace, I, Artaxerxes, will war against him or them with those who share my views. This will I do by land and by sea, with ships and with money.[9]

No Greeks objected here. Objections came quickly, though, when the full details were revealed. The primary terms of the King's Peace were the allocation of mainland Greece to Sparta and the Greek city-states of Asia Minor to Persia. While the former was a return to existence prior to the war, the latter was a staggering indignity. The Spartans had repeatedly promised the Greeks of Asia Minor that they would liberate them from the Persians and restore them to their brothers across the Aegean. Indeed, this had been one of Agesilaus' main marketing points as he prepared for the Spartan invasion of Persia in 396. The Greeks of Asia Minor were livid at the prospect of returning to Persian rule, but they held no serious negotiating power.

Antalcidas and his Persian allies next targeted the Corinth-Argos union. While it had been an interesting experiment as an alternative to outright conquest, Sparta had no interest in sharing the Peloponnese with a larger, more powerful city-state. They demanded the dissolution of the union. The Argives were incensed, but with no sustainable militaristic position against Sparta they had few options. They voiced their discontent, but Agesilaus – who had been watching the peace conference like a hawk without so far being involved – had choice words for the Argives and the Corinthian oligarchs who supported the Argos-Corinth union. Mustering all the laconic eloquence and solemnity of which he was legendarily capable, Agesilaus demanded they disband the union. It was as if his words had wings, and Xenophon describes the immediate response of the Argives and Corinthians: 'The terror of both was so great that the Argives marched out of Corinth, and Corinth was once again left to herself; whereupon the "butchers" and their accomplices in the deed of blood determined to retire from Corinth, and the rest of the citizens welcomed back their late exiles voluntarily.'[10]

Shockingly, the next item of the agenda was the very existence of the Boeotian Confederacy. In fact, Thebes and her claims to Boeotia became the primary discussion point of the King's Peace. On its face, this was an odd candidate to be the most-discussed part of the negotiations to end a pan-Aegean war in which Thebes had been essentially inactive for seven years. But Agesilaus' deep-rooted frustration at Thebes over the offences at Aulis had not waned over the long course of the war, and he was singularly responsible for targeting Thebes in the negotiation. The conflict centred upon the signing of the agreed oath. Thebes anticipated signing the treaty and taking the oaths on behalf of the entire Boeotian Confederacy, with no consultation – after all, no other Boeotians were present at the negotiations. Agesilaus, however, had no interest in this arrangement. He pointed to the specific use of the word autonomous (or 'independent') in the peace terms, which reiterated that 'the rest of the Hellenic cities [Artaxerxes II] thinks it just to leave independent, both small and great.'[11]

Agesilaus declared that unless Thebes relinquished claims over the rest of Boeotia, he would not accept the peace treaty. This was an astonishing demand, and one that no other Greek league or symmachy had to endure, least of all the Spartans who would be keeping their Greek empire and certainly not allowing any meaningful 'autonomy' for other cities. The shellshocked Thebans could only muster a minor appeal before being dismissed outright by Agesilaus and sent on their way. The Theban ambassadors thus complied and returned home, but Agesilaus wasn't done. Xenophon describes how 'Agesilaus, out of hatred to the Thebans, took active measures at once.'[12] He ordered a Spartan infantry unit to begin to march towards Boeotia, just in case the Thebans refused to comply with his demands. It proved unnecessary, however, because the Thebans acquiesced. They saw no solution but to recognize the independence of the Boeotian city-states and formally disband the Boeotian Confederacy. It was a sputtering end to the great federal state. As Xenophon describes it, the Thebans 'were forced to accept the truce unconditionally, and to recognize the autonomy of the Boeotian cities.' For now, the Spartans had no reason to attack Thebes. This would not last for long, however.

Despite its weaknesses, the King's Peace was a groundbreaking treaty for the classical world. It was the first *koine eirene*, or 'common peace,' in Greek history and would form a blueprint for future treaties. In orchestrating the end to such a complex war, Antalcidas had – perhaps inadvertently – designed a brilliant diplomatic tool in the common peace. He had included all Greek city-states in some capacity, arranged customized terms for each one, confirmed their legitimacy and autonomy, and did not advantage city-states based on military strength. While the final two points were present in writing only in the King's Peace, the model was nevertheless forged and would be replicated in future peace treaties. Antalcidas' journey in Spartan diplomacy culminated in this crowning achievement, and Sparta stood stronger for it. Despite the odds, Sparta stood alone – if wounded – atop the Greek city-states.

While the Corinthian War was less a victory for the Spartans and more a bloody stalemate, they nevertheless survived in the most effective position of all the Greek city-states, and even outlasted genuine Persian interest in Greece. From 387 on, the Persians became more concerned with internal matters and finally decided Greek politics might not be worth the chaos. Content with their stranglehold on Greek cities in Asia Minor, Persia now left the mainland of Greece entirely to Sparta. This, of course, was the problem. The anti-Spartan confederacy had failed to dethrone Sparta, and succeeded only in provoking its rage. Sparta now framed its entire imperial apparatus towards the ruthless oppression of the states that had defied them. The walls of Athens had been dismantled and its harbour burned, but Athens was always a favourite target of the Spartans. It was Thebes, though, that was most squarely in the crosshairs of Sparta and her triumphant, vengeful king Agesilaus.

Agesilaus had finally become the incarnate Agamemnon he had tried to channel at Aulis. His victories in Asia Minor and unquestionable dominance over the mainland of Greece now caused him to feel empowered and unrestrained. His task of humiliating Thebes, especially, was not yet finished and he would pursue it at all costs. The Spartan empire would soon occupy Thebes and the Cadmea, and choke the life out of the feeble remnants of the Boeotian Confederacy. But as we will soon see, such an empire was predicated on a rapidly diminishing resource: the Spartan hoplite.

Chapter 3

Sparta's Flawed Imperial Architecture

The Spartiate and the Spartan Social System

Despite its victories in the Peloponnesian and Corinthian Wars, the Sparta of 387 BC had no business claiming an empire over Greece, or anywhere else. This was not because of a decline in their martial prowess or diplomatic acuity, both of which remained as strong as ever. Nor was there any degradation in the educational quality of the *agoge* and, furthermore, they generally did not face the same civil conflict over the ideal form of government that conflicted most Greek city-states. Instead, Sparta faced a simple statistical challenge: she could not produce citizens at a fast enough pace.

The Spartiate was the essential unit of Spartan society. The only citizens of the state with fully endowed legal rights, the Spartiates were the backbone of the military system. Only Spartiates could become ephors and join the council of five oligarchic leaders, or be one of the two kings who alternated religious and military command. Only the Spartiates could vote in the popular assembly or be appointed to the council of elders known as the *gerousia*. In fact, Spartiates made up the entirety of Sparta's unique governmental system, which blended oligarchy, democracy, and monarchy in a jumbled but highly effective fashion. To become a Spartiate – which was also to become one of the *homoioi* meaning 'equals' or 'peers' – was no simple matter, however. It took twenty-three years of rigorous military education, beginning at age seven in the *agoge* training camp, and later as a hoplite, living in the communal barracks until age thirty. Surviving this upbringing was no easy feat, but those who came through were fiercely loyal to the state, expert warriors, and thoroughly compliant to the rigid Spartan social hierarchy. Successful service in the Spartan state earned the peers a plot of land to farm and own for their rest of their life.

Spartiates, quite simply, could not be easily replaced. All the core positions in government were held by them, though often after they retired from active duty in the military. And, of course, the renowned Spartan army was composed primarily of Spartiates. The heavy infantry hoplites, the core of any Greek militia in the classical era, was almost exclusively made up of them. Sparta's great military machine owed its success directly to the fact that they could field full-time soldiers in the Spartiates, who held no other employment and trained year-round for battle. By contrast, in Athens and other Greek city-states, the hoplites were part-time soldiers and part-time farmers, only going on campaign around the planting and harvesting seasons.

The Spartiates were not the full extent of Sparta's military, though. Three other categories of the population existed: the *perioeci*, the helots (*heilotes*), and the *neodamodes*. The *perioeci* or 'those dwelling nearby' were the light infantry and sailors. They were not citizens of Sparta but second-class citizens from about 25 cities across Messenia, Laconia, and the southern Peloponnese, merchants and craftsmen who had been conquered and subjugated by the Peloponnesian League to serve the Spartan state. Because Sparta was economically isolationist and allowed no outside trade, the *perioeci* filled the roles of artists, traders, and manufacturers while holding no political power.

Perhaps the most significant sector of the Spartan population was the helot. Made up of the enslaved people of Messenia and other neighbouring regions of Sparta, the helots were the skirmishers and light infantry of the military. They had a still more important role in Spartan culture as manual labourers in the fields, whose labour was responsible for the production of all the state's food, since outside trade was forbidden. The helots were serfs to their land, brutally oppressed by the Spartan citizens and holding absolutely no political rights. The helots' submission was the very bedrock of Spartan society. As a show of force, the Spartan government began each new year by formally declaring war on the helots. A secret police force called the Crypteia existed purely to spy on the helots and ruthlessly suppress any signs of resistance. Young Spartans in the *agoge* were required to murder a helot to earn citizenship. This systematic and psychological oppression was orchestrated in large part to sustain Sparta's military supremacy and the economy, but the Spartans also realized the true nature of the helots' situation – they vastly outnumbered the Spartiates.

Helots were, of course, equally aware of this reality and took every opportunity to revolt. Helot rebellions became an annual event at certain moments in Spartan history but were at all times the primary threat to the state. The Spartans feared a successful helot revolt more than internal conflict over political structures or even outside invasion by Athens. The events following the catastrophic earthquake of 464 rooted this idea in the mind of the Spartiates: more than 20,000 residents were killed in the disaster and the helots seized their chance and almost succeeded in overthrowing the entire Spartan regime. Sparta had to beg for help outside the Peloponnese, which led ultimately to Athenian interference on behalf of the helots. After more dominoes fell, the result was the formal outbreak of the Peloponnesian War four years later.

The ancients did not stay silent on Sparta's treatment of the helots. Plutarch remarked that the Spartan slave system was 'a most savage and lawless practice.'[1] Plato described how the system was 'of all Hellenic forms of slavery the most controverted and disputed about.'[2] Thucydides captured the Spartan fear of helots in the aftermath of the 464 earthquake: 'Indeed fear of their numbers and obstinacy even persuaded the Lacedaemonians to action…their policy [was] at all times…governed by the necessity of taking precautions against them.'[3]

Sparta's *stasis* struggle was not one of political philosophy but a matter of liberty, with helot revolts peppering its history every few years. The state's merciless oppression of the helots continued because they knew that their entire social and now imperial structure would collapse without the production of the helot masses. Where Athens had naval trade and colonial interests, Sparta had helots. If she lost the helots, as Athens had lost her navy after the Peloponnesian War, then she would not recover as Athens had. All domestic and foreign policy in Sparta was first considered through the prism of helot subjugation.

The final group in the Spartan social pyramid was also the newest. The *neodamodes* were former helots who had been freed and granted more rights. Literally translated as 'those who are newly of the people', the *neodamodes* are little discussed in Greek texts, suggesting the model of liberating helots had not long been practised by the Spartans. The first appearance of freed helots fighting for Sparta is in 424, when the celebrated general Brasidas received a group of 700 helots as reinforcements, there being no Spartiates available.[4] These soldiers served with such distinction that they earned the nickname of the Brasideoi after their commander, and three years later were given both their liberty and a new social class. Within a few years, this model of emancipating helots to guarantee more soldiers, and even heavy infantry, became standard in Sparta's military.

It is difficult to determine the demographics of *neodamodes* by the early fourth century, or even to know if the trend survived long past Brasidas. There was a practice of granting helots their freedom and promotion to a social status somewhere above helot but below *perioeci*. Brasidas granted this honour following successful service, but by the Corinthian War helots were freed prior to their military service and committed to several years of fidelity. Xenophon and Plutarch mention *neodamodes* sparingly, but never clarify their role in descriptions of Spartan society and battle. Xenophon refers to the *neodamodes* as 'the enfranchized' and offers little in the way of description, but he does consistently distinguish *neodamodes* from helots, Spartiates, *perioeci*, and other Spartan groups.[5] Xenophon identifies thousands of *neodamodes* over the course of the early fourth century, indicating that the movement Brasidas started had quickly become grafted on to the design of Sparta's army and the production of new soldiers.

Sparta had other sources of residency and even citizenship in the state – but not for males. Women, though granted a higher status here than in other city-states, could not don the armour of a hoplite but held citizenship and important advisory and family roles. For all the virtues of Spartan women, they could not serve on the battlefield. Spartan society saw the primary purpose of women as the head of the family, to give birth to and raise the next generation of Spartiates – who would in turn serve honourably as hoplites and defend the city-state. Gorgo, the wife of the king Leonidas, famously answered that, '[Spartan women] are the only women that give birth to men'[6] when asked why Spartan women tended to rule over men. In many ways, such a statement was the culmination of centuries of cultural norming and struggle in Sparta. The problem was, there were fewer and fewer men.

Oliganthropia and the Spartan Paradox of Hoplites

Brasidas took the radical step of liberating helots out of desperation, because he was acutely aware of the most pressing problem faced by Sparta's brittle empire: population decline. Spartiates simply could not be created at a rate fast enough to keep up with warfare and earthquakes, no matter how impressive the Spartan army was. If the Spartans were to maintain their hegemony over the Aegean, they would need new sources of soldiers. The heavy infantry hoplites, especially, were threatened due to the diminishing number of *agoge* graduates who could serve and survive in campaigns. Brasidas had reckoned that loosening the exclusivity of Spartan citizenship would help in the crisis, but it was only a temporary relief. In the 330s, Aristotle pinpointed the issue when describing the fall of Sparta's empire: 'Although the country is capable of supporting 1500 cavalry and 30,000 heavy-armed troopers, they numbered not even a thousand. And the defective nature of their system of land-tenure has been proved by the actual facts of history: the state did not succeed in enduring a single blow, but perished owing to the smallness of its population.'[7] To emphasize his argument, Aristotle invented a new word to describe that 'smallness of population', *oliganthropia*. Meaning 'the lessening of people', *oliganthropia* was an exclamatory statement of affairs.

A statistical survey of Spartiates from the Persian Wars to the Theban-Spartan Wars helps illustrate the population crisis (see Table 3.1). Herodotus names 8,000 male citizens of Sparta in 480,[8] which is generally accepted as a baseline number. If we track the appearance of Spartiates in major battles, then Herodotus begins our count a year later with 5,000 Spartan hoplites at the battle of Plataea, in 479.[9] At Pylos in 425, the number of Spartan peers had declined to 2,755 in action. Two decades later during Agesilaus' invasion of Persia, he took an unclear number of *perioeci* and helots but likely brought a Spartiate numbering around 1,000.[10] The year after that, at the battle of Nemea, Xenophon tells us that there were 1,800 Spartiates, and at Leuctra in 391, there were under a thousand Spartiates.

Sparta was shrewd enough to not put all its best soldiers in one location, of course, and so spread the peers across multiple armies. While the army generally hovered around a total of 10,000 soldiers, the proportion of Spartiates within that number dropped at every measurement. In the sixty years from Plataea to Mantinea, there was a 58 per cent decrease in the

Spartiate count at major battles. From Mantinea to Leuctra, there was a further 52 per cent decline. In the century from Plataea to Leuctra, the reduction amounts to an astonishing 80 per cent. No empire could withstand such a steep decline in its citizenship. This was especially true for the Spartan structure, where the fall was localized to the sole social class enfranchised to own property or hold office. Compounding the matter was the increasing number of helots. Helot population is notoriously difficult to track, as few ancient historians give any specifics of helot society beyond recognizing their large numbers. What is clear is that the helots increased at a fast pace, even as the Spartiates declined. Herodotus famously claimed there were seven helots for every Spartiate during the Persian Wars.[11] However, there is a wide range of understanding by modern scholars on this ratio, ranging from 7:1 to 20:1.[12] As with the proportion of Spartiates to *perioeci*, the helot population grew to vastly outnumber the Spartan peers. The Spartan ephors and *gerousia* were clear on this existential threat. Brasidas' bold practice of liberating loyal helots was an effective approach, but had a limited reach. This internal struggle was, perhaps, the primary motivation for the imperial visions of Lysander and Agesilaus. The only solutions to maintaining the Spartan social state, and therefore her vast empire, was to either loosen the standards for Spartiates or to rely more and more on non-citizen soldiers. Both options were deeply unappealing to the Spartan leadership, and they saw the only solution as leaning further into their hegemony over Greece – if Sparta could hold on to it.

Table 3.1. Spartan Oliganthropia

Year	Battle	Spartiate Population	Approx. Perioeci Population	Approx. Ratio of Spartiates to Perioeci
479	Plataea	5,000	5,000	1:1
425	Pylos	2,755	4,400[13]	5:8
418	Mantinea	2,100[14]	3,375	5:8
395	Sardis	~1,000	unknown	unknown
394	Nemea	1,800[15]	3,000	3:5
375	Tegyra	~700	unknown	unknown
371	Leuctra	Less than 1,000[16]	2,150	1:2

Note: This chart is an expansion of the excellent work of Thomas J. Figueira outlining Spartiate population decline.[17]

Sparta's Imperial Model

Sparta's 500-year dominance over Greece evaporated like water in the summer heat, but it was not sudden. By the dawn of the fourth century BC, Sparta had oppressed the Peloponnese for generations and all of Greece for a generation. Greeks had grown resentful.

The Spartans had held sway over Greece for three decades through the Peloponnesian League, but they technically could not claim the category of 'empire'. In its strict definition, an empire must dominate the domestic politics of their conquered and client states. Prior to the reign of Lysander, Sparta had relatively little interest in such policy and instead prioritized compliance and tribute. The Peloponnesian League did not micromanage the affairs of the Greek *poleis* in the way Athens' empire had, nor even to the extent of Persian foreign policy and their satrapy system. Instead, they preferred to maintain a military presence and a contribution to the Spartan hegemony via tribute and military aid. Sparta occupied conquered cities with military garrisons, sent ambassadors to broker alliances, and enforce treaties. For city-states within their hegemony, and often beyond, they also bolstered the local oligarchic factions. Athens and Corinth both experienced such treatment at the hands of Sparta in the period after the Peloponnesian War.

Sparta enforced its dominance with ruthless aggression. Any scent of rebellion had to be quelled, as were the helot rebellions of Messenia. Examples abound: the razing of Athens after the Peloponnesian War, the brutal dismantling of Elis which dared defy the Peloponnesian League in 400, or the trial against Plataean rebels in 427. Spartan hegemony demanded that any and all insurgency was immediately and utterly stamped out.

Frustratingly, Sparta was quite inconsistent in her treatment of client states, who found it very hard to predict when they would benefit from Sparta's hospitality or suffer under her boot. Spartans proclaimed themselves defenders of traditional Greek values, yet repeatedly allied with Persia against fellow Greeks when it suited their interests. They promised liberation for the Greeks of Asia Minor yet abandoned them to Persia. They declared liberty from Athenian tyranny as a justification for the Peloponnesian War, but after their victory installed oppressive regimes across the Aegean. Worst of all, Sparta celebrated autonomy for all Greek cities in the King's Peace, but defined autonomy in 'creative' ways, as they immediately set about breaking up rival symmachies such as the Boeotian Confederacy.

Despite disavowing democracy, Sparta maintained relationships with democracies when convenient – as was the case with Elis, until that state became troublesome and had to be put down. Spartan support often wavered, even with their interventionism. In both Corinth and Argos during the Corinthian War, Sparta encouraged and funded oligarchic factions, but provided inconsistent aid and selectively sent reports only when convenient to their own war effort. The result was a failed democracy in Argos and a bloodbath in Corinth in 392, when pro-Spartan oligarchs murdered a different group of pro-Spartan oligarchs. Sometimes, the Spartans even overthrew pro-Spartan oligarchies if they showed too much independence, as the citizens of Phlius discovered to their cost in the 380s.

While the divergent worldviews of foreign policy in Sparta had largely subsided, with Agesilaus and the imperial vision victorious, fissures remained and the ephors vacillated between differing governmental approaches to their subjects across the realm. Chaos tended to reign while both Sparta and their client states tried to discern precisely how Sparta wished to govern. As Paul Cartledge describes it, 'The Spartans…imposed autonomy as and where it suited them.'[18] This is well illustrated by their system of tribute. Unlike tribute to the Athenian or Persian empires, Sparta's tribute system bordered on improvisation, and Greece took notice. Sparta's hegemony also offered only unreliable protection; while city-states could see Athenian ships sailing in and out of their harbours to offer protection, they were forced to trust the Spartans based on the presence of a treaty and local garrisons. Few found comfort in those. Worse, Sparta's absence of a mercantile and trade system meant they could offer client states no materials or goods in return for the tribute. For city-states that had enjoyed access to the vast naval trade network of Athens or the fabled riches of Persia's Royal Road, Sparta's 'empire' returned paltry benefits. Spartan hoplites might protect them from invasion – if they deigned to appear – but they could not put food in bellies or silver in coffers.

Lysander's radical new model of harmosts and decarchies had been a brief foray into Athenian-style imperialism, and given time and a greater commitment by the ephors it might have persuaded the Aegean world that

Sparta could maintain her empire more consistently. But the course of the Corinthian War had convinced the ephors that their historic model was far preferable. Agesilaus' moves soon after the King's Peace of 387 clearly demonstrated that no more Lysandrean reforms would be coming to Spartan foreign policy. And Agesilaus had taught his traditionalist approach to his fellow king, the impressionable young Agesipolis who helmed the Agiad monarchy of Sparta.

Spartan dominion featured one more method of control worth analysing: the forced reorganization of conquered states. Provoked by the audacity of the anti-Spartan confederacy of the Corinthian War, Agesilaus and Agesipolis were out for blood – and unfortunately for Thebes, Corinth, and Athens, they had never been more empowered than after the King's Peace. Xenophon begins one chapter of his *Hellenica* with a vivid description of Sparta's thirst for vengeance:

> Indeed the late events had so entirely shaped themselves in conformity with the wishes of the [Spartans], that they determined to go a step farther and chastise those of their allies who either had borne hard on them during the war, or otherwise had shown themselves less favourable to Lacedaemon than to her enemies. Chastisement was not all; they must lay down such secure foundations for the future as should render the like disloyalty impossible again.[19]

The first on the list was Mantinea. In 385, just two years after the King's Peace, the Spartans determined to make an example out of the central Peloponnese city-state. It was an odd choice, but considering the dissolution of both the Boeotian Confederacy and the Argive-Corinthian union, Sparta had already relegated many other Greek states during the King's Peace – and were likely unwilling to take on the relative strength of Athens and the reemergence of naval power that would soon become the Second Athenian League. Since the end of the Corinthian War, Athenian ships had become increasingly prevalent across the Aegean, as she sought to remake her seafaring empire. Two years after that war Sparta was hesitant to take on Athens, but still decided that someone must be publicly disciplined in order to reinforce her dominance over Greece. Mantinea's cardinal sins lay in a minimal contribution to the Corinthian War effort and her routine trading with Argos. Sparta's ambassadors stated their true intentions, though, in a letter that revealed the insecurity of their regime. They wrote, 'But, more than that… we note the jealousy with which you eye any good fortune which may betide our state; the extravagant pleasure you exhibit at the sudden descent of some disaster.'[20]

It is likely that Mantinea was a symbolic choice. In 418, after an embarrassing display for Sparta in their loss at Pylos, the first battle of Mantinea had been a dramatic victory that reestablished the dominance of Spartan hoplites in the Peloponnesian War. It had been a turning point in the last phase of the war, and a tremendous morale boost for Sparta. Several decades later, upon the expiration of the treaty that followed that first battle of Mantinea, Sparta needed another victory of the sort to remove all doubt they now controlled the mainland of Greece. Curiously, Agesilaus argued against Mantinea as the example, pleading that they had been loyal allies to Sparta and, more importantly, his own father Archidamus. The stubborn ephors delegated command, therefore, to the other Spartan king Agesipolis who marched on Mantinea in the early fall of 385. Usually well out of campaign season, the fall was a strategic choice and Agesipolis deliberately waited until after the harvest. This might seem counterintuitive, considering the Mantineans would have ample food stores to survive a long siege by the Spartans. But Agesipolis was more concerned with the fall flood season. Instead of trying to starve the Mantineans through a traditional siege, he dammed the Ophis River that flowed through the city.

By stopping the flow of the river at the city walls, Agesipolis 'caused the water to rise above the basements of the private dwellings and the foundations of the fortification walls.'[21] The city walls soon began to crack and fold, and desperate attempts by the Mantineans to keep them upright found little success. Within days, Agesipolis had negotiated the surrender of Mantinea.

The siege of Mantinea was also significant for an unforeseen reason. The Spartans, often needing reinforcements due to the declining Spartiate population, had called for support from several subjugated states including Thebes. The Thebans, seeing few options in their current state, sent a contingent of soldiers that included two promising young commanders named Pelopidas and Epaminondas. Pelopidas came from a distinguished family, and was in appearance and ability the pinnacle of a Theban hero. Dashingly handsome, erudite and intelligent, cunning in battle, and wise beyond his years, Pelopidas was on his way to a legendary career. Epaminondas was cut from the same cloth, though from a less noble family. Both were also fiercely patriotic to Thebes, and it would have been painful for them to serve as lowly infantrymen in Sparta's army when they had formerly commanded armies for the Boeotian Confederacy. Despite their hatred for their Spartan overlords, Pelopidas and Epaminondas were men of integrity and followed the orders they received to support Sparta.

In one of the skirmishes at Mantinea, Pelopidas found himself wounded and at risk of his life. His colleague Epaminondas fought through the ranks of Mantineans to rescue him, and in so doing changed the fate of Greece (see figure 3.1).

> Pelopidas, after receiving seven wounds in front, sank down upon a great heap of friends and enemies who lay dead together; but Epaminondas, although he thought him lifeless, stood forth to defend his body and his arms, and fought desperately, single-handed against many, determined to die rather than leave Pelopidas lying there.[22]

Surprisingly, the two friends were in turn saved by the Spartan king Agesipolis. Had Agesipolis known what saving the two Theban commanders would mean for his beloved Sparta, surely he would have let them perish. Pelopidas and Epaminondas survived the battle and, within a decade, would be directly responsible for the rapid ascension of Thebes and the destruction of Sparta. We will return to their narrative shortly.

For now, Sparta was victorious and exercised her new favourite imperial practice of reorganizing the conquered city-states. The ephors now did with the Mantineans as they had done with the Boeotians, the Argives, and the Corinthians – the state was divided into four local villages, each with its own autonomous government.[23] The citizens were even required to demolish their own homes and rebuild them in their new village. It was a radical reforming of the entire *polis*. Sparta symbolically sent an ambassador for each of the four villages, showing that they formally considered each a new city-state and the former *polis* of Mantinea was now a thing of the past. This Mantinean adventure demonstrates how Sparta had redefined Greek

EPAMINONDAS SAVES PELOPIDAS' LIFE IN BATTLE.

autonomy in the wake of the King's Peace. While the treaty celebrated the independence of the local city-state, in reality Sparta was taking great liberties with the actual words: 'the rest of the Hellenic cities he thinks it just to leave independent, both small and great.'[24] Sparta now thought that the best way to champion the autonomy of Greek city-states was to make sure they fit the 'small' category rather than the 'great' – even if it meant making that city-state smaller by force.

The Spartan Conquest of Thebes

Since the King's Peace of 387, Thebes had been in turmoil. Like Corinth and so many other Greek city-states before, the city was rotting due to its factionalism between those yearning for oligarchy and those fighting for the rights of the lower classes. This civil conflict was part of what the Greeks knew as *stasis*, and nearly every major Greek city-state suffered from it at some point in the classical era. In Thebes, the *stasis* centred on the city's role in the Boeotian Confederacy and, of course, how they should adapt to the hegemony of Sparta. The Theban oligarchs were pro-Spartan, while the democrats, led by Ismenias, championed independence from Sparta and a historic Theban role as leaders of Boeotia. The Thebes of 382, however, had a feckless democratic faction and had made virtually no progress in achieving autonomy from Sparta's empire. The oligarchs sensed they could bring an end to the *stasis* in short order, and were vigilant for an opportunity to formally align Thebes, and Boeotia at large, with Sparta.

Two years after Mantinea, the Spartans set about subduing other city-states far away from the Peloponnesian League, starting with Olynthus in Chaledice in northern Greece. Another symbolic example, both of the length of Sparta's reach and a harkening back to the Peloponnesian War with a parallel to the nearby battle of Potidaea, Olynthus might seem to have been an unusual choice. However, it was already the headquarters of another regional symmachy that threatened Spartan power. The Chalcidian League had been formed around 430, late in the Peloponnesian War, and was still expanding across northern Greece. They were now absorbing smaller cities and seizing most of Macedonia, ousting the king Amyntas III. Amyntas, along with the smaller cities of Akanthos and Apollonia, pleaded for Sparta to intervene and restore their territories. Sparta cared little for the petty squabbles of northern Greece, but would not abide the rise of another confederacy that might eventually challenge their hegemony. They marched on Olynthus in 382. The Spartan ephors had determined to dismember the Chalcidian League as they had the Boeotian Confederacy, the Delian League, and so many other Greek alliances.

The ephors gave the command to one Eudamidas, who was given a unit of 2,000 *neodamodes*, *perioeci*, and skirmishers.[25] In a notable example of Spartan *oliganthropia*, no Spartiates were sent. Perhaps because of the absence of these Spartiates, Eudamidas struck a deal with the ephors that his brother, Phoebidas, would bring reinforcements several weeks later, once his vanguard had begun the campaign. The road from Sparta to Olynthus snaked through the great crossroads of central Greece and the Spartan soldiers journeyed past Thebes on their trip north. Phoebidas led the hoplite reinforcements past the Theban walls, and opted to make camp not far from the city, near its gymnasium. Phoebidas surely intended to give a show of strength, but during his posturing the pro-Spartan oligarchs in Thebes called for a summit.

Since the King's Peace, the relationship between the Thebans and the Spartans had not changed substantially. Thebes despised Sparta for breaking apart the Boeotian Confederacy, and for specifying that Thebes could not maintain authority over Boeotia. But Sparta had subsequently appeared to move on from singling out Thebes, even if Agesilaus' personal feelings had not abated. The Thebans had contributed military aid during the past five years, and had adequately appeased their Spartan overlords by not attempting to reassert themselves over their Boeotian neighbours. In 382, by every measurable standard Sparta had no particular concerns about Thebes other than a general suspicion that she might one day seek to remake the Boeotian Confederacy. Plutarch claims that the Spartans 'ostensibly treated the Thebans as friends and allies, but they really looked with suspicion on the ambitious spirit and the power of the city.'[26] The Spartans hated the democratic faction of Thebes, but not so much that they planned to intervene more in Boeotian politics.

This is why, when the Spartan general Phoebidas diverted his army's march through Boeotia and attacked Thebes, the Greek world – and even Sparta's own government – was completely blindsided. Phoebidas' summit with the pro-Spartan oligarchic faction of Thebes had not gone as the Spartan had expected. That faction's leader, Leontiades, was locked in a bitter rivalry with the democratic leader Ismenias over the future of a city that no longer led the Boeotian Confederacy. Rudderless without dominance over their Boeotian allies, the *stasis* of Thebes depended upon how they decided to define themselves politically. For a half decade now, neither democrats nor oligarchs had found any success. Leontiades felt this held Thebes back, limiting the opportunities for the city to make a bid for a greater slice of Greece's resources. He therefore seized the rare moment when a unit of Spartan hoplites could directly intervene. Leontiades approached the Spartan commander, offering Theban aid in the Olynthian War and, of course, eternal glory for the name Phoebidas – he would be the first Spartan to conquer the mighty Thebes.

Phoebidas, of course, had not planned to incidentally conquer a major Spartan rival on his way to Olynthus. The ephors had not been consulted, an invading *mora* (army of invasion) not assembled, and no religious sacrifices had been made. The Spartan assault on Thebes in 382 was, according to the majority of ancient sources, an entirely unplanned endeavour.[27] Tempted by the chance for glory, however, Phoebidas agreed to march on the Cadmea and take Thebes in the name of Sparta's empire. The trouble with Phoebidas singularly remaking Spartan imperial policymaking was that he, to put it charitably, lacked a strategic mind. Xenophon concurs with this assessment, remarking that, 'To do a brilliant deed was far dearer to [Phoebidas] than life; on the other hand, he had no reasoning capacity, and would seem to have been deficient altogether in sound sense.'[28] Nevertheless, with the aid of Leontiades, he pretended to break camp and continue the trek north to Olynthus, but instead headed straight to the Theban citadel on the Cadmea.

The Theban senate – and its armed guard – was meeting at that moment, but not in the usual meeting place on the Cadmea. Thebes, like much of Greece, was in the midst of celebrating Thesmophoria, a fertility festival in honour of the goddess Demeter. For the several days of festivities, the usual government buildings on the Cadmea were occupied not with bureaucrats and hoplites, but with women and priestesses. Moreover, it was a suffocatingly hot summer day, and most citizens had remained indoors trying to keep cool. Hardly a soul was in the streets as the Spartan hoplites climbed the Cadmea. It was a cunning move by Leontiades, who surely knew that such an opportunity was rare. The Spartan hoplites faced almost no resistance. They took Thebes so quickly and efficiently, that even the Thebans did not notice. It took Leontiades, mounted on horseback, to issue a surprise decree to the Theban senators:

Sirs, the Lacedaemonians are in possession of the citadel; but that is no cause for despondency, since, as they assure us, they have no hostile intention, except, indeed, towards any one who has an appetite for war. For myself, and acting in obedience to the law, which empowers the polemarch to apprehend all persons suspected of capital crimes, I hereby seize the person of Ismenias as an arch-fomenter of war. I call upon you, sirs, who are captains of companies, and you who are ranked with them, to do your duty. Arise and secure the prisoner [Ismenias], and lead him away to the place appointed.[29]

Thus Ismenias was arrested and the Theban federal government was dissolved. Thebes adopted the oligarchy that Sparta was fond of assigning to its client states. About 300 democrats from the party of Ismenias fled in exile to Athens, where they would await a chance to retake their city. In a matter of minutes, Sparta had taken Thebes, installed a pro-Spartan oligarchy led by Leontiades, secured reinforcements to win the Olynthian War, and eliminated one of their most powerful rivals. The Spartan hoplites made a garrison in the Cadmea, occupying Thebes as a conquering army, not merely as hegemon over it. The next item on the agenda was for the Spartan ephors to be told this shocking move had actually happened.

Leontiades himself journeyed to Sparta to persuade the Spartan ephors of the wisdom of this manoeuvre. He gave a pathetic justification, that forfeiting all Theban autonomy would mean Thebes was no longer a threat and would henceforth yield to Sparta. He is quoted by Xenophon as saying: 'You need fear Thebes no longer. One brief dispatch in cipher will suffice to procure a dutiful subservience to your every wish in that quarter, provided only you will take as kindly an interest in us as we in you.'[30]

Nevertheless, Sparta was horrified at the conquest of Thebes and occupation of the Cadmea, as was Greece at large. It shattered all diplomatic norms. Thebes had not rebelled or antagonized Sparta since the King's Peace, but had instead dutifully met all requirements of the Spartan empire. Surviving under Sparta's hegemony had always been unpredictable, but the fact that a major city-state could be completely wiped out almost on a whim was a line that had not been crossed in recent memory. It was a thoroughly embarrassing incident that threatened to cancel out Thebes as a major player in Greek politics. Plutarchy aptly summarised the response of the wider Greek world to Sparta's conquest of Thebes: '[It was a] foul deed of seizing the Cadmea in a time of perfect peace, and all the Greeks were indignant and the Spartans displeased at the act.'[31]

There was one voice applauding the actions of Phoebidas and the downfall of Thebes. King Agesilaus had to conceal his joy at the sufferings of Thebans. His hatred of Thebes had still not subsided – a demonstration of how great men often refuse to tolerate the smallest of slights. Agesilaus not only counselled Leontiades before his speech to the ephors, but also publicly supported the occupation of the Cadmea. To the Spartan assembly, Agesilaus said that Phoebidas' actions should be judged by the only rubric that mattered: whether they benefited Sparta. In a short speech he argued that if it had diminished Sparta's standing the move would have deserved condemnation – but it had not. Agesilaus put it simply, 'the sole point you have to look to… is whether what has been done is good or evil [for Sparta].'[32]

Every ancient historian from Plutarch to Xenophon to Diodorus agrees that this stunning move was met with horror and displeasure across Greece, and even within Sparta. Greece had understood the heavy-handed deconstruction of Athens after the Peloponnesian War, but Thebes was no parallel. This was not enough for Sparta to reverse their actions, however. The ephors may have been horrified, but Phoebidas had undeniably strengthened Sparta's military position by eliminating a major rival. Sparta determined that, despite the offences of destroying a neutral and autonomous city-state during a time of peace that should have been under their protection, it was easier for them to move forward with military occupation of Thebes to ensure the city's response would not risk the hegemony's stability. Spartan hoplites occupied the Cadmea for the next three years. It was the only full-scale military occupation that Sparta had executed since the occupation of Athens. The Thebans were irate, even those who had supported the oligarchic party. But they also knew that as things stood they lacked the firepower and political unity to overcome the Spartan garrison on the Cadmea.

Phoebidas was given a hefty fine, and his reputation tarnished for the rest of his career, but suffered no other punishments. That, alone, was a message that the rest of Sparta's empire understood. There would be no repercussions for Spartan malfeasance. And, despite claims for her to honour the promises of autonomy given in the King's Peace, Sparta would act as she saw fit, while her Greek underlings would be at the mercy of this unpredictable and disorderly regime. Things were made worse by the fact that Sparta installed a Lysandrean-style harmost in Thebes. This was not unusual in itself, but they empowered the harmost to govern all of Boeotia, not just the city of Thebes. Sparta – who had been so insistent about breaking apart the Boeotian Confederacy in protest at Theban claims over Boeotia – now reversed her position and agreed that Thebes was in fact in charge of Boeotia. But only, of course, when Sparta directly benefited from it.

Among those Thebans exiled to Athens was the young commander Pelopidas, who was a staunch supporter of Ismenias and the democratic party. Along with 300 allies, the Thebans had no choice but to plot for a hopeful return to their city where they could overthrow not only the Spartan conquerors but also the traitorous oligarchical faction who had sold out their home. The other young Theban statesman, Epaminondas, remained behind in Thebes, vowing to fight the puppet government of Sparta and prepare for the inevitable moment of weakness on the part of the Spartans.

In 382, Sparta was at the apex of her power. Ruling by brute force across the entire Greek world, they now controlled the very definition of a Greek city-state and reshaped entire *poleis* at their whim. Agesilaus, though no longer the dominant politician in Sparta, had achieved his imperial vision and established a Peloponnesian League that stretched across all Greece – despite the painful absence of Persia. The intra-Spartan squabbling over imperialism was at last settled, with Agesilaus' vision of a traditionalist Spartan hegemony fused with Lysander's Athenian-style empire. Sparta was alone in celebrating this, however. The rest of Greece felt as though they were now helots in Messenia. At the heart of the matter was Sparta's betrayal of her earlier commitment to Greek autonomy. Despite waxing eloquent about their adherence to the promises made to all Greek city-states in the King's Peace, the Spartans had once again returned to the domineering ways that had caused the Corinthian War. A Spartan empire would never achieve stability or predictability, and therefore could not govern effectively.

Pelopidas and Epaminondas, however, were determined that this centuries-old cycle had to end once and for all. The Spartans had trampled on the Greek notion of autonomy enough. While Sparta held the Cadmea now, in just three years Thebes would field a massive, innovative army that would liberate Thebes and then directly challenge not only Sparta's empire, but her very existence.

Chapter 4

The Saviours of Thebes: Pelopidas and Epaminondas

Pelopidas and Epaminondas: Warrior-Statesmen

Ancient Theban history was rich in mythological heroes like Cadmus, Heracles, and Oedipus. The Thebes of the fourth century BC had not one but two men who were cut from the same cloth. When reading the ancient historians, it is hard to avoid the impression that Pelopidas and Epaminondas were the pinnacle of Theban culture and virtue, who were directly responsible for the rise of the Theban hegemony and for shattering the power of Sparta, not just in Boeotia but across Greece. Surely the sources exaggerate generously at times, but it is clear that these two men rank easily among the most formative and successful figures of classical history. Plutarch dedicated two full chapters of his *Parallel Lives* to the men, though his *Life of Epaminondas* has been lost to the sands of time. In the *Life of Pelopidas*, Plutarch – himself a Boeotian – summarises the importance of these two Thebans:

> And the true reason for the superiority of the Thebans was their virtue, which led them not to aim in their actions at glory or wealth, which are naturally attended by bitter envying and strife; on the contrary, they were both filled from the beginning with a divine desire to see their country become most powerful and glorious in their day and by their efforts, and to this end they treated one another's successes as their own.[1]

Both were born around 420, and raised in a Thebes that had been neutered of her prestige and influence over the Boeotian Confederacy. Though they were from the aristocratic class, they grew to adulthood in the shadow of Thebes' secondary role in the Peloponnesian War, followed by her failed attempt to topple Sparta in the Corinthian War. By 386, both had been conscripted into reinforcement roles in Sparta's army while commanding their own units.

During the siege of Mantinea, in 385, both fought for the Spartans and nearly died. As we previously saw, Pelopidas was rescued by Epaminondas – himself twice wounded – and both fought valiantly until the Spartan king Agesipolis himself had to save them. The action was dripping with gallantry and courage, but also was entirely unnecessary. The Thebans surely were not needed to support Sparta's army against the Mantineans, but as vassals of Sparta they had no choice. And, of course, their efforts for the Spartan cause would go unrewarded as the Cadmea was soon to be occupied by Spartan hoplites. That moment at the siege of Mantinea, however, crystallized the relationship between Pelopidas and Epaminondas. The two would go from that moment to form a bond deeper than friendship. The Greeks termed such a relationship *philoi*, a profound bond between companions based on reciprocity and shared social and personal obligations. Ancient Greek *philoi* transcended modern friendship, with a basis in support and fidelity. The friends were expected to help each other in everything from finances to political support to military aid. Greek legal codes counted *philoi* as reliable witnesses and often forbade one to testify against the other. Their fates and their identities were tied together.

Pelopidas and Epaminondas were certainly *philoi*, if not something more. Their friendship involved all the hallmarks of this deep companionship, and given their high-ranking positions in Thebes they were mutually concerned in their many social, cultural, and political obligations. Tracing their narratives will help us to understand their pivotal role in remaking Thebes into the new Greek superpower of the early fourth century.

Pelopidas

Perhaps no man better represented the moral and intellectual virtues of a Theban citizen more than Pelopidas. The ancients write of him as though he were the distillation of Boeotia's culture and identity into a single man and often rank him among the greatest of the Greek heroes. Plutarch, a Boeotian himself, was perhaps the biggest advocate of Pelopidas as a hero straight from the tales of Homer. He dedicated one of the biographies in his

Parallel Lives to Pelopidas, comparing him to the Roman general Marcellus, hero of the Second Punic War and rival to Hannibal.

The Roman historian Cornelius Nepos struggled to find the words to describe Pelopidas:

> I am in doubt how to give an account of his merits; for I fear that if I undertake to tell of his deeds, I shall seem to be writing a history rather than a biography; but if I merely touch upon the high points, I am afraid that to those unfamiliar with Greek literature it will not be perfectly clear how great a man he was.[2]

Pelopidas did not avoid all criticism though. Discussing the great commander in contrast to Marcellus, Plutarch remarks how men such as he 'were careless of their own lives, and recklessly threw them away at times when it was most important that such men should live and hold command.'[3] His worst sin may have been dying when Greece needed him most, but Pelopidas had accomplished much by the time of his death. He was born in Thebes some time around 420. He was the son of an aristocrat named Hippoclus but was orphaned at a young age, probably his early teens. Pelopidas inherited great wealth and never wanted for anything. He hardly even wanted his own money, apparently, being prone to philanthropy, out of both service to his fellow Thebans and a commitment to virtue – he gave away most of his estate to the underprivileged in Boeotia.

Pelopidas was concerned about the impact of his inherited wealth on his soul and repeatedly gave away his money. He was determined to be the master of his wealth, lest it should become his master.[4] He even convinced many fellow aristocrats in Thebes to donate to the less fortunate. In one memorable tale, Pelopidas' friends chastised him for his generous nature and reminded him that money was, in fact, a necessary thing. Pelopidas shot back a quip worthy of the Spartan laconic tradition: 'Yes indeed, necessary for Nicodemus here' – pointing to a beggar close by.[5] Still, he was not exclusively concerned with benevolence, his true motivation included a healthy care for his own reputation. Plutarch remarks how he was often 'ashamed to let men think that he spent more upon his person than the poorest Theban.'[6]

While his lifelong friend Epaminondas took a shine to philosophy and the life of the mind, Pelopidas was reported to have primarily focused on physical training. A natural athlete, he trained in the gymnasium daily and prepared for combat. This is not to say that Pelopidas avoided intellectual or academic rigour – his later career as a statesman clearly showed impressive skills in rhetoric, logic, and eloquence. Pelopidas' education was likely in the tradition of Greek *paideia*, bringing up young people with the aim of preparing them to be citizens, first and foremost, who contribute to the political and cultural life of the state. The Greeks aimed to form the minds of their students so that they would in turn promote virtue and excellence in their community and help their *polis* flourish.

The Thebes that Pelopidas grew up in, though, was far from flourishing. It was also a far cry from the city-state that had once been a prosperous champion of the Boeotian Confederacy and ruled over all of central Greece. Pelopidas' formative years would have been during the final decade of the 400s, at the very tail end of the Peloponnesian War. During his teens, Pelopidas watched the Spartans finally defeat Athens and he may have been among the many Thebans calling for that city to be outright destroyed, the common sentiment across Greece in 404. If so, he would have been most disappointed when Lysander opted instead to install the Thirty Tyrants to dismantle the last vestiges of democracy.

During his twenties, Pelopidas was among the Theban patriots who rebelled against Sparta's oppressive regime and he served as a hoplite in the Theban phalanxes of the Corinthian War. Although his exploits during these years are no longer in the historical record, Pelopidas would most likely have gained substantial command experience at the battles of Nemea or Coronea. Thebes, though, would retreat back to Boeotia each time – once again sidelined from the main action of Greece.

All the ancient sources present Pelopidas as fiercely patriotic and unwavering in his passion for Thebes – often at the cost of all his personal interests or relationships. Plutarch emphasizes that 'he neglected his private interests to devote his whole time to the state,'[7] explaining why he never married. Pelopidas was married to the state of Thebes and the notion of restoring her glory at the top of the Boeotian Confederacy. And this is why, in 382, when Phoebidas and the Spartans conquered Thebes and occupied the Cadmea, Pelopidas emerged as the face of Theban resistance. Pelopidas was the youngest of the Thebans to be exiled to Athens. Accompanying him were 300 others who detested the Spartan occupation of Thebes and would work tirelessly to find a way to liberate their city. Among the exiles were two significant names: Gorgidas and Melon. Gorgidas was an adept military commander who would soon become known as the founder of the Sacred Band of Thebes. Melon, meanwhile, was a skilled statesman who happened to be very close friends with a man named Phillidas – by 379, three years into the Spartan occupation of Thebes, Phillidas was a double agent working as the chief assistant to a Spartan general in the city. The beginning of a coup to retake Thebes was forming.

Epaminondas

Back in Thebes, Epaminondas was laying the foundation for a rebellion. But to truly understand his key role in retaking Thebes from Sparta, Epaminondas' backstory is essential, as he blazed a trail no less impressive than his blood brother Pelopidas. Epaminondas was born in Thebes some time between 420 and 410. Although not in quite as grand a social class as Pelopidas, he was nevertheless a bonafide member of the Theban aristocracy. Epaminondas' ancestry was said to trace back to the very first Theban aristocrats – the Spartoi warriors whose seeds had been planted by Cadmus himself.

Despite such an honourable lineage, Epaminondas had little wealth. Plutarch remarked that 'poverty was hereditary and familiar'[8] to Epaminondas, unlike his wealthier friend Pelopidas. For Epaminondas, riches came instead from the proper formation of his mind and body – a true Greek *paideia*. In the Theban tradition, Epaminondas was trained in everything from athletics to theatre, from rhetoric to philosophy. The philosophy of Pythagoreanism was particularly transformative for the young man. The mathematician and philosopher Pythagoras (mostly nowadays known for his mathematical theorem) founded the school of thought in the sixth century BC in Italy. By the fourth century, Pythagoreanism was among the most popular religions in Greece; it fused philosophy, science, maths, and religion into a syncretic faith whose followers worshipped the Pythian Apollo as often as they deciphered mathematical calculations. It was a curious balance of mathematics and mysticism and it quickly captured the hearts of many Greeks. At its core, Pythagoreanism promotes balance, teaching that the universe operates according to principles of harmony and proportion and that all truth can be expressed mathematically. In practice, this means that the human soul could migrate into other living beings after death, and therefore we should purify our souls in preparation. A strict diet, an unwavering moral code, and more rigorous practices created a byzantine system of laws to debate and to navigate. For Epaminondas, this simplified matters: if he could master his own body and find order in the chaos of the universe, then he could also master the chaos of Greek politics and diplomacy. Pythagorean political philosophy espoused aristocracy – perhaps advocating for those who were enlightened by Pythagoreanism – which certainly shaped Epaminondas' political vision for Thebes.

For noblemen like Epaminondas and others who could afford it, the Greek model of education in the fifth and fourth centuries was tutoring by a private teacher. The teachers, known as sophists, taught rhetoric, logic, music, astronomy, mathematics, poetry and, above all, the pursuit of *arete* – virtue or excellence of all kinds. Epaminondas' tutor was Lysis of Tarentum. A wizened old man, revered for his expertise on Pythagoreanism and its philosophy of harmony, Lysis was the author of multiple influential books including (according to at least one major historian) *The Golden Verses*, a text of 71 moral exhortations, so essential to Pythagoreanism that we might proclaim it the Pythagorean creed.

By the 390s, Thebes had become a refuge for many philosophers. Though not as famous for its intellectual and philosophical contributions as its Athenian neighbours, the Thebans had a great many influential philosophers and sophists, and offered relative safety in the Greek world during the Peloponnesian and Corinthian Wars. Lysis had survived a purge of Pythagoreans in southern Italy and fled to Thebes, where he now made his living teaching the children of the aristocracy and happily accepted their silver. Lysis himself had been the student of a Theban philosopher named Philolaus, a man so prestigious in classical Greek philosophy he resembles a Theban Socrates. Philolaus was an influential leader of the Pythagorean movement and often ranked among the most formative Pythagoreans – alongside Pythagoras himself. His key legacy was in astronomy, where he was possibly the first Greek to argue for heliocentrism, the idea that the sun (or at least a body which he called 'The Great Fire') and not the earth was at the centre of the cosmos, and that everything else rotated around it. What's more, in later life Philolaus was a contemporary and colleague of Plato, and is recorded by Diogenes Laertius as the author of a major text, now lost to time, that Plato himself bought and read on a journey to Sicily.

Other major Theban philosophers of the 390s included Simmias and Cebes, who were two of the interlocutors in Plato's dialogue *Phaedo*. Known to the ancients as *On the Soul*, this Platonic dialogue in which Simmias, Cebes, and others debate with Socrates himself, explored the nature and immortality of the human soul. Of particular interest might be the dialogue's setting in Socrates' prison cell, the day before he is to die for his crimes of corruption of Athenian youth and atheism. Despite being overshadowed, the inclusion of these Theban philosophers indicates that the Thebes of the 390s was by no means lacking in intellectual and philosophical firepower. Their main challenge was marketing – nearly all of the surviving historical sources on history, literature, and philosophy come from Athenian authors.

Keenly aware of Thebes' fertile academic soil, Epaminondas was determined to not waste the opportunity to learn from a sage like Lysis of Tarentum. Epaminondas' father allowed Lysis to live in the family home while tutoring the adolescent boy, who took full advantage of his tutor. The Roman biographer Cornelius Nepos wrote:

> [Epaminondas] was so attached that in his youth he was more intimate with that grave and austere old man than with any of the young people of his own age; and he would not allow his teacher to leave him until he so far surpassed his fellow students in learning, that it could readily be understood that in a similar way he would surpass all men in all other accomplishments.[9]

Epaminondas, of course, was also trained in the physical and warrior arts of ancient Greece. Proper training of the body in the gymnasium was just as essential as proper cultivation of the mind for a Greek *paideia*. Epaminondas apparently favoured not brute strength but agility in combat. Nepos wrote how the young man considered 'the former… necessary for athletes, but that the latter would be helpful in warfare.'[10] It was a strong sign of his future interest in unorthodox and unpredictable military strategy.

By his early adulthood, Epaminondas was regarded as a paragon of virtue and character in Thebes. He was the embodiment of *paideia*, combining physical beauty with virtue and eloquence. Many ancient historians extol his qualities at length:

> [He was] temperate, prudent, serious, and skilful in taking advantage of opportunities; practised in war, of great personal courage and of high spirit; such a lover of the truth that he never lied even in jest … he was self-controlled, kindly, and forbearing to a surprising degree, putting up with wrongs, not only from the people, but even from his friends; he was most particular in keeping secrets, a quality which is sometimes no less valuable than eloquence, and he was a good listener.[11]

As with Pelopidas, admiring anecdotes about Epaminondas abound. In one story, he rebuffs a bribery attempt from the Persian ambassador, choosing Thebes over his own fortunes.[12] In another, his charity to those in need was so substantial that even his own friends could not tell the difference between his possessions and theirs, since he gave away so much of his wealth and property. He was known to never conclude a theological or philosophical discussion, ensuring he always stayed to the end of the dialogue to maximize his learning.

Of course, not all historians agreed. Xenophon harboured not only a deep preference for his Spartan patrons, but also a dislike for Thebes and its leaders. In fact, Epaminondas and Pelopidas, as influential as they were in the early fourth century of Greece, are suspiciously absent from his history. They are missing almost entirely from a painfully brief narrative of the liberation of Thebes in 379 in Xenophon's *Hellenica*, the landmark history of the era. And sadly, Plutarch's biography of Epaminondas is one of the few *Parallel Lives* lost to time. While we have some references and quotes, the full manuscript has not survived.

Unlike his friend Pelopidas, Epaminondas eschewed marriage and a family life. He was instead singularly focused on public service, his true passion, and on military duty. Keen to deploy his Pythagorean-inspired eloquence, Epaminondas soon became Thebes' leading orator. In Athens, many famous orators dotted the fourth century including Demosthenes, Isocrates, and Lysias. Thebes had its share of orators, but only a limited reputation for the classical virtue of rhetoric. Cornelius Nepos shared the common perspective on Theban oratory: 'for [the population of Thebes] possesses more bodily strength than mental ability.'[13] But Epaminondas was among the precious few, in Athens or in Thebes, who matched his martial skills with excellence in oratory.

Despite his commitments to the life of the mind, he was even more pledged to military prowess. Epaminondas most likely began his illustrious military career during the Corinthian War in 395. At this time, he would have been around 20 years old and possibly given a minor command due to his aristocratic heritage. Little information is available on his early exploits for the Theban army, but it is clear that he was highly successful and distinguished himself with skill and valour. Epaminondas served first against the Spartans in the Corinthian War, and then under their command in the various lesser conflicts following it, as the Spartans sought to quell uprisings from their subjects. The first narrative of Epaminondas in combat takes place at the siege of Mantinea, where he famously rescued his ally and friend Pelopidas.

In warfare, Epaminondas would soon earn a reputation for strategic thinking and cunning tactics, as he put the full weight of his Pythagorean-honed intelligence into action. He was not bound to the rigid traditionalism of Greek warfare and tactics. Heavy-armoured hoplites fighting in slow-moving phalanxes had won the Persian and Peloponnesian Wars, but Epaminondas was enraptured by the innovations of the Athenian general Iphicrates and his use of light infantry and skirmishers. At the battle of Lechaeum outside Corinth, in the latter years of the Corinthian War, Iphicrates deployed an unpredictable style of combat predicated on the use of *peltasts* – light infantrymen with small shields and shorter spears to be thrown at the enemy. The peltasts of Athens had a host of new techniques and equipment, including smaller shields, lighter armour, and lightweight boots. The advantage was, above all else, speed. The Athenian peltasts attacked quickly, confusing the Spartan enemies who managed to do little else but lumber around in clumsy pursuit of them. The Athenians destroyed a full *mora* of Spartan hoplites, and their success began a slow and steady transformation of Greek warfare that would eventually climax with the massive reforms of Philip II of Macedon and the Macedonian empire that Alexander the Great would inherit.

Epaminondas knew that if Thebes were to survive the challenges of the fourth century, he would need to lead its army. While Iphicrates was technically a rival from Athens, Epaminondas nevertheless took good notice of his ability to destroy an entire Spartan *mora* in one fell swoop. Epaminondas began to implement similar reforms in the Theban army, along with a number of his own new strategies. He never once lost sight of the critical nature of military innovation to Thebes' survival, and considered it his primary mission. Once, when challenged by a political rival who claimed Epaminondas' reputation was due to his skills at warfare rather than politics, he issued a devastating retort:

> You are deceiving your fellow-citizens by using the wrong word, when you dissuade them from war; for under the name of peace it is slavery that you are recommending. As a matter of fact, peace is won by war; hence those who wish to enjoy it for a long time ought to be trained for war. Therefore if you wish to be the leading city of Greece, you must frequent the camp and not the gymnasium.[14]

The apparently charmed life of Epaminondas came to an abrupt halt when the Spartans conquered Thebes in 382. The treacherous acts of Phoebidas in the seizing of the Cadmea transformed the city overnight, hollowing out the social class structure as all those who had dared to publicly oppose Sparta over the years left for exile in Athens. In the newly occupied Thebes, Epaminondas suddenly became its foremost citizen. He was not considered a threat by the pro-Spartan government, possibly because he was careful to give every outward sign that he held no political ambitions and they believed him to be focused on philosophy. They were, however, sorely mistaken. During this period, Epaminondas worked tirelessly to inspire younger Thebans with patriotic values and prepare them for the coming rebellion. Plutarch notes how Epaminondas spent three full years instructing youngsters in the ethos and virtues of proper Theban citizenship.[15] But mere allegiance to the cause would not be sufficient to win the city its liberty, and Epaminondas knew it, so he also trained the youth of Thebes in combat. He made a habit of spending time at the gymnasiums of the city, pushing the young men to their limits in wrestling and martial skills. Knowing they had to stand against the Spartans as well as succeed in their own training in the *agoge*, Epaminondas pulled no punches. He challenged them at every occasion, proclaiming 'their cowardice made them the slaves of the men whom they so far surpassed in bodily powers.'[16]

And so Epaminondas continued in Thebes, corresponding covertly with Pelopidas and the Theban rebels dwelling in Athens. From the moment the Cadmea was captured by the Spartans, the Thebans began plotting to retake their beloved capital. Three years of networking, preparing, planning, bribing, training, spying, and praying would soon come to a climax.

Athens in 382 BC

The Theban patriots exiled to Athens in 382 found a city that was at a turning point in its legendary history. At the same time the Thebans found there unlikely friends for their cause – largely due to the fact that Athens had experienced a similar situation just two decades earlier. In 404, after Sparta conquered Athens at the conclusion of the Peloponnesian War, many Athenian democrats went in exile to Thebes. Thebes hosted them, offering limited support more out of a distaste for Sparta than an enthusiasm for Athens. Eventually, these Athenian exiles retook their city and overthrew the oligarchs, restoring their traditional form of government. By 382, the roles had been reversed and it was Theban exiles fleeing Spartan oppression who sought safe harbour in Athens. Pelopidas and the Thebans yearned for a similarly successful outcome in retaking their city following the years of exile.

The democracy of Athens had already endured several evolutionary cycles despite being little more than a century old. Different democratic forms had been instituted and had flourished, only to be subsequently subverted. Beginning with the proto-democracy of Solon, Athenians had already experienced multiple manifestations typically driven by powerful politicians and military threats: the attempt to diffuse political power across social classes in the reforms of Cleisthenes, the early populism of Themistocles following the Persian Wars, the hegemonic years of Pericles, the oligarchy of the Thirty Tyrants following Sparta's conquest of Athens in 404, and most recently the reemergence of Athenian democracy and her naval empire under the leadership of Thrasybulus.

Thrasybulus was the latest and greatest Athenian democrat. Just as the Thebans now aspired to do, he had ousted the occupying Spartans in 403 and, slowly over the next decades, remade Athens into something that now came close to her former glory. It had not been easy, however. Thrasybulus and his fellow rebels, dubbed the Phyle rebels after the first location they reconquered from Sparta, inherited an Athens that no longer had a true harbour at Piraeus – the Spartans had burned it – had no city walls, almost no triremes, and possessed very few colonies or even allies across the Aegean islands. Since the days of Themistocles in the 470s, the heart of Athens' strength had been naval power. What originally had been a scheme to defend against the Persian invaders had morphed into an outright thalassocracy. The pinnacle of Athenian naval supremacy came with the Delian League, a symmachy founded on the island of Delos in 478. The Delian League's stated purpose was to eliminate Persian presence in the Greek world by pooling resources among the Greek city-states, reconquering all Persian-held territory, and then sharing the bounty at a treasury, headquartered on Delos. The league's actions would be determined via democratic means and power decentralized.

Of course, within a few years Athens realized that her ships vastly outnumbered the rest of the league combined. Not long after its formation, the Delian League became little more than a formality and was functionally replaced by the Athenian Empire. Athens administered the Delian League as if it were the city's personal piggy bank, raiding the funds to pay for grand building projects in Athens such as the Parthenon. In 454, the treasury of the Delian League was simply moved to Athens, acknowledging what had already been the case for decades. Athens ruled the Aegean with an iron fist, 'liberating' Persian-held cities only to force democracy and Athenian-style rule on them. Athenian leadership over the Delian League matched Sparta's ruthless grip on the Peloponnesian League. City-states were strictly monitored and rebellion was not tolerated. Islands like Thasos and Naxos tasted harsh retribution for daring to push back. The island of Melos and the city of Mytilene experienced particularly severe treatment under the guise of democracy. The Athenian voting assemblies debated destroying each of them and voted in favour – an example of the brutal nature of their democratic system. All city-states in the Delian League were forced to pay a heavy tax, contribute ships to the Athenian fleet, forfeit their legal cases to Athenian courts, and install democracies.

The Delian League's territories stretched from Thrace to the Cycladic Islands, the entire coast of Asia Minor, all the way up to Byzantium and the Black Sea. No city-states in either Boeotia or the Peloponnese joined the Delian League. As a result, power across Greece was largely shared between the Delian League, the Peloponnesian League, and – in distant third place – the Boeotian Confederacy.

By the Athenian Empire's destruction in 404, Greece had certainly had enough of Athenian imperialism, which is why the resurgence of Athens' naval empire three decades later is a shock. The full re-emergence of Athenian naval power took place in the early 380s, but the roots of its revival stretch back to before the end of the Peloponnesian War. After the Athenian disaster at Sicily, when they lost most of their legendary navy, Athens floundered in its war against Sparta. The Athenian admiral Thrasybulus, however, laboured tirelessly to secure strongholds of Athenian democratic power in Aegean islands. During the oligarchic coup of Athens in 411, when democracy was briefly overthrown, Thrasybulus protected the Athenian fleet and a new seat of democracy at Samos. Then during the Corinthian War, when ironically Athens was fighting against Spartan tyranny, Thrasybulus realized the significance of holding colonial territories. He soon brought many islands and ports back into the control of the Athenian navy, including Thasos, Samothrace, Tenedos, Lesbos, and cities near Byzantium and Chalcedon. Within just two years Athenian ships were trading across the Aegean at a similar rate to their glory days under Pericles, in the Athenian Golden Age. Trading ships and mercantile goods flowed through the harbour of Piraeus once more, in a respectable if diminished quantity. Athens was reborn as both a naval and political power. Thrasybulus, however, did not live to see it. He died in 388 during a skirmish at Aspendus on the southern coast of modern Turkey, when the Athenians sought to colonize the territory. While Athens was indeed resurrected, she had still only a shadow of her former glory. Despite a reputable navy, a strong army, and an important voice in diplomacy, she no longer dictated terms.

One example of the rapid yet cautious empire-rebuilding of Athens took place in 384, when a new diplomatic arrangement was made with the island of Chios. An historic member of the Delian League, Chios had famously revolted against Athenian oppression in 412 and joined the Spartans. Now eager to return to the Athenian side, Chios brokered a deal with Athens that carefully outlined economic and political terms to appease all parties involved in the King's Peace. Perhaps acknowledging the delicacy of having a former Spartan ally located very near to Persian territories in Ionia, the treaty was worded to mollify any tension:

> They will uphold like the Athenians the peace and the friendship and the oaths and the existing agreement which the King swore and the Athenians and Spartans and the other Greeks, and have come [announcing] good things for the People of Athens and the whole of Greece and the King...[17]

Such deference to Sparta and Persia mattered little in the long run. Persia in the mid-380s was already alarmed at the alacrity with which Athens was clawing back relevance in the Mediterranean. It was a prime motivator in Persia's fateful decision to flip sides in the Corinthian War and join the Spartans, turning the tide of the entire war and sealing the fate for the anti-Spartan confederacy.

Culturally, in the last few decades Athens had survived not just the stunning loss of the Peloponnesian War but a thoroughly destructive series of aftershocks related to that devastating defeat of the Athenian worldview. Perhaps nowhere is this more evident than in the realms of philosophy, theatre, and literature. One titanic event was the trial and death of Socrates in 399. In a kangaroo trial, Athens prosecuted Socrates for the high crimes of corruption of Athenian youth and for atheism. The trial was the climax of a generation of frustration with the rising influence wielded by Socrates, the 'gadfly' who challenged and embarrassed the Athenian elite, yet won the hearts of the youth and the philosophers.

Hatred for Socrates and his incessant questioning of the Athenian cultural and political system stretched at least a few decades back as shown in Aristophanes' *The Clouds*. A popular comedic play where Socrates persuasively convinces a young student to throw away his potential with trivial philosophical pursuits such as measuring the distance of a flea's jump, it was likely representative of Socrates' deep unpopularity with the intelligentsia of Athens. His trial and death, though, led not to the extinguishing of his Socratic Method and social movement, but instead to its renewed vitality.

Present at the trial of Socrates was a star pupil of his, a young aristocrat named Aristocles who had been tapped for political greatness in Athens. Better known to history by his wrestling nickname of *Plato* ('broad-shouldered'), this young philosopher was so moved by the words and actions of Socrates that he abandoned his political career and devoted himself to the life of the mind. In his countless philosophical works, from *The Republic* to *The Apology*, Socrates was the main character in Socratic dialogues addressing the great truths, such as 'what is beauty?' and 'what is piety?' Plato would, of course, go on to found The Academy in 387 not far from the Acropolis. A centre of learning and enquiry that would be the bedrock of scientific and intellectual advancements for centuries, the Academy boasted none other than Aristotle among its many students.

While philosophy's star burned bright, the Athenian government was experiencing quite the opposite experience. Numerous literary and theatrical references paint a picture of government as corrupt, incompetent, and avaricious – even during the reign of Thrasybulus. In the 391 play *Assemblywomen*, the playwright Aristophanes imagines a world where women take on the mantle of magistrates in Athenian democracy to solve the issues that men have so often failed at. Playing on social class inequality and the shortcomings of democracy, Aristophanes harshly critiqued Athens' values at the height of the Corinthian War. This was a thread the playwright picked up a few years later in 388's *Wealth*, where he tackles the plight of commoners and others who watch the lives of privilege being enjoyed by the wealthy. At the play's end, the gods are infuriated at the lack of attention paid them, as the sacrifices of the Athenians have been made only in the name of wealth and materialism. In short, Athens remained a hotbed of rebelliousness and civil strife. While they were on the upswing in many regards, they struggled with the same bouts of dissatisfaction over inequality in political opportunities and distribution of land and wealth. Most critically, they still had not resolved their issues with democracy. Some yearned for the democratic ideals of Pericles and the Athenian Golden Age, but many preferred a more pragmatic oligarchy.

Pelopidas and the Theban exiles who fled to Athens in 382 had entered into this unique cultural moment, and it shaped their own preparations to take back Thebes. Athens would survive not only the Corinthian War but also the vice-like grip of Spartan hegemony that followed. After 387 and the King's Peace, Athens continued her slow but steady increase in economic and political significance. But she knew enough to keep her head down in the era of Spartan vengeance across Greece. As the historian Robert Morstein Kallet-Marx puts it, the Athenians 'scrupulously avoided any conflict with Sparta'[18] until at least 379/378, when they were thrust back into the centre of the conflict. For now, Athens would try to kindle the flame of resistance while not outwardly provoking Spartan ire.

Chapter 5

The Liberation of Thebes

Seeds of Rebellion

At the start of 379, Sparta was at the apex of its power and its hegemony had few if any challengers. With Thebes safely subdued, the Cadmea occupied, and Athens content to slowly rebuild her naval empire across the Aegean, Sparta had little reason to suspect anyone would rise against her. By the middle of that year the Spartans had even gained more territory, with the submission of Phlius and Olynthus after lengthy sieges. Xenophon lavished much praise on Sparta's undisputed power over Greece in 379:

> On every side the affairs of [Sparta] had signally prospered: Thebes and the rest of the Boeotian states lay absolutely at her feet; Corinth had become her most faithful ally; Argos, unable longer to avail herself of the subterfuge of a movable calendar, was humbled to the dust; Athens was isolated; and, lastly, those of her own allies who displayed a hostile feeling towards her had been punished; so that, to all outward appearance, the foundations of her empire were at length absolutely well and firmly laid.[1]

And yet, by the close of 379 Sparta would be reeling from the loss of Thebes and, more importantly, a potent message had been sent to all of Greece that rebellions against Sparta could now be successful.

While not as famous as its counterpart, the battle of Leuctra in 371, the liberation of Thebes from Spartan occupation in 379 was the turning point for Sparta's hegemony over Greece. Never before had a major city-state so convincingly ousted their Spartan overlords and thoroughly removed their tentacles from both city and countryside. It was a black eye for Sparta's empire, the first public sign that Sparta was not invincible and her hegemony not inevitable. The pro-Spartan historian Xenophon summarised the liberation of Thebes succinctly: 'a bare score of the fugitives were sufficient to destroy their government.'[2] The historian Charles Hamilton took a similarly critical approach, describing the rebellion as 'the first overt challenge to Sparta's hegemony.'[3]

The story of how Thebes toppled the Spartan occupation is, however, a winding and unpredictable one. The most interesting account comes from Plutarch, though not from his *Parallel Lives* where we get most of our record of the fourth century outside of Xenophon. (Xenophon's *Hellenica* skims over the events of this period – likely due to his Spartan patronage and sympathies.) In his *Moralia*, Plutarch penned a brief Socratic dialogue called *De genio Socratis* or *On the Genius of Socrates*. The setting is Athens, summarising the retaking of Thebes shortly after its success, and the cast of interlocutors includes philosophers and co-conspirators alike discussing the events. These characters include the prominent Theban philosophers Cebes and Simmias, a Pythagorean named Theanor, and Caphisias, the brother of Epaminondas (though he sadly appears nowhere else in classical literature).

Plutarch was a highly trained philosopher, and his execution of a Socratic dialogue worthy of Plato's own writings is admirable as he addresses the primary purposes of the discussion, with ethical questions about the nature of spirits and the conscience. But Plutarch was also a Boeotian and a patriot, and doubtless made sure to present his homeland in a charitable light. From his narrative, along with less accurate but still helpful histories from Diodorus Siculus and Cornelius Nepos, we can piece together the dramatic liberation of Thebes. Before turning to the events of the retaking of Thebes, it is important to recall that Phoebidas had not been without assistance when he took the Cadmea in 382. A contingent of pro-Spartan and pro-oligarchy Thebans had invited the Spartans in, with Leontiades as their primary leader. The Spartans had reinforced the garrison in the city in the years since, and Phoebidas had been fined and removed from his command – but not executed, due to the intervention of Agesilaus. Phoebidas had instead been demoted to the harmost of neighbouring Thespiae. His replacement in Thebes was Lysanoridas, who ruled as an oligarch along with at least two other Spartans, Herippidas and Arcesus.

Leontiades and the Theban oligarchs had, of course, tried to eliminate the exiled democrats in the three years since the Cadmea's capture. While

Leontiades' threatening letters to the Athenian government had failed to have any effect, he and the oligarchs were singularly determined to extinguish any democratic opposition to their grip on Thebes. He sent waves of assassins after all the exiles in Athens, but succeeded in killing only one: Androcleides. Androcleides was among the most prominent of the exiles, and had been second only to Ismenias in the party of Theban democrats – or rather federalists – who had struggled in the *stasis* of Thebes. Ismenias and Androcleides had their heyday in Thebes in the 490s and 480s, and Androcleides was influential enough to have been bribed by the Persians in 495, when Persia was rallying support for the Corinthian War. Thus it was he who had been the Theban most responsible for his city's entry into that fateful war, whose outcome had led to its subjugation under Sparta's boot.

The story begins at the house of Charon, a nobleman of Thebes, who had offered his home as a safehouse for the stealthy return of the Theban exiles. Charon had remained in Thebes throughout and, like Epaminondas, kept in covert contact with the exiles in Athens. On the appointed day in December 379, a cadre of men entered Charon's home. Among them were Pelopidas, Melon, Damocleidas, and Theopompus. They had set out from Athens likely individually, but soon banded together as a group of about twelve, dressed as hunters, bringing equipment and even hunting dogs. By the time they reached Thebes, they had swapped disguises to appear as peasants. They entered the city in broad daylight, with the agreement to meet at Charon's house.

Not all the rebels had entered Thebes covertly, however. A commander named Pherenicus remained outside the city, within striking distance, with reinforcements. Most of the men felt this unnecessary; they had made contingency arrangements for the care of their families after their death.[4] Indeed, the revolutionaries had plenty of reason to suspect the Spartans were on to their plan. They had witnessed Spartan squads prowling about the countryside and multiple times thought they had been seen. Moreover, there was no shortage of leaks back in Athens and many suspected a mole had been passing information to the Spartan harmosts. Some of the Thebans believed they were walking into a trap. Their caution was wise; as we shall soon see, most of the concerns about Sparta becoming privy to their schemes were indeed true.

Undeterred by rumours, Melon had maintained his correspondence with Phillidas, the clerk for the Spartan *polemarchs* or chief magistrates of the pro-Spartan government in Thebes, and had secured the use of Charon's house. But when final arrangements were confirmed with Charon earlier that morning, one conspirator got cold feet and furtively ordered a messenger to visit Pelopidas and Melon, demanding a delay in the plan. Had this message been delivered, the scheme might very well have been delayed or even cancelled – but the Fates decreed that a marital squabble was to save Thebes. The courier was not able to saddle his horse, as his wife had forgotten to put out the equipment. He was enraged and the pair began a furious argument, leaving the courier so distracted he simply abandoned the message. The plot therefore continued, and that lovers' quarrel may have saved the day for Thebes.

By nightfall of the next day the entire crew had infiltrated Thebes, and nearly fifty conspirators were gathered at Charon's home, preparing to take back the city. This might have set a suspicious scene for the Spartans, seeing so many known Theban democrats and patriots in one location. However, social gatherings at Charon's home, and the homes of other members of the conspiracy, were by no means unusual – and that was by design. For several years now, the Theban patriots had been strategically hosting and publicizing social events and parties. Apart from the normal revelry and merrymaking, the parties often turned into philosophical discussions as a further cover. Many events took place at the home of Simmias the philosopher, and the rebels were even bold enough to invite Leontiades and Archias, the leaders of Thebes' pro-Spartan oligarchs.[5] They occasionally agreed to attend, and Archias especially loved hearing Simmias' tales of foreign lands. Thus nothing would appear unusual about a party at Charon's home on this December night.

In order for the gathering to garner as little suspicion as possible, Plutarch recounts that the first half of the evening was taken up with a philosophical dialogue on the nature of Socrates' *daemon* and divine intervention. Using the Theban revolution as a backdrop, Plutarch explores how Socrates cultivated virtue and how that relates to his *daemon* (a spirit that offers guidance and protection for humans while serving as a mediator to the divine). As the Socratic dialogue developed, yet another wrinkle appeared in the conspirators' plan. Their champion Epaminondas had, allegedly, lost heart and was mourning his tutor Lysis at his graveside instead of joining the revolutionaries. Epaminondas' brother Caphisias was forced to spring to his defence when the rebels realized that Epaminondas might fail to come. On account of his education and devotion to Pythagoreanism, Epaminondas was accused of thinking himself 'superior in virtue to all other Boeotians' and 'not keen or eager' to help the men who are braving danger for their country.'[6] Caphisias passionately refuted such claims, and gave a lengthy speech explaining his brother's fidelity to the cause:

> unless driven to it by extreme necessity, [Epaminondas] will put no countryman to death untried, but will gladly join forces with all who endeavour without resorting to civil bloodshed and slaughter to set our city free. But since the majority are against him, and we are already engaged in this course, he would have us allow him to await the favourable moment for intervention, remaining innocent and guiltless of bloodshed. Thus interest as well as justice will be served. For, he contends, no distinction will be drawn in the actual fighting… [the soldiers] will not lay their swords aside until they have filled the entire city with slaughter and destroyed many of their personal enemies.[7]

The matter was not able to be properly settled before two special guests arrived at the party to join the conspirators. The new arrivals were none other than the polemarch Archias and the Spartan commander Lysanoridas, the two leaders of Spartan-occupied Cadmea. Despite their internal quibbling the rebels' plan was now irreversible, for the next step in the plot was to eliminate these important Spartan military commanders.

Archias had actually served alongside Leontiades as the Theban leaders of the new Spartan-friendly regime. They were equal in rank, but diverged starkly in leadership styles. Leontiades was scrupulous and measured in all his actions, preferring to think strategically and keep up proper appearances for the honour of both Thebes and Sparta. Archias, meanwhile, was ruled by his baser instincts and given to the usual vices of the social elite: drinking, adultery, and licentiousness. And this was precisely the Theban rebels' gambit.

Phillidas, meanwhile, was in company with the Spartan polemarch Archias, in order to carry out his own assignment for the evening. He had been tasked with getting Archias inebriated at a different venue where, after an evening of drinking and carousing, the polemarch would be delivered into the conspirators' hands for swift execution. This did not present a particularly challenging task and Archias was easily seduced by the idea of holding a private party, fortuitously timed as there was on that day a festival of Aphrodite to celebrate. Thus Archias left Charon's to host his own party after just a brief participation in the philosophical discourse. It was a short journey to his home, which was most likely located near the safety of the Spartan-fortified Cadmea. But Archias had not been gone for ten minutes when the entire plan almost unravelled. A loud rap on the door shocked the conspirators, who did not expect any more partygoers. Worse, when the door was opened there were two city guards loyal to Sparta and working directly for Archias. Shortly after arriving home, Archias had despatched them to go back in order to ask some questions of Charon.

The entire group of Theban rebels thought that was it – the end of their plan. And they could have been right. The guards had been sent to question Charon about a suspicious group of people seen at his home that very evening. Archias had probably received a report from the Spartan patrols in the countryside who may have seen what looked like Theban hunters afoot, a rather suspicious sight during the early winter. Some Spartans mistrusted the party in any case, where so many guests had connections to radicals like Epaminondas, and thought they might be part of a cabal against the government. Of course, they were entirely correct in their suspicions and were in exactly the right location to devastate the rebels' scheme – but Charon played his role well enough to allay their fears.

Charon stepped out into the chilly night air to speak with the guards. They were demanding that he accompany them to Archias immediately. While he spoke with them, the forty-seven remaining revolutionaries panicked. As Plutarch narrates in *Life of Pelopidas*:

> All were at once convinced that their enterprise had been revealed, and that they themselves were all lost, before they had even done anything worthy of their valour.[8]

With daggers drawn, the conspirators were ready to begin the slaughter of Spartans in Thebes that very moment. Most unexpectedly, however, Charon returned. He had successfully delayed the abrupt collapse of their revolution, convincing the guards he was following close behind them and would report to Archias of his own volition. Astonishingly, Charon did just that. It would have been a tempting option to ignore the request and continue with the revolutionary plan, but he believed that speaking with Archias would buy the conspirators vital time. Charon therefore made his way to Archias' home, where Phillidas had arranged for beautiful escorts and drinks to distract his master. Phillidas had actually had no prior confirmation that the plan was going to take place on this day, but at Charon's house he had managed to speak privately with Caphisias to find out if the other guests were indeed the Theban rebels. Upon being told they were, he remarked, 'I did well, then, to prepare for today the entertainment in which I am to receive Archias into my house and make him an easy prey for our men at a drunken banquet.'[9]

Nevertheless, the meeting between Charon and Archias got off to a rocky start. Archias immediately told Charon that he had heard there was collusion among certain Thebans who might try to overthrow the city. Still, his suspicions were easily allayed – Phillidas had already successfully plied him with wine and Archias was eager to return to his drinking and debauchery, happy to ignore any hints of subterfuge in his city. But before he could do so, the seeds of revolution were yet again nearly foiled. A letter arrived at that very moment from an Athenian spy, who had learned of the plot from the Theban exiles in Athens. Archias was handed the letter and directed to open it instantly, because it was of the highest importance. Indeed, it contained all the details of the Theban revolution and would have alerted the Spartans to the whole scheme.

Archias, however, responded in the manner that had characterized his entire career as a commander of the Spartans and traitor to Theban federalism: he went back to the party. He never even opened the letter – instead he placed it under his pillow and quipped, 'serious business for the morrow.'[10] The saying became a Greek proverb and Archias, of course, never lived to see the morrow or the letter's contents.

The Liberation of Thebes

After a harrowing number of near-misses, the plan had now accelerated beyond containment. The time was at hand and the revolutionaries decided to act immediately. Two squads were formed to accomplish one simple goal: execute as many Spartan leaders in Thebes within the next hour as possible. One team would head off to assassinate Archias and his minions, while the other led by Pelopidas himself would eliminate Leontiades at his home.

There was a price for Charon, however, that meant putting his own son at risk. He offered the conspirators custody of his son, a boy no older than fifteen, as a pledge of fidelity to the cause of Theban liberty. Charon knew the gravitas of this moment in the history of Thebes, and also that this would be a rite of passage for his boy to claim manhood. Shortly before his son departed with Pelopidas' strike force Charon said this:

> This is my only child, and very dear to me, as you know; I place him in your hands, adjuring all of you in the name of gods and daemons: if it should appear that I have played you false, kill him, show no mercy. For the rest, face what has befallen like the brave men you are; do not surrender your bodies to unmanly and inglorious destruction by your bitterest foes, but fight back, keeping your souls unconquered for your country's sake.[11]

Melon led the squad to assassinate Archias, together with Charon and four other men. Their strategy was to infiltrate the Dionysian festivities at Archias' home that Charon had just left and where Phillidas was ensuring the wine never ceased to flow and the women attended every guest. The plan, however, included one unusual feature – they were to wear women's clothing, posing as courtesans until the fateful moment. Below their robes they were fully armoured, with breastplates, and wearing hoods to obscure their faces. They only needed to buy a few moments in the drunken crowd. The men donned their disguise and surreptitiously entered the party. Once inside, they were presented by Phillidas to great merriment from the crowd, who had been eagerly awaiting a fresh crop of entertainers. Melon took the lead, advancing towards their primary target, Archias, and sliding forward with his hand on his sword. One guest, perhaps less inebriated than his colleagues, then caught a glimpse of Melon's face – he grabbed hold one of his arms and shouted, 'Isn't this Melon, Phillidas?'[12]

It was the official start of the revolution: Melon, still fully dressed in woman's attire, now darted at Archias with his sword raised. Archias tried

A field in Boeotia in early spring. Here, the Boeotians grow their famous golden wheat. (*ID 44475936 © Eric Cauchi | Dreamstime.com*)

Plains outside Thebes, Greece. These agrarian hills are covered with golden wheat at harvest time. (*ID 106819629 © Emmanouil Pavlis | Dreamstime.com*)

Sparta today, with some remains of the ancient city where the mighty Spartan military machine was forged. (*ID 159525490 © Leonid Andronov | Dreamstime.com*)

A Greek vase depicting the foundation of Thebes. On the journey to find his missing sister, the mythical hero Cadmus fought and defeated a dragon. Afterwards, he planted the dragon's teeth in the soil. The teeth sprouted into soldiers who became the very first Thebans, and the city was founded shortly thereafter. (*Marie-Lan Nguyen via Wikimedia Commons/CC BY-SA 4.0*)

Ruins of the Cadmea in Thebes. This was the great citadel that also served as the cultural and political nexus for the Thebans. In 382, the Spartans captured the Cadmea and subjugated Thebes, to the shock of all Greece. This event led to the rise of Pelopidas, Epaminondas, and the Sacred Band and, ultimately, the demise of Sparta's hegemony after the Theban victory at Leuctra. (*olexdj via Wikimedia Commons/ public domain*)

Another view of the ruins of the Cadmea in Thebes. (*VladoubidoOo via Wikimedia Commons/CC BY-SA 4.0*)

A Greek soldier wearing a *pilos* helmet of the fourth century BC. This pointed style of helmet was worn by the hoplites at the battle of Leuctra in 371. (*Marie-Lan Nguyen via Wikimedia Commons/CC BY 2.5*)

The modern city of Naxos on the island of Naxos, Greece. Here, the battle took place in 376 between the Athenians and the Spartan fleet. The Athenians, and a young upstart lieutenant named Phocion who would later lead Athens himself, soundly defeated the Spartans. (*ID 82175224 © Mila Atkovska | Dreamstime.com*)

The plains near the small village of ancient Leuctra where the great battle took place in 371 BC. (*Elżbieta, 'Valley of the battle of Leuctra' via Vici.org/CC BY-SA 3.0*)

The Theban victory monument (*tropaion*) at the site of the battle of Leuctra. This is not the original, it has been rebuilt many times over the centuries. The Roman orator Cicero even lamented the building of a new monument during the Roman Republic. The first permanent trophy bore a statue of a hoplite. The modern reconstruction includes some original stonework. (*George E. Koronaios via Wikimedia Commons/ public domain*)

This Theban coin from the fourth century was cast in honour of the battle of Leuctra. Many such coins were minted by Epaminondas himself in the national celebration over Sparta's defeat. (*O.Mustafin via Wikimedia Commons/ public domain*)

The ruins of ancient Messene. Founded by Epaminondas during his invasions of the Peloponnese, the city-state became a refuge for the former helots of the Spartan empire. (*ID 295226939 © Antonios Karvelas | Dreamstime.com*)

The painting *Pelopidas' Death* by Andrey Ivanov. Painted in 1805 in the Russian Neo-Classicist style, it depicts Pelopidas, surrounded by the Sacred Band of Thebes, on his deathbed, having fallen in battle in Thessaly in 364. (*Wikimedia Commons/public domain*)

Pierre-Jean David d'Angers' sculpture *Death of Epaminondas*. Created in 1811, this relief sculpture shows the mortally wounded Epaminondas at the battle of Mantinea in 362. Members of the Sacred Band of Thebes visibly mourn his death. (*VladoubidoOo via Wikimedia Commons/CC BY-SA 4.0*)

The Lion of Chaeronea monument that celebrates the Sacred Band of Thebes. Until they were wiped out at the battle of Chaeronea against Alexander the Great and the Macedonians, the Sacred Band was the greatest fighting force in Greece and had never been defeated in almost four decades. (*ID 286676657 © George Stamatis | Dreamstime.com*)

to respond in kind, but drunkenly stumbled up and then fell back down. He was easy prey for Melon's sword. Melon's fellow assassins acted with equal alacrity, quickly killing all the revellers at Archias' home, including a high-ranking commander named Philippus who was cut down by Charon. One man, the bureaucrat who had recognized Melon, was almost shown mercy as he was holding a sacred spear that was used in Theban civic ceremonies during this feast of Aphrodite, which was the ostensible reason for Archias' party. While one assassin hesitated over the man's fate, another struck him down, proclaiming vengeance and Theban liberty:

> Lie there with these you toadied to: may you never wear the chaplet when Thebes is free and never sacrifice again to the gods before whom you have invoked so many curses on your country in your many prayers for her enemies.[13]

The coup to liberate Thebes was not yet finished. Next on their hit list was Leontiades. The man perhaps most responsible for Thebes' subjugation to Sparta, he had been the one to personally invite Phoebidas and the Spartan legion to conquer the Cadmea in 382. Leontiades, though, would be a much more formidable opponent than the lazy and drunken Archias.

Leontiades was, as ever, at home with his wife and family, but it was not a long journey for Pelopidas' team. Leontiades had not avoided the evening's many events – he had been at the party earlier, at Charon's home, and had even shared a private word with Simmias the philosopher. Evidently he had found it a tiring affair, for when the Theban revolutionaries arrived at his house they found the lights off and everyone asleep. They knocked loudly several times, hoping to surprise Leontiades at the door and attack him. But sleep was deep for Leontiades and his family that evening and for a long time no one answered. After many minutes, a servant of Leontiades blearily rose and unlatched the door. The Theban conspirators stormed through, trampling the servant and making quite a clamour. This alerted Leontiades to their presence, and he quickly ran to his bedroom door knife in hand, ready to defend his home and family. Plutarch recounts how this counter-move might have worked if only Leontiades had not failed to shield the lamps he had lit – if he had done so he might have been able to keep out of sight in the darkness. As it was the assassins saw him plainly and leapt forward, daggers raised. Leontiades managed to kill one of his attackers before Pelopidas bested him. Thus Pelopidas, the great hero of Thebes, vanquished Thebes' greatest traitor.

The conspirators soon fanned out through the city, eliminating as many Spartan commanders and pro-Spartan Thebans as possible. Word spread quickly as the uprising gathered pace. Epaminondas joined the fray, bringing with him the bands of youth he had trained for this very moment. Old men joined them, dusting off their spears which had not been used perhaps since the Peloponnesian War. Phillidas made his way to the prison, still posing as a pro-Spartan bureaucrat, and tricked the guards into letting him inside. He slew the jailers and released all the prisoners, adding greatly to the ranks of the revolutionaries. By now, the soldiers in the streets were calling for all Theban citizens to join the fight and see that the tyrants were dead. So many Thebans spilled out into the streets that they had to break into blacksmith shops and storefronts to find proper weapons for them. It was now a true revolution.

Word was sent back to Athens that the plan was succeeding. All the remaining Theban exiles immediately began making their way back to Thebes, eager to liberate their homeland. Pherenicus and the others who had waited outside the city now provided much-needed reinforcements. Plutarch describes the near-beauty of the chaos: 'The city was all in a flutter of excitement, there was much noise, the houses had lights in them, and there was running to and fro.'[14]

The Spartans responded in kind, the few officers in the Cadmea, realizing the rising threat, sending for reinforcements from Plataea. Most Spartan commanders would also have ordered a counter-attack, but the shock tactics of the Theban conspirators had worked well and confusion reigned. The 1,500 Spartan soldiers in the Cadmea remained paralysed and uncertain. Meanwhile, the Thebans had predicted the Spartan call for reinforcements and had already despatched cavalry from the city. Supported by a small contingent of men from Athens, they were perfectly situated to meet the Spartan auxiliaries, given Plataea's location between Thebes and Sparta. They easily neutralized the threat: no aid would come for the Spartans trapped in the Cadmea.

Even Xenophon, normally reserved in presenting any Spartan weakness and always eager to champion a Spartan victory, could not whitewash what happened next. Instead of further resistance, the Spartans on the Cadmea surrendered. Xenophon describes how the Spartans remaining in Thebes 'agreed to evacuate the place if the citizens would allow them a safe-conduct to retire with their arms.'[15] The Theban commanders accordingly gave their oaths, promising a safe exit from the city if the Spartans surrendered the Cadmea. For the Spartan soldiers, it was a far cry from Leonidas and the 300 who fought to the last man at Thermopylae.

And it made no difference in the end. When the frenzied Thebans saw their oppressors walking freely out of the city, they could not contain themselves. The mob attacked the Spartans, putting many to death. Not satisfied with that, they even began to murder the Spartan children, as the families tried to leave. The small number of Athenians who had joined the cause took pity on the remaining Spartans – a rare sight indeed – and managed to smuggle them out of the city.

By daybreak, when the fighting had at last ceased, Epaminondas and Pelopidas convened an assembly of Thebans and any Boeotians, the *damos*, to celebrate their victory. Garlands, hymns of praise and jubilation, and tears of joy abounded in the Cadmea as they rejoiced at the restoration of Theban independence. The three years of Spartan oppression were over. Thebes would not be conquered again for nearly fifty years, when Alexander the Great himself would march on the Seven-Gated city. For the present, Thebes belonged once again to the Thebans.

Chapter 6

The Sacred Band of Thebes

Advent of the Boeotian War

The Thebans had little time to bask in their new liberty. The Spartan king Cleombrotus now marched on the city with an army, determined to make the Theban uprising a mere footnote in history, not a full-fledged revolution. Cleombrotus had recently ascended to the Agiad kingship in Sparta, after his brother Agesipolis had died of an illness during the neverending Spartan campaign against Olynthus. While Thebes had been able to earn a surprise victory, the Olynthians had been successful at withstanding a lengthy siege from the Spartans. The Olynthians had succeeded in creating a stalemate, but like the Boeotian Confederacy before them had been forced to dissolve their symmachy, the Chalcedonian League. Sparta was now determined to ensure Thebes was next.

Cleombrotus brought a full Spartan *mora* with him, marching from the Peloponnese to Boeotia and resting in Plataea, which had remained loyal to Sparta. This was Cleombrotus' first major command and he had received the honour only after it was declined by an ageing Agesilaus. By now Agesilaus had given more than forty years of military service to Sparta, making him nearly sixty years of age. He had fought against the Olynthians but had apparently decided – quite shockingly – to put his anti-Theban sentiments aside, preferring to rest in the bucolic Laconian countryside.

This was, of course, not the entire story. The challenge of Olynthus had rattled the Spartan empire, and now the stunning democratic coup in Thebes threatened her supremacy over Greece in a way that had never before happened. While Agesilaus would have surely relished the opportunity to crush Thebes at such an opportune moment, and to satisfy his decades-long grudge at least temporarily, cooler heads prevailed. For Agesilaus, the only advantage to the Spartan occupation of Thebes had been the humiliation of the rival city-state. He nevertheless realized that the abrupt conquest of Thebes by Phoebidas had sent a deeply disturbing message to the rest of Greece that Sparta could decide to destroy your city on a whim, and treaties or agreements made no difference. For Agesilaus to support a campaign against the Thebans now would be tantamount to supporting tyranny, and giving in to the imperial vision of Lysander that he had fought so hard against.

It was now the dead of winter and snow was dusting the Boeotian wheat fields. Cleombrotus led a brief, moderately successful campaign to retake some territory, fighting against Athenian peltasts loyal to the Theban cause. The border fortress of Eleutherae, straddling the Attican-Boeotian line, had already been taken by Theban patriots, and so Cleombrotus – perhaps eager to impress in his first major command – boldly took his army over Mt Cithaeron. But after two weeks of fighting, Cleombrotus succeeded in retaking only the city of Thespiae. Recognizing he had achieved all he was destined to, he departed back to Sparta, leaving a man named Sphodrias as harmost of Thespiae.

Though he had no way of knowing it, this was Cleombrotus' most fateful decision and may well have sealed the destruction of Sparta's empire. Sphodrias was a capable commander, and had spent most of his career in the inner circle of the Spartan kings. Nobody was likely to think much about his selection for harmost. Sphodrias, though, harboured burning ambitions to make more of himself. Plutarch describes him as a warrior of undisputed reputation, but 'full of vain hopes and senseless ambition.'[1] The Thebans decided they could exploit that vanity.

After the revolution in Thebes, Pelopidas had overseen the election of new boeotarchs for Thebes. The *damos* had elected three men – Pelopidas, Melon, and Charon – to this rank as a reward for their roles in liberating the Cadmea. At this time, the title of 'boeotarch' was merely an honorific, since the Boeotian Confederacy remained defunct. The election of three new boeotarchs, however, signalled Thebes' ambition to eliminate the Spartan presence in all of Boeotia, not just Thebes and the Cadmea. Pelopidas' master plan was to liberate central Greece town by town and harmost by harmost, by any means necessary. His preferred methods were conquest, insurrection, or manipulation.

Thespiae would be taken by manipulation of its harmost Sphodrias. Pelopidas and Gorgidas sent a messenger, laden with gold for the requisite bribery, to present Sphodrias with an ambitious proposal. It was suggested that he should use his 10,000 Spartan hoplites to attack the Athenian harbour of Piraeus. The Theban envoy, pretending to be a Spartan sympathiser, seduced Sphodrias with visions of Sparta hailing him as a hero – surely with such a conquest under his belt, the Spartan ephors would at long last recognize his true worth to their empire.[2] The example of Phoebidas was especially alluring for Sphodrias – Phoebidas had earned a name for himself with his seizing of the Cadmea, and suffered virtually no repercussions. The quickest way for a Spartan commander to climb the career ladder, it seemed, was to capture an allied city-state without the ephors' permission.

Accordingly, come nightfall, Sphodrias and his force left Thespiae and marched on Athens. The gates to the Piraeus were apparently unguarded, and the superior Spartan numbers should have made quick work of the lacklustre Athenian defences. But sadly for Sphodrias almost nothing went to plan. He had misjudged the distance between Thespiae and Athens, and the sun began to rise before they even reached sight of the city walls. Their night-time raid no longer possible, Sphodrias opted to press on. However the Athenians of course saw the approaching army and had time to man their defences. Sphodrias' men raided houses and farmlands, but found little of substance and realized they would never take Athens.[3] When the invading Spartans saw their tactical advantage lost, Sphodrias' leadership skills were found lacking and 'the hearts of his soldiers failed them.'[4] He had little choice but to go back to Thespiae with a dismayed army and no bounty.

That might have been the end of Sphodrias' expedition, except for yet more bad luck. There was an envoy of ambassadors from Sparta in the city of Athens that morning, who – since Sphodrias had not shared his plans with the ephors – had not been informed of the Spartan assault on the city. They were quickly arrested by the Athenians and brought to a hasty trial. Pleading their case, the Spartans assured the enraged Athenians that they had not sanctioned the attack, saying: 'You will hear before long… that Sphodrias has paid for his behaviour with his life.'[5]

The ambassadors surely meant these words and had every reason to believe that the ephors would ruthlessly punish Sphodrias for his reckless actions.

Phoebidas had received only a slap on the wrist, but they were confident that Sphodrias would be judged much more harshly, given his colossal failure at a precarious moment for Sparta's empire. Athens sent ambassadors to Sparta to ensure that Sphodrias received the death penalty, and the men were satisfied to find themselves apparently redundant upon arrival in Laconia; Sphodrias had already been indicted on charges and the Spartan public was enraged at his behaviour.[6] A guilty verdict was all but certain. However, before justice could be served, Sparta's two kings intervened. As a longtime friend of Sphodrias and the one that appointed him harmost, Cleombrotus' actions are perhaps understandable, if not defensible. Agesilaus, however, issued a stern rebuke to the courts and overrode the verdict using his royal powers. It was a rare move, but legal under Sparta's constitution.

Agesilaus' motives are somewhat obscure. Plutarch and Xenophon both recount his son's friendship with the son of Sphodrias as the primary motivation. Agesilaus, a devout family man who was known to do anything for his children, argued at length with his son Archidamus about the trial and deliberated over his intervention. Agesilaus originally declined to exonerate Sphodrias, but changed his mind after several public confrontations from his son, even one outside the Spartan mess hall. Archidamus made no attempt to justify Sphodrias' actions in Athens, but appealed instead to a simple thesis: putting Sphodrias to death would kill yet another Spartan hoplite and accelerate *oliganthropia*. As Archidamus put it, 'Sparta needs such soldiers.'[7] Whether Agesilaus truly agreed with this demographic argument or whether he acted out of love for his son – or perhaps his hatred for Thebes – matters little in the end. Sphodrias was declared innocent. All of Greece was outraged. Even Xenophon, ever reserved in anything that could be construed as criticism of Sparta and especially of his beloved Agesilaus, could not withhold judgement. He labelled it a 'miscarriage of justice.'[8]

The conquest of Thebes in 382 had already left a dark stain on Sparta's reputation, but the effect of Sphodrias' feckless attempt to conquer Athens was like a tinderbox. Athens immediately declared war on Sparta and joined Thebes' nascent rebellion against Spartan tyranny. Before this, Athens had been content to offer covert support and sympathy for Thebes, but after the verdict on Sphodrias, she demanded retribution.

By 378, the Theban-Spartan Wars had truly begun. This first phase would be known as the Boeotian War and would last from the revolution in Thebes to the battle of Leuctra. As Plutarch described it, the Boeotian War became 'the war which broke down the pretensions of Sparta and put an end to her supremacy.'⁹ It would be the greatest challenge to Sparta's empire yet. And it all could have been avoided if not for Phoebidas and Sphodrias.

Formation of the Sacred Band of Thebes

Though they now had Athenian support, Thebes was focused solely on the war effort against Sparta. Despite their momentum, it was still an uphill battle. Sparta maintained her supremacy across land and sea and her army was rarely even challenged in a pitched battle. Spartan dominance on the battlefield was the result of exceptional training, subjugation of the helots, and the *polis*-wide cultural focus on the *agoge* structure. Thebes could not yet match Sparta's military might in outright combat. So in 378 the Thebans created an elite military unit of shock troops that doubled as a symbol of Boeotian glory. It soon became the most legendary fighting force of the ancient world: the Sacred Band of Thebes.

The origins of the Sacred Band of Thebes lie in an odd mixture of Platonic philosophy, ancient Greek sexuality and romance, and Greek martial culture. At its heart, the Sacred Band of Thebes was a highly-trained unit of 300 hoplites who specialized in assault tactics, served as the vanguard of the Theban army, and whose primary purpose was to ambush and break the formation of the enemy, then eliminate their best soldiers by any means available. These were not the heavily-armoured hoplites of a century before. In the Greek language, they were known as a *lochos* – a 'war-band' or tactical unit of soldiers. The Sacred Band of Thebes is thus the *Hieros Lochos*, where *hieros* means sacred or holy. (Modern English terms such as hierarchy or hieroglyphics all come from this word.) A *lochos* was, curiously, also a common unit in the Spartan army. In Sparta, the *lochos* was the second largest military unit at approximately 144 men and formed a quarter of the primary Spartan unit, the *mora*, which was around 600 men, commanded by a polemarch. A full Spartan army would be composed of six *morai* under the leadership of the general or king.

The Sacred Band of Thebes, however, numbered a more mythologically-oriented 300 men. For the ancient Greeks, this seems to have represented the ideal number for a tactical unit. The most famous story of 300 Greek soldiers is certainly the last stand of the Spartans at Thermopylae, where Leonidas and his 300-strong bodyguard kept the Persians at bay for long enough, before dying gallantly, to secure the independence of all Greece. A century earlier, a famous battle that took place between Argos and Sparta determined the entire war, when each city named 300 champions to fight against each other, instead of full armies of men. Both events stand tall in Greek military and cultural history, making the selection of 300 Thebans to the Sacred Band all the more significant. The defining feature of the Theban force was that the 300 men were constituted of 150 pairs of lovers who fought alongside each other in battle. This romantic bond between the members of the *lochos* was not only its hallmark, but more critically the connective tissue that forged them into a cohesive and deadly unit. That love also ensured each pair of warriors fought not just for victory, but for each other's very lives. The Theban general Pammenes described how, 'Homer's Nestor [in *The Iliad*] was no tactician when he urged the Greeks to form in companies by clans and tribes, "That clan might give assistance unto clan, and tribes unto tribes," since he should have stationed lover by beloved.'[10]

In his dialogue *The Symposium*, Plato discusses the nature of love and its role in the pursuit of a good life. Normally, a citation from Plato helps us uncover a greater truth or Socratic question that we can apply to a later development. In this case, however, Plato was a contemporary of the Sacred Band of Thebes and, perhaps, is even speaking of these Thebans when writing. Most historians agree that *The Symposium* was written in Athens in the 370s, during the Boeotian War and the Sacred Band of Thebes' rise to fame. He discussed the ideal structure of an army, and how they can be properly motivated – not only for their highest good but also for the love of their city and their own beloved. He proposed that if men could stand alongside their lovers, they would be all the keener to fight, wielding spear and shield for both victory and the protection of their beloved:

And if there were only some way of contriving that a state or an army should be made up of lovers and their loves, they would be the very best governors of their own city, abstaining from all dishonour, and emulating one another in honour; and when fighting at each other's side, although a mere handful, they would overcome the world. For what lover would not choose rather to be seen by all mankind than by his beloved, either when abandoning his post or throwing away his arms? He would be ready to die a thousand deaths rather than endure this. Or who would desert his beloved or fail him in the hour of danger? The veriest coward would become an inspired hero, equal to the bravest, at such a time; Love would inspire him. That courage which, as Homer says, the god breathes into the souls of some heroes. Love of his own nature infuses into the lover.[11]

To understand this devoted partnership, we must first consider the spectrum of Greek sexuality and love. Unlike the narrower categories of modern definitions, the Greek concepts of sexuality were fluid and multifaceted. Traditional gender roles in this patriarchal culture often demanded that women were monogamous and faithful to their spouse, especially those not in the upper social classes. For Greek men, however, the primary standard was not fidelity to a wife but a dominant and active sexual role that maintained their masculine honour and social status. The Greek concept of *eros*, or romantic and passionate love, was therefore a matter not just of personal piety and goodness, but of civic virtue. Another Greek word translated into English as 'love,' *philia*, meaning deep friendship and intimacy, involved reciprocal care and concern for another person's flourishing. *Philia* was considered essential for both personal happiness and life in the Greek *polis*. It was the bedrock of political alliances, military bonds, and philosophical relationships. Like many same-sex partners in ancient Greece, the members of the Sacred Band of Thebes merged *eros* with *philia*.

It is well-known that same-sex love for Greek men often took the form of pederasty between an older male and an adolescent or young boy. This was particularly true in the upper echelons of society, and such a relationship was valued culturally as an educational experience, with the older partner serving as a kind of sage and mentor. Examples abound in Greek literature and history: the philosopher Socrates and the Athenian statesman Alcibiades, the Spartan leaders Lysander and Agesilaus, and Achilles and Patroclus in *The Iliad*.

While the city-state of Thebes practiced pederasty like most of Greece, there is no evidence that the Sacred Band was built on this model. In fact, one might argue that its arrangement is uniquely anti-Spartan. Sparta had embedded pederasty into their state educational system, the *agogé*, as an essential rite of passage into adulthood and citizenship. As Thebes pushed back against all things Spartan, the formation of the Sacred Band immediately after the revolution of 379 suggests that it was set up directly to fight the Spartans and create a counter-identity to the Spartan hoplite. The pairs of lovers, therefore, were all two adult males with no age distinction, in contrast to the Spartan model. For this reason, Cartledge describes the Sacred Band as a 'complete anathema to Sparta'.[12] As ever, anti-Spartan sentiment coloured all aspects of Thebes in the early fourth century.

The most famous example of the deep intimacy two fearsome warriors could share is found in Homer's *Iliad*, with Achilles and Patroclus. While *The Iliad* never failed to shape Greek culture, the specific dynamics of the relationship between the great hero Achilles and his close friend Patroclus is never elucidated by Homer, and even in the ancient world there is much disagreement on the nature of their love. The Athenian playwright Aeschylus argued they were romantic lovers and even based an entire trilogy of plays on their relationship, the *Achilleis*. Multiple later Greek authors claimed the relationship was pederastic. Xenophon, in his own version of *The Symposium*, instead described their intensely devoted bond as deep friendship and loyalty, but with no romantic entanglement.

No matter the particulars, it is clear that Achilles and Patroclus were the model of Greek *philia*. Both of them were also, of course, the model of a Greek warrior. Famously, Achilles refused to fight for most of *The Iliad* out of protest against his mistreatment at the hands of the Greek king Agamemnon. Patroclus, in a bid to encourage the Greeks, dresses as Achilles and enters the fray, with both Trojans and Greeks assuming Achilles himself had returned, given the two looked and fought so similarly. Patroclus' use of Achilles' armour sparks the fiercest fighting of the battle, and he succeeds in killing many renowned warriors during his brief fighting stint. When Patroclus is finally killed by the Trojan hero Hector, Achilles enters into a frenzy of grief and rage over the loss of his partner. He returns to the battlefield himself, inflicting carnage on all in his path (even a river god who dares to get in his way). At last Achilles kills Hector in combat and for a long time refuses to honour his corpse in the customary tradition, until his anger at last abates in the final book.

The entire plot of *The Iliad* here turns on the love that Achilles and Patroclus share, and despite their many faults they are seen as its primary heroes, overflowing with Greek virtue. Their romantic bond became the idealized version of the combined *eros* and *philia* between fellow warriors. The Sacred Band of Thebes, in essence, was designed to be an entire military unit of Achilles-Patroclus partnerships. The results spoke for themselves: they never lost a battle in forty years.

First Adventures of the Sacred Band

The Sacred Band was headquartered on the Cadmea and given special privileges by the state. Their lodging and food were provided in exchange for the protection of Thebes, and as a result they were often called the City Band. A day in the life of a member of the Sacred Band of Thebes entailed a rigorous daily training regimen that often included equestrian exercise, dance, wrestling, and fighting. By living and training together, the Sacred Band sought to strengthen their bond. Beyond these descriptions, the ancients are silent on the matter of the Band's public life. We can surmise, however, that the men were Boeotians in strong standing with the state and who were passionately committed to federalism – certainly not the oligarchy that Sparta had tried to impose. They were doubtless excellent soldiers and of the aristocratic class. Had they not been in this elite force, they would have served in the cavalry or hoplite ranks alongside their peers in the middle and upper classes.

What is rather unclear, however, is the selection of the soldiers. Was their romantic attachment a prerequisite for joining and did new members join in pairs? Or were they chosen exclusively for their martial prowess, then assigned a partner upon enrolment in the Sacred Band? Were their partners in the Sacred Band their only partners, or were they married to a woman as well? If one man grew too old for the Band, would his companion find a new beloved or also leave the squadron? Ultimately, these questions cannot be answered from the available evidence. We do know that Xenophon described the partnerships of Thebans in general as 'man and boy [being] yoked together as if they were married people,'[13] but this would not necessarily be the norm just in Thebes, but rather a unique practice of the Boeotians.

In the final analysis, we know simply that the Sacred Band of Thebes emerged in 378 and quickly established itself as the greatest military unit in Greece for the next four decades. The secret to their success seemed to be the unique companionship experienced by its members. Plutarch summarised the thesis behind the Band's formation, that 'a band that is held together by the friendship between lovers is indissoluble and not to be broken, since the lovers are ashamed to play the coward before their beloved, and the beloved before their lovers, and both stand firm in danger to protect each other.'[14]

Their first commander and founder was Gorgidas, the former exile to Athens and member of the resistance movement against Sparta. Gorgidas was now a boeotarch alongside Melon, Charon, and Pelopidas and was likely the man who had the vision not only to create the Sacred Band, but who instituted all of its unique characteristics and training. Under his military leadership, though, the tactics of the Sacred Band were lacking. He strategically distributed the members of the Band through the front ranks of his phalanx. This spreading out of his elite fighters raised the performance of the entire phalanx, but it limited the effectiveness of shock troops as they were not focused on a single target.

The first known outing of the Sacred Band was in support of the Athenians in the spring of 378. Having recently declared war on Sparta in response to the scoundrel Sphodrias, Athens sent a commander named Chabrias to watch the roads into Boeotia from the south. He was a hero of the Corinthian War and held the distinction of never having lost a single battle. The orator Demosthenes described him as a name worthy of the most triumphant Athenian leaders, saying: 'When he commanded you none of your enemies has any trophy over you and him, while you have many over many enemies, under his command.'[15] Chabrias took a unit of hoplites, as well as lightly-armoured mercenaries in the style of peltasts, the favourite soldier of fourth-century Athens, following their smashing success under Iphicrates in the Corinthian War. With these troops, Chabrias manned the fort at Eleutherae – one of the most ancient garrisons in the region and strategically located near one of the few passes through the mountain range that formed a natural boundary for Boeotia, Attica, and the path from the Peloponnesian peninsula where Sparta was located. The towering Mount Cithaeron blocked most of this path, but the Spartans were confident they could overcome the challenge.

After the underwhelming expedition from the Spartan king Cleombrotus and his abject failure that was the Sphodrias affair, the Spartans had begged their far more competent king Agesilaus to lead a new series of invasions into Boeotia and Attica. Sparta was clearly beginning to worry about Thebes' growing power, and believed that the 'magnitude of the war called for a first-rate leader'.[16] If the mighty Agesilaus could not suppress the upstart Thebans, then no Spartan could. Agesilaus set off with a massive army of nearly 20,000 soldiers and 1,500 cavalry northwards, to the outskirts of Mount Cithaeron, where he soon came up with the Athenians and Chabrias, together with Gorgidas and the Sacred Band of Thebes in their first known appearance. The Athenians and Thebans held the higher ground, and were positioned on a ridge above the much larger Spartan army. This being their only tactical advantage, they intended to use it to the fullest extent.

After the customary light skirmishing, Agesilaus fully expected direct engagement in a pitched battle. He anticipated leveraging his overwhelming cavalry numbers to a quick, efficient victory. Instead of the order to advance, however, Chabrias commanded his phalanx to halt. He instructed his men to rest their shields on their knees and point their spears outstretched at the Spartans. In this stance they remained, in full battle lines atop their higher ground, looking down on the Spartans with expressions of contempt. It was a show of deep disrespect, directed not just at the Spartans but at the most famous general in all of Greece. And, since it came from an army composed of mere mercenaries from Athens and pairs of lovers from Thebes, it somehow seemed more scandalous than losing an actual battle.

After some time spent processing the scene and its possibilities, Agesilaus commanded the Spartans to retreat. He was confident in their discipline and uniformity, but also recognized that advancing up the steep ridge to meet the enemy would result in unsustainable losses. To the dismay of the ephors and his advisors, Agesilaus actually gave up on conquering Thebes during this campaign. He settled for rampaging across the countryside in order to destroy crops, starve the Boeotians, and push Thebes' allies back towards Sparta. In this, he found great success and his actions forced the Thebans to attack him the following spring. However, he failed to reconquer any meaningful Boeotian territory.

Meanwhile, the stance that the Athenians and the Sacred Band adopted to look down on Agesilaus and his men entered into legend. Word spread quickly of this position and all of Greece was soon gossiping about it. For this victory, Chabrias earned himself a statue in Athens and he asked that it display him in a particular pose to commemorate the glorious moment. The Athenian sculptors honoured his request and the resulting statue became so well-regarded that adopting the pose became quite a trend. The Roman historian Cornelius Nepos begins his brief biography of Chabrias with discussion of this very position, noting how 'athletes, and artists as well, adopted appropriate attitudes for the statues which were set up in their honour when they had won victories.'[17]

So the Sacred Band's first adventure saw little fighting, but did establish them as a symbol of anti-Spartan resistance and exemplars of a disciplined, highly trained military unit. The Theban army, likely with the Sacred Band leading the way, continued to liberate Boeotian city-states over the next few years. Their next attempt after the showdown with Agesilaus was at Thespiae, but they failed to take the city though they did bring justice to Phoebidas. Gorgidas and the Theban army assaulted Thespiae several times, taking smaller fortresses but not the main city. Phoebidas, now harmost of Thespiae, marched out to meet the Sacred Band of Thebes in battle. He fought valiantly, but by the end of the day the formidable Spartan who had conquered Thebes was killed in combat against the Sacred Band.

Gorgidas led the Sacred Band admirably, but within a year of the defeat of Phoebidas, the Band came under the leadership of Pelopidas and their tactics were transformed. Pelopidas was a man of great cunning, who succeeded in using the Sacred Band as the bedrock of Thebes' military ascendancy. Shortly after the revolution for Thebes finished in 379, Pelopidas bagan systematically conquering the Boeotian cities and liberating them from Spartan rule. He would become Thebes' most famous commander and would go on to be elected boeotarch every year for the following fourteen years until his death.

Over the next three years under Pelopidas' leadership, from 378 to 375, the fighting skills of the Sacred Band of Thebes became a sight to behold.

Their martial excellence and each man's unwavering devotion to his partner forged a unique offensive force that was unlike any other military unit in Greece. They fought not just to protect their beloved, but also to impress him and even compete with him. Time and again they struck fast, hard, and unpredictably against the Spartans. Plutarch gives an artistic sketch of the Sacred Band in action:

> For just as horses run faster when yoked to a chariot than when men ride them singly, not because they cleave the air with more impetus owing to their united weight, but because their mutual rivalry and ambition inflame their spirits; so he thought that brave men were most ardent and serviceable in a common cause when they inspired one another with a zeal for high achievement.[18]

Despite this, for the Sacred Band and the Theban military as a whole, there was precious little time for standard training. Years of Spartan occupation and the sudden shift to rebellion had given Theban forces little time to prepare against opponents who had been training for war since childhood. Instead, training for the Thebans took place on the battlefield. After the revolution of 379 the battles had been nonstop, so that the Theban hoplites hardly needed to practise formations or troop movements. Fascinatingly, Lycurgus, the author of the Spartan constitution, actually prohibited repeated engagement with the same enemy for exactly this reason: through habitual conflict their foes would learn how to better fight the Spartans and potentially how to beat them.[19]

When Agesilaus returned from one of the many fruitless campaigns against the Thebans, the Spartan diplomat Antalcidas quipped a line worthy of inclusion among the wittiest Spartan quotes: 'Indeed, this is a fine tuition-fee which thou art getting from the Thebans, for teaching them how to war and fight when they did not wish to do it.'[20] The moment surely reveals Antalcidas' soreness over the recent dissolution of his peace treaty that had ended the Corinthian War. That treaty was, of course, no longer relevant. The Boeotian War was now raging across Greece.

The Second Athenian League

While the Thebans were busy slowly but surely rebuilding the Boeotian Confederacy, the Athenians had similar ambitions to reconstitute their old empire. We have covered the resurgence of Athenian colonialism across the Aegean Sea, but the outbreak of the Boeotian War and the Spartans' failed attack on Athens' harbour by Sphodrias had lit a fire under the Athenians. Sparta had threatened their very existence yet again, and flagrantly violated treaty after treaty. By 378, Athens was in open conflict with Sparta's increasingly vulnerable hegemony, but such defiance was not sufficient either for their bloodlust or their long term strategic planning. Their aim was the complete re-establishment of Athenian thalassocracy. A naval empire as vibrant as the Delian League would provide not only the fleet needed for military engagements, but also a stable source of grain, foodstuffs, and other supplies that Athens depended on when the Spartans invariably burned the Attic countryside. Moreover, it would bring Athens a more influential place at the diplomatic table and, perhaps, a bulwark against the rising tide of Thebes and their rapid successes under Pelopidas. And with public sentiment across Greece souring on Sparta after their abuse of their subjects, Athens found plenty of willing allies in city-states and islands.

This new Delian League is now known to historians as the Second Athenian League. In order to convince sceptical Aegean city-states that Athens had, at very long last, learned her lesson on how to treat allies, the Athenians created a new imperial model distancing themselves from the corruption of the old Delian League. Their recruiting pitch was simple: we were once your oppressors, but now we stand with you as fellow victims of Spartan tyranny. The Athenian ambassadors found many states willing to lend their support, who apparently preferred the devil they knew in Athens, as opposed to the increasingly unpredictable Spartans. The league's earlier supporters, prior to the outbreak of the Boeotian War, had included Chios, Thasos, Samothrace, Tenedos, and Lesbos. These were excellent additions to any naval symmachy, but much larger and wealthier cities such as Byzantium, Rhodes, and Mytilene all rejoined the Athenians' naval empire during the recruitment drive that followed the Sphodrias affair.

The Second Athenian League's formal origins are found in a new constitution, entitled the Decree of Aristoteles. Discovered on a stele in the Athenian agora near a sacred statue of Zeus, the decree paradoxically boasted both of Athens' imperial might and her humility. The stele outlined not just the contractual parameters of the Second Athenian League, but clearly outlined its limitations. In fact, most of the document was an intricate description of elaborate legal provisions, crafted to avoid any repetition of Athens' exploitation of the Delian League.

The first matter was to explicitly proclaim that there would be no economic exploitation by the Athenians, no agriculture outside Attica (to protect members from Athens' historic passion for stealing grain), and no imperial occupation by their soldiers. The decree made this crystal clear in its opening clauses:

> So that the Spartans shall allow the Greeks to be free and autonomous and to live at peace, possessing securely all their own [territory]…the People shall resolve: if any[one] of the Greeks or…the islanders…wishes to be an ally of the Athenians and the allies, it shall be permitted to him, being free and autonomous, living under the constitution which he wishes, neither receiving a garrison or a governor nor paying tribute, on the same terms as the Chians and Thebans and the other allies.[21]

The second, but equally important, matter dealt with was to hold sacrosanct the independence and autonomy of each member state. Apart from offering a litany of technical clauses allowing states to reject or appeal against particular policies, the Decree of Aristoteles designed a council, called a *synedrion*, that would give all members – except Athens – an equal voice and vote. Athens not only had no vote at all, but the other allies could vote on Athenian properties. No longer would Athens seize territories across the Aegean as she wished, nor would she charter the course of the alliance by herself. All policies would have to be approved by the council.

The matter of finances was especially critical. The Athenians had, both figuratively and literally, robbed the coffers of the Delian League to the extent that the treasury on the island of Delos was little more than Athens' piggy bank. The Second Athenian League ensured this would not recur by transforming the standard tribute system into a *syntaxis* – a communal contribution to the League, distinguished by its optional nature, and exclusively controlled by the council at large, with no Athenian input. The *syntaxis* was immediately successful in its ability to garner support for the formation of this new league and persuade hesitant allies that Athens could now be trusted. It caused the Second Athenian League, however, to never stray far from poverty. Over the next few decades, Athens and the league were little more than paupers in comparison to their predecessor the Delian League. In 455, Xenophon would write a book investigating the Athenian financial system's failures and how it failed to overcome 'the pressure of poverty on the masses'[22] in its relationships with its allies. But irrespective of the high price Athens paid, the Decree of Aristoteles was a shining example of how Athens had steadfastly committed herself to better treatment of her allies – for now.

As was common in other symmachies, mutual protection was paramount. The decree demands the states protect each other from attackers, and explicitly names Athens as being required to assist in all cases. The stele reads, 'If anybody attacks those who have made the alliance, either by land or by sea, the Athenians and the allies shall support the latter both by land and by sea with all their strength as far as possible.'[23] What's more, the decree specifically affirms the King's Peace of 387, both to emphasize Athens' commitment to the treaty's promise of autonomy for all Greek city-states and also to underscore to Persia that this new symmachy would not challenge the King of Kings. The Decree of Aristoteles concludes with an itemized list of the more than sixty city-states and islands that joined this new Second Athenian League.

At every level of its design, the new league was the inverse of the old. Where the Delian League protected Greek interests against Persia, the Second Athenian League targeted one Greek state and gave special accommodations to Persia. Where the Delian League had tribute, land seizures, and hegemony, the Second Athenian League had optional tax collection, guaranteed territorial autonomy, and a true democracy. But while Athens was successful in persuading new states to join the new League, keeping them in it was another matter. Their most pressing need was financial. Shipbuilding and wages quickly ate away at their accounts, and the Athenians were not yet ready to exploit their new allies as they did at Delos generations earlier. The solution was found in a new tax model for Athens.

For generations, the Athenian liturgical tax system fuelled the state and civic life (liturgy in Greek literally meant 'work for the people'). It was the responsibility of a handful of wealthy elites to pay the taxes that met virtually all the costs of running Athens. Instead of being seen as a burden, it was often viewed as an honour to be selected for the privilege of taxation and was not typically met with dismay. Each of these wealthy men was also required to fund the construction and wages for a trireme, strengthening Athens' naval foundation. After the collapse of the Athenian empire, however, even the wealthiest Athenians could not afford to keep the state running.

Thus in 377, under the archonship of Nausinikos, the tax system was redesigned for the new circumstances of the Second Athenian League and the war effort against Sparta. The taxpayers were again chosen from Athens' upper echelons, as determined by property ownership, and allocated into groups of about one hundred. These tax consortiums were known as the *symmoria* or the 'sharing together'. Each was responsible for a particular tax portion in Athens that year, on a rotating basis and based on the civil and military demands of the day. They shared the financial burden corporately among them, lessening the individual impact and allowing flexibility to spread major costs across multiple citizens or even *symmoria*.

This innovative approach quickly proved a boon to the merchants and shipbuilders of Athens and the Aegean islands. The funding of triremes remained with the new system, and ships were added annually to the Athenian fleet and the Second Athenian League navy. Moreover, the *symmoria* stimulated trade and commerce. Merchants poured into the Athenian harbour at Piraeus to capitalize on the opportunities opened up by the remade naval empire. They did need cash, however, and new systems of moneylending emerged to meet the demand. Loans were made available to ships sailing from Athens, where more favourable interest rates encouraged trade. Additionally, the design of maritime loans was changed to offer an early form of insurance for lost ships and cargo, and though it came with high risk it allowed for a substantial increase in trade deals of medium size. The wealthiest Athenians saw no advantage, but it greatly increased commercial opportunities for the merchants and middle classes. These innovative financial moves became the bedrock of Athens' fiscal recovery from the devastation of the past wars.

Athens was now properly ready for another full-scale war with Sparta. And the timing was prescient, as in 377 Agesilaus marched on Attica and Boeotia yet again.

Chapter 7

Three Harrowing Years
of the Boeotian War, 377–375

Agesilaus' Campaigns of 377

The King's Peace of 387 had included strong emphasis on the preservation of autonomy for all Greek city-states. It was this agenda that Agesilaus was prosecuting in 377 when he led another expedition into Boeotia, determined to end the reconstitution of the Boeotian Confederacy. His argument was that by absorbing the Boeotian city-states back into the confederacy under Theban leadership, Thebes was violating the King's Peace and undermining the autonomy of those cities. Whether Agesilaus actually believed this or whether he was pursuing vengeance was not relevant.

Agesilaus sent word ahead to the Spartan garrison at Thespiae that they should occupy the pass through the Cithaeron mountain range into Boeotia. This pass, the Dryoscephalae, was always strategically significant for Greek trade and military campaigns, but was now taking on a special pre-eminence in the annual Spartan invasions of Boeotia. The Spartans were facing increasing challenges in navigating the pass without being attacked by the Thebans or Athenians. Whoever controlled the Dryoscephalae controlled access to Thebes.

As spring began in 377, Agesilaus marched towards the pass from the Spartan homeland in the Peloponnese. After the last campaign's focus on Thespiae and the troop movements that he had ordered before his departure, the Thebans expected Agesilaus' attentions to again be focused on Thespiae as the forward base for his eventual assault on Thebes herself. The cunning Agesilaus anticipated their thoughts, however, feinting towards Thespiae before turning sharply northeast towards the heartland of Boeotia, close to the city of Thebes itself. The Thebans were caught completely off guard, having fortified the entire road to Thespiae further north and west, so Agesilaus trekked ahead happily unhindered to the farmlands southeast of Thebes. Once they had crossed the earthworks and barricades at the village of Scolus along the Asopos River, the Spartan army was shielded by the forbidding landscape of the region. The geographer Strabo once described the cruelty of the rugged crags and rocks of Scolus, quoting a common saying of the Boeotians: 'Neither go to Scolus thyself nor follow another thither.'[1] To make matters worse for the Thebans, Agesilaus had marched at double speed, covering twice the distance a Spartan army typically averaged in a single day. He and his army now set about ravaging the countryside to the east of Thebes, destroying all that he could while always keeping the city walls on his left side.

Once aware of Agesilaus' trickery, the Thebans moved quickly to the Spartans' rear, hoping to force a decisive battle that would end the campaign. As in their previous encounter with Agesilaus, the Thebans occupied the high ground and therefore had a significant advantage if the Spartans were to attack. But regrettably for Thebes, Agesilaus had anticipated the situation. He refused to meet the Thebans in combat, and instead began retreating rapidly towards the walls of Thebes, which were within sight. Keeping up his inclination to compliment Agesilaus on every possible occasion, Xenophon declares this manoeuvre 'a stroke of genius'.[2]

It was a brilliant move, of course. The Spartans sprinted towards Thebes, while the Thebans raced along the top of the hill overlooking them. Without breaking speed, the Thebans volleyed spears down at the defenceless Spartans, striking several including a polemarch. Undaunted, the Spartans continued their headlong rush, the prize that was Thebes growing ever closer on the horizon, while the Thebans had to change course as their ridge came to an end. Agesilaus capitalized on this opportunity, ordering his light infantry, the Skiritai, to attack the Theban rearguard. Still, the majority of Theban forces made it to the city walls in time to repel the invaders, even as the Spartans cut down the luckless men at the tail of their ranks. At the walls of Thebes, the Spartans halted and withdrew. Though it was not a real battle – and they had been outsmarted – the Thebans celebrated this skirmish as a triumph and erected a memorial trophy at the site.

Sparta had earned a moral victory, but would soon pay dearly for it. On the way back, after using his cavalry to eliminate some Thebans who had tried to harry the retreating Spartans, Agesilaus again made his way to the city of Thespiae. While Thespiae had been the stronghold of Spartan presence in Boeotia these past few years, it was now in turmoil. Pro-Theban forces in the city had staged their own rebellion and were in open conflict with the pro-Spartan faction. Agesilaus, however, refused to intervene and declined the oligarch's request to execute several supporters of the Boeotian Confederacy. He did assist in quelling the civil strife in the city, then returned to Sparta by way of Megara, burning Boeotian farmland all along the way. But while he was in Megara, one of his legs suddenly became swollen and congested, violently painful and inflamed. Worse still, the affliction was in his previously healthy leg – the other had been lame from birth. Agesilaus had earned much of his fame precisely because he had overcome these physical limitations in his many victorious campaigns.

Xenophon says that a blood vessel had burst in Agesilaus' leg, causing such swelling that he had to be carried home to Sparta on a litter. Whatever it was, he was in overwhelming pain and unable to move for long stretches of time. In fact the injury so crippled the great general that Xenophon, his most ardent supporter, now labels him 'a bedridden invalid'.[3] It took a surgeon who journeyed all the way from Syracuse to alleviate Agesilaus' pain. The surgeon succeeded in draining excess blood and fluid from his leg via an incision at the ankle, and while the injury took months to heal Agesilaus was eventually able to return to the twin arenas of the battlefield and Spartan politics.

Life was not proving rosy for the Thebans, however. In his campaigns through Boeotia, Agesilaus had burned vast acres of wheat fields and destroyed the entire crop yield for the region. The war had eliminated two years of harvest and starvation was imminent. The Thebans sent ambassadors to the port city of Pagasae in Thessaly with a fortune of ten talents (approximately 600 lbs of silver/gold) to buy grain. The fact that Thebans had to outsource their grain was painful enough, as the golden fields of Boeotian wheat were a source of their pride and livelihood, but the fact that they were forced to humble themselves to their ancient rivals the Thessalians was much worse. They secured several ships' worth of grain and prepared to sail back to Boeotia.

However, an ambitious Spartan harmost named Alcetas, from the nearby city of Oreus on the large island of Euboea, decided to make a name for himself just as Phoebidas and Sphodrias had done. He sent three triremes that captured the grain ships, together with 300 Theban sailors whom he promptly imprisoned in his citadel in Oreus.

While the Thebans languished in his prison, Alcetas celebrated his upcoming promotion with a riotous party that would have made Bacchus envious. During the festivities, he became enraptured with a young servant whom he took back to his quarters. The 300 Thebans seized the moment to break out of the citadel's prison, start a revolt that overthrew the Spartan garrison in the city, and finally take back their grain ships. Instead of the Boeotians facing starvation the situation was now radically changed – the Thebans had liberated another city from Spartan rule and opened a viable trade route with Thessaly to provide grain for the duration of the war. For the rest of the Theban-Spartan conflicts, the supply of wheat was not a major issue in Boeotia.

Once again, a rogue Spartan commander had changed the course of history due to an absence of traditional Spartan discipline. Phoebidas had started the war with the conquest of Thebes, Sphodrias had drawn Athens into the war with the attempted conquest of Piraeus, and now Alcetas had squandered a golden opportunity to end the war by wrecking the Spartan blockade of Thebes' grain supply.

The Battle of Naxos, 376

The following spring of 376, the Spartans were not able to wage a land campaign due to the relegation of Agesilaus. They turned instead to their other king, Cleombrotus. He began another invasion of Boeotia and marched north, but as he came to the mountain pass at Cithaeron, he began to realize the futility of another such assault on Thebes. A brief skirmish with the Thebans and Athenians at the pass cemented this view, and he retreated back to Sparta and called a council.

Cleombrotus now offered a new strategy – though not one that scaled back Sparta's hostilities against the rebellious Thebans and Athenians, lest 'faintheartedness… soon lead to their being absolutely worn out by the war.'[4]

He proposed that instead, the Spartans shift their offensive actions towards Athens and her nascent naval empire, figuring that Sparta could attempt to drive a wedge between the new allies in the Second Athenian League and their former overlords in Athens. Furthermore, Cleombrotus argued that the two years of assaults on Thebes had been ultimately in vain, as even the mighty Agesilaus had failed to overcome the treacherous geography of a land invasion into Boeotia.

Cleombrotus' motivation was probably questionable. By the year 376, he had developed a reputation for avoiding direct combat that was not unearned. He had been the first Spartan general to respond with full force to the Theban revolution of 379, but despite having a full army of Spartan hoplites he only lasted sixteen days on campaign in Boeotia. He had withdrawn despite tactical advantages, and may have put an end to the Boeotian War before it truly began. From that moment, he would never surpass – or even approach – Agesilaus in the eyes of the Spartan assembly. His actions in 376 were not much better, and his refusal to enter the pass at Cithaeron did him no favours. The proposal to pivot to a naval war had sound strategy behind it, but many Spartan ephors viewed it as simply another attempt to avoid direct confrontation with the Thebans. Nevertheless, the council accepted his proposal, and set their sights on strangling Athens and her maritime trade. With a foothold in Athens, the Spartans could march unfettered into a Boeotia bereft of allies. They therefore decreed the organization of a fleet of 60 triremes and appointed a commander named Pollis to lead it.

Pollis was a capable admiral and had travelled far across Greece, which was unusual for natives of Sparta, which normally sequestered its citizens from the outside world. He is most infamous, perhaps, not for his naval exploits but for his involvement in a scheme against the philosopher Plato. Pollis had been tasked with killing or enslaving the philosopher after Plato had frustrated the wishes of the Syracusan tyrant Dionysius. Dionysius had invited Plato to Sicily to visit the renowned city of Syracuse a decade before the Boeotian War. Plato was one of many cultural leaders that Dionysius had brought to Sicily in an effort to bolster his public image and surround himself with the most famous men of the day. But Plato had his own agenda, wishing to enhance his knowledge of philosophy and test his political theories in practice by potentially converting the tyrant to his ideals of just rule.

Dionysius had heavily insinuated to Plato that there was a possibility the philosopher could install a version of his ideal form of government in Syracuse. That ideal is set out in his dialogue *The Republic*, in which he proposes a state where citizens are assigned roles not based on wealth or class, but on the character of their soul. In his model, the state is ruled by philosopher-kings, a select few whose souls are governed most by reason. These individuals are chosen for their intelligence, strategic thinking, and virtue. Those whose souls are most influenced by willpower or spirit are given the roles of auxiliaries, the warriors and soldiers who protect the state and enforce the philosopher-kings' maxims. The vast majority of the population, though, would be the producers. Their souls are ruled by natural desires and appetites, and that drive causes them to constantly create things, whether it be art or produce or buildings. The producers provide the material needs of the state. Above all, the Republic of Plato is designed to promote justice, and these strict social classes ensure that the state would prosper and achieve that goal.

Of course, Plato was offering this model purely as a thought experiment – until Dionysius approached him. Dionysius was all too happy to encourage Plato to map out how Syracuse could convert to this model of government, until Plato informed him that he would not be classed as a philosopher-king. This was unconscionable to the tyrant, who now viewed Plato as a threat to his authority and put him on a ship going back to Athens. The captain of Plato's ship was none other than the Spartan Pollis, and he had been ordered by Dionysius to kill the philosopher en route. Dionysius did suggest an ironic alternative to the death sentence, though, which was for Pollis to sell the philosopher into slavery. This, he said, might be appealing to Plato as he would be 'quite as happy, being a just man, even if he should become a slave.'[5] Pollis obligingly sold Plato into slavery on the island of Aegina, not far from Athens. Of course, as we now know he would manage to make his way home to Athens and continue to work at his Academy. Outside of Sparta, this enslavement of history's greatest philosopher was Pollis' most famous accomplishment.

Pollis sailed with the shiny new Spartan fleet to the island of Naxos in the central Aegean Sea. One of the most strategically located islands in the Aegean and a major trading port between the Ionian coast and mainland

Greece, Naxos was often a bellwether for control of the sea. The feisty residents of Naxos also had a complex relationship with the Athenians. The island had been the target of a failed invasion by a rogue Persian satrap in 499, and the satrap had opted to appeal to the Greeks for aid rather than return home to face punishment. Athens was the main Greek city-state to respond and became allies in the Ionian Revolt, where cities up and down the Ionian coast fought back against Persian tyranny. Eventually, Athens provoked Persia too far by burning the Persian regional capital, and Darius the Great responded by initiating the first Persian invasion of Greece. Naxos was expected to show gratitude to her Athenian 'rescuers' so was one of the first states to join the Delian League in 478. But just seven years later she became the first state to secede from the League, citing the all-too-common complaint of Athenian imperial oppression. Athens responded by conquering the island and demanding a brutal annual tribute.

A century later in September 376, the Athenian fleet was sailing to Naxos again. This time, however, their primary motivation was not tribute or suppression, but trade. Pollis had found fast success in choking off sea trade into Athens. Following the orders of Cleombrotus and the ephors, Pollis had used the Spartan navy to cut off access to almost all major trade ports in the southern Aegean and Cycladic islands. Spartan ships lurked around every island from Aegina to Ceos to Andros, so that Athenian trade vessels could only journey as far as the southernmost tip of Euboea – not nearly enough for supplying the bustling metropolis. Grain trading remained Athens' lifeblood, and without action the city would soon begin to starve. The situation was desperate.

Naxos was one of the best-placed islands for grain trade in the Aegean. Athens' control of the sea lanes and of strategic sites like Naxos was therefore essential, not only for her imperial ambitions but for the very survival of her population. With this as justification, Athens sent her greatest commander, the hero Chabrias. Fresh from his success against Agesilaus alongside the Sacred Band of Thebes, Chabrias proved as adept at naval warfare as he was at conducting land campaigns. After ensuring a particularly large shipment of grain made it safely into the Athenian harbour of Piraeus, Chabrias set his sights on Pollis and the Spartan fleet. He sailed to Naxos with a fleet of 83 triremes.

Chabrias was an excellent admiral, but nevertheless the Athenians hoped they would only need to fight the Naxians and be able to take the island before the full Spartan fleet arrived. They brought 20,000 soldiers and siege engines, aiming to quickly destroy the storied walls of Naxos. Naxos, though, was famously difficult to conquer – as the Persians could confirm. Chabrias had begun to besiege the city and was on the way to success, but he ran out of time and Pollis arrived with the Spartan fleet of 65 triremes before he could fully take the island. Chabrias left his soldiers to continue the siege, and set off in his trireme to direct the combat. Chabrias was never one to hesitate when it came to bloodshed – Plutarch describes his tendency to rush headlong into battle and his violent temperament: 'His spirit was excited and all on fire, and he would rush on with the boldest at too great a hazard.'[6] The land battle with the Naxians was all but forgotten by Chabrias when the Athenian ships met the Spartan fleet just outside the island's harbour: the battle of Naxos was underway.

The two sides arranged themselves in lines facing each other. The site of the battle was the Strait of Paros, between the island of Naxos and its neighbour Paros. The strait was about 20 kilometres at its widest and generally considered safe water for trade. While the Aegean Sea's formidable Meltemi winds can whip up waves of a metre or more here in the summer and early fall, the passage was navigable for seasoned captains. Much of the trade between Ionian Greece and the mainland went through this very strait. On the peninsula that overlooked the spot where the seabattle took place stood the majestic Temple of Apollo, silhouetted against the sky in the city of Naxos.

Pollis' fleet was outnumbered, but that was familiar territory for the Spartans. While the Spartans were not historically seafarers like the Athenians, Corinthians, or Phoenicians, their expertise in military strategy and discipline was more than sufficient for them to create a formidable navy. Their fleet was funded by a mixture of Persian subsidies, which had decreased substantially over the years, and tribute from their allies in the Peloponnesian League. While their *agoge* training did not focus on nautical warfare, they had plenty of qualified strategic thinkers such as Lysander, Callicratidas, or Agesilaus' half-brother Teleutias. And, of course, the Spartans never lacked slaves to man their triremes – the helots handled that duty.

Naval warfare had not changed substantially since the end of the Peloponnesian War in 404, and Athenian and Spartan triremes had met in combat at multiple major battles over the past three decades, including the decisive battle of the Peloponnesian War at Aegospotami and the battle of Cnidus during the Corinthian War. In naval battles of the fourth century, the mighty trireme still reigned supreme. These vessels with their three banks of oars were designed for a lethal combination of speed and force. They were 120 feet long, and had a crew of 170 oarsmen rowing in unison. In addition to a commander and several crewmen, each trireme also had a small force of marines who provided protection and could jump aboard an enemy ship for close combat.

Trireme warfare was fundamentally about ramming your opponent with the bronze beak of the vessel, which acted as a battering ram and could smash through the wooden sides of a ship easily. The ram could weigh as much as 1,000 pounds and was known as the *embolon*, which translates to 'wedge' – a name that encapsulates the purpose and function of the deadly weapon. Since the advent of the trireme in the early 400s, many men had died when an *embolon* ripped the sides of their ship apart. They drowned in the chaotic waters of the Aegean Sea or were put to death by enemy spears. There simply was no more deadly sea vessel in the ancient world than a trireme captained by a veteran commander.

There were two primary manoeuvres in trireme warfare: the *diekplous* and the *periplous*. In the *diekplous*, the trireme went full speed at the enemy lines and broke through the front ranks, opening a gap that allied triremes then poured through. In the *periplous*, a trireme sailed directly past the opposing ship, then looped back round in a J-shape to attack from behind. More complex tactics included staging a 'double-attack' where two triremes hit an enemy ship at once, or even pulling the oars inside the ship and sailing on fast, directly along the side of an enemy trireme, thus snapping off the enemy's oars and leaving them helpless in the water. The goal of trireme warfare was to ram or disable enough enemy ships to create a chaotic melee that forced the opposition to retreat. Athens had found particular success with their practised perfection of weaponizing triremes, from standardized tactics to building the necessary infrastructure to deploy triremes en masse.

The design of the trireme was an upgraded version of the Archaic period's *pentekonter* – a substantially smaller galley with one row of oars and just fifty rowers. The earliest triremes were likely brought to Greece from the great seafarers of the Levant, Phoenicia, and were first used by the Corinthians. The Corinthian navy had been the best of the Greeks for generations until it was eclipsed by the Athenian navy, during the Persian Wars of the early fifth century. Under the visionary leadership of their statesman and admiral Themistocles, the Aegeans had built a world-class trireme fleet in just a few years. Their navy not only secured them victory in the Persian Wars, but also laid the foundations of the Delian League and the Athenian Golden Age. It was these Athenians who perfected the trireme design and made it the gold standard war vessel of the Mediterranean. But now, the Athenians were fighting for their own survival against the historically land-based Spartans.

Similar to hoplite warfare, the strongest fighters were usually placed on the right wing. The Spartans adopted this traditional formation with Pollis positioning himself on that side. Facing him on the Athenian left wing was an accomplished, veteran captain named Cedon. Also commanding his own ship was one of Cedon's lieutenants, a promising young captain named Phocion. At just 25 years old, Phocion was already on the fast track to the upper echelons of Athenian statecraft. He had an excellent pedigree for an Athenian politician, being a former student of Plato and a close friend of Xenocrates, the future leader of Plato's Academy. The battle of Naxos was Phocion's first taste of war, and he was eager to prove himself. He had intentionally sought a command under Chabrias, primarily to learn from his military genius and leadership, but with the bonus of advancing his political career by being at the forefront of major conflicts under Athens' top general. Chabrias himself positioned his own trireme in the rather unorthodox centre, alongside 'the strongest part of the fleet.'[7]

Just before the battle began, Chabrias set in motion a cunning scheme that would have impressed the crafty Athenian admiral Themistocles or even Odysseus himself. He ordered the Athenian triremes to discreetly lower their flags, making it more difficult to identify the Athenian ships amongst the more than one hundred triremes. The historian Polyaenus described how the Spartan captains, searching for Attic flags, actually sailed directly past the Athenian triremes without recognizing their enemy. The Spartans would have surely realized their mistake – but not in sufficient time to counter the inevitable Athenian attack.[8] The Athenian subterfuge offered no advantages for the Athenian ships on the left flank, however. Pollis sailed his ships straight at Cedon and the Athenian triremes in what seems to have been a *diekplous* manoeuvre. The Spartans quickly gained the upper hand, and began systematically smashing the Athenian ships. Pollis recognized the flagship of the admiral Cedon and sailed straight for it, personally killing Cedon and sinking his ship in what Diodorus described as 'a brilliant contest'.[9] The rest of Cedon's triremes were scattered.

The young Phocion, however, was still holding his position on that side. He stayed and fought fiercely against the Spartans, refusing to cede the left wing. Little detail is given about Phocion's actions, and the significantly lacking sources on the battle of Naxos make it impossible to reconstruct what precisely occurred. It is clear, though, that Phocion's bravery at least delayed the Spartan advance. Chabrias and the stronger Athenian triremes in the centre were given sufficient time to send reinforcements. They arrived quickly enough to stop the complete collapse of the Athenian formation, which bent but did not break thanks to Phocion's heroism. In his *Life of Phocion*, Plutarch says, 'the battle raged hotly and the issue was speedily decided.'[10] Phocion earned his stripes at Naxos and leveraged it well; he would go on to become perhaps the greatest politician in Athens during the fourth century.

Meanwhile, at the other end of the battlefield, Chabrias' clever flag tactic was starting to give the Athenian triremes a clear advantage. The Spartan commanders were still looking for Attic flags and sailed past ships without them, allowing the Athenians to execute a *periplous* manoeuvre and attack the hapless Spartans from behind. As Chabrias had ordered, the *periplous* included a series of 'double ramming'[11] attacks, where two Athenian triremes simultaneously rammed into one Spartan ship. The Athenians had an easy time picking apart the Spartan triremes – which were easily identifiable as by this point in the battle the Spartan triremes were the only ships flying a flag at all. Any ship with a flag was hunted down and destroyed by the merciless Athenians. Chabrias' reinforcements soon repelled the enemy ships on the left flank, and with that the Spartan lines were broken entirely.

The Athenians had overcome the early Spartan momentum and made good use of their superior numbers to gain a much-needed victory, that not only helped the war effort but also secured the flow of grain back into Athens – and, most importantly, back into Athenian bellies. Chabrias' cunning, Phocion's courage, and the triumphant return of Athenian trireme warfare all created a special alchemy at the battle of Naxos and it was a resounding victory for the Athenians. Naxos was the first time Athens had fought a sea battle without the aid of other Greek ships in a generation. More critically, it was their first major naval victory since the Peloponnesian War.

Chabrias elected to not pursue the retreating Spartan ships. Eighteen Athenian triremes had been destroyed and the dead were given full burial honours. On the Spartan side, 24 ships had been lost and eight more were captured by the Athenians. Chabrias, along with the newly minted hero Phocion, sailed back into Piraeus with the captured Spartan triremes brimming with grain for the starving population. The Athenians celebrated the victory, but were perhaps short-sighted in appreciating its significance. The battle of Naxos was the first pitched battle of the Boeotian War and was a smashing success for the anti-Spartan allies. After several years of skirmishing and prolonged invasions of Boeotia, the war had finally seen its first battle, and it was one the Spartans lost decisively.

The Battle of Alyzeia, 375

By June of 375, the Thebans were looking to exploit any flagging of Spartan energy. As campaign season drew near, all of Greece expected another Spartan invasion of Boeotia – and this time the triumphant return of Agesilaus to the head of the army. Moreover, the Spartans planned to ferry hoplites across the Gulf of Corinth to avoid the challenges they had faced with the pass at Cithaeron over the past few years. Rather than confronting this unpleasant reality, the Thebans now thought of a new plan. Much like their clever manipulations during the Sphodrias affair, they aimed to get the Athenians to do their dirty work. They sent ambassadors to Athens to request that the Athenian fleet sail round the entire Peloponnesian Peninsula to the opposite side of the Isthmus of Corinth. Their thinking was that the Spartans would not be able to manage the dual tasks of raising a large army of invasion while keeping a firm grip on their allies in the Peloponnesian League, and at the same time keep their boot on the helots. The Thebans also began to foment dissent and rebellion among helot cities in the Peloponnese. It initially had limited effect, but would grow steadily. This would be the start of a grand Theban strategy to force the Spartans to constantly pick their poison between raising armies and quelling helot revolts. It was the tactic that would end the Spartan empire.

The Athenians agreed to the plan and Timotheus, son of the great admiral Conon, was given command of this expedition around the Peloponnese. Conon had been the most accomplished Athenian admiral of the past few decades, and had masterminded victory after victory during the Corinthian War. Intriguingly, his loyalties had not just been to the Athenian navy – Conon also led Persian and mercenary navies. In the disastrous Athenian defeat at the battle of Aegospotami that ended the Peloponnesian War, Conon was the captain of one of only nine Athenian ships that survived the battle. Fearing retribution from the Athenians, or from the Spartan-allied Thirty Tyrants who now governed Athens, Conon self-exiled to Cyprus and then into Persian territory. He spent the next decade in mercenary work. During the Corinthian War, however, Conon's leadership of the Persian fleet led to his grand homecoming to Athens. He returned to rebuild the walls of the city and the harbour at Piraeus, and to reclaim the Athenians' position as a naval superpower. Conon quickly became the undisputed leader of Athens, setting the city back on the track to imperial power and ensuring her long-term survival after the catastrophic losses against Sparta.

Conon's son Timotheus, therefore, had big shoes to fill. And he went on to do exactly that in time. The Athenian orator Isocrates would later describe Timotheus as one of the greatest Athenian generals and 'superior to all the rest' for his acumen in strategy and leadership.[12] This was his first major command as a *strategos*, one of the annually elected Athenian generals, and he was given a sizeable fleet of 60 triremes to sail to the Gulf of Corinth. Circumnavigating the Peloponnese, however, was no easy feat. The city of Corinth had essentially built its entire commercial empire through helping traders avoid it, constructing a paved road across the Isthmus of Corinth so that merchants could simply travel by land instead of risking the sea voyage. There were precious few safe harbours on the journey and tempestuous weather was virtually guaranteed. Those ships brave enough to attempt it could complete the journey in 10–20 days if the weather was fair and the gods were appeased. As triremes were built for coastal navigation and were inherently unsuitable for long-distance, open-sea going, Timotheus' ships would be forced to hug the treacherous, steep cliffs all the way round.

The geographer Strabo claims the cape of Malea, at the very southern tip of the Peloponnesian Peninsula, was the most dangerous part of the journey. Many ships had been destroyed by what the Roman poet Statius called 'foaming Malea's dreaded headland'.[13] Many of those that survived were battered off course by the howling winds. Most strikingly, Malea was the very place where Odysseus had been swept away to the land of the lotus-eaters in *The Odyssey*, on his fateful journey back to Ithaca. It was so feared that the sailors of Greece had a proverb for it: 'But when you double Malae, forget your home.'[14]

Timotheus, however, was blessed by the gods and made the journey with minimal delay. Along the way, he seems to have exhibited exceptional skills at conquest and diplomacy. He added to the Second Athenian League substantially by bringing into the fold the islands of Corcyra and Cephalonia, the Molossians of Epirus, and multiple cities on the coastal region of Acarnania. They all joined in quick succession after Timotheus showed that the Second Athenian League was fully committed to the promised light imperial touch – having conquered Corcyra, he changed no laws, put no man to death, and did not occupy the city. Once word of this spread, the rest joined the Athenian cause and cut all ties to the Spartans. Athens' new empire was rapidly expanding.

The Spartans got word of Timotheus' successes, and despatched their own fleet to meet him in combat. A Spartan navy of 55 triremes was given to the admiral Nicolochus, a man 'of consummate boldness'[15] who might rival Timotheus' impressive skills. Despite his success, Timotheus had not yet arrived at the Gulf of Corinth to blockade the ferrying of Spartan soldiers into Boeotia. Racing against the clock, Nicolochus aimed to intercept him before he could reach the gulf in time to thwart yet another Spartan invasion of Thebes. The Spartan fleet found Timotheus at the city of Alyzeia on the western coast of central Greece. Alyzeia was an Acarnanian city situated at the mouth of several key trade routes along the western coast of Greece, and was a natural location for Timotheus to target in order to expand the new Athenian naval empire. It was not a tall order to persuade any Acarnanian to stand against the Spartans. They were longtime enemies of Sparta and the Peloponnesian League, and had been staunch supporters of Athens in the Peloponnesian War.

When Nicolochus saw the Athenian fleet, he wasted no time in launching an attack. In fact he was so eager for the battle that he ordered the assault before his full fleet was in place, as they were still awaiting the arrival of six triremes from Ambracia which had been delayed. The two sides would be almost even, a rarity for Sparta in battle, with 55 Spartan triremes against 60 Athenians.

Timotheus was not to be caught by surprise. That morning, expecting the Spartans would arrive soon, he ordered all his triremes to be decorated with myrtle to celebrate the festival of Skira, a sacred holiday in Athens honouring the conclusion of the calendar year in June. The men believed that their holy day's patron goddess, Demeter, would offer them divine protection and give them a competitive advantage over their Spartan opponents. In his first battle command, Timotheus decided to employ some traditional Athenian trickery, as Chabrias had done with the flags at the battle of Naxos. The Spartans had arranged their triremes in the customary single line, and were waiting for the Athenians to make the same formation. Instead, Timotheus kept 40 of his triremes back from the fight and sent only 20 smaller vessels out to meet the Spartans. While lesser in number and size, these were fast ships manned by local Acarnians who knew the waters here intimately. Their orders were to harass the Spartans through constantly shifting tactics, creating maximum unpredictability and chaos. The Spartans pursued the Acarnian vessels as they darted back and forth, undoubtedly eliminating a few of the little ships.

This went on for quite some time, and after about an hour the Spartan rowers began to tire. Meanwhile, the bulk of the Athenian trireme crews remained fresh, simply watching from the sidelines. Timotheus judged his moment carefully and when he saw the Spartan oars begin to slow he ordered the full Athenian fleet to engage.[16] The Athenians made quick work of the exhausted Spartan ships and won the engagement decisively. Timotheus returned to Alyzeia and immediately built a trophy on the shore to commemorate the victory.

The battle of Alyzeia was not yet over, however. The delayed Spartan triremes from Ambracia had finally arrived and a vengeful Nicolochus, having survived the first assault, was now intent on punishing Timotheus. His remaining Spartan ships reinforced by the Ambraciot triremes, Nicolochus was eager for a second round. The Athenian vessels were by now beached and undergoing repairs from the battle they believed had ended, so were caught off guard. Scrambling to meet the Spartan ships, the Athenians barely managed to send out a small squadron. Timotheus, though, refused even to leave land and give the Spartans the dignity of another battle. When Nicolochus finally realized that Timotheus would not commit to another engagement, he gave up and departed. Trying to control the narrative, Nicolochus erected his own trophy on a neighbouring island to honour his 'victory' at Alyzeia.

Timotheus was now able to reach the Gulf of Corinth and hinder Sparta's plans for transporting hoplites into Boeotia. This not only required the Spartans to change their invasion plans, it also cemented the Athenians' renewed naval supremacy in Greece. Timotheus remained on the western coast to oversee the new additions to the Second Athenian League and to ensure that Sparta would not invade Boeotia by sea. Not all was going well for the Athenians, however, despite their rousing success at Naxos and Alyzeia. Naval empires were expensive, and they were rapidly running low on funds. The Delian League had the luxury of demanding more tribute from its peons, but the Second Athenian League was constitutionally forbidden from such a step. Timotheus was forced to take out loans on his own account, supplying the army under his own line of credit.[17] Plutarch recounted how Timotheus' 'naval superiority was undisputed, but he was forced to send to Athens for moneys.'[18] It foreshadowed the financial crisis that would one day bring down the Second Athenian League.

The year 375 had so far been resoundingly successful for the Thebans and Athenians in the Boeotian War. Their ability to prevent successful invasions of Boeotia and their two naval victories at Naxos and Alyzeia had left the Spartans wrongfooted. Total victory was in sight, but the Thebans had yet to meet the Spartan hoplites in a pitched battle on land. That was truly the Spartan strength, and the Thebans could only avoid direct land combat for so long. Later, in 375, the battle of Tegyra would be the first real test of the Theban military and the Sacred Band of Thebes.

Chapter 8

The Battle of Tegyra and the Peace Conference of 374

The Battle of Tegyra, 375

By 375, emboldened by the failure of repeated Spartan invasions, Pelopidas had led the Sacred Band of Thebes to liberate much of Boeotia, as part of a broader Theban strategy to free as many cities of the Boeotian Confederacy as possible. The Band was undefeated in direct combat and a fearsome enemy, but Pelopidas employed them cautiously and focused solely on cities that were weakly garrisoned or susceptible to attack. This had not limited their success. Quite quickly Thebes had regained many city-states back into her fold. More resistant cities such as Orchomenus, Plataea, and Thespiae were still occupied by the Spartans, but Pelopidas was nevertheless having some success against them. He and the Sacred Band won skirmishes outside each city, diminishing Sparta's grip and even assassinating a harmost or two. Yet the Thebans stuck to hit-and-run and guerrilla tactics, still avoiding direct confrontation with a full Spartan army and never risking a formal engagement.

But the Thebans could not avoid a pitched battle with the formidable Spartan hoplites for much longer. In the spring of 375, Pelopidas' network of spies discovered that the Spartan regiments in Orchomenus were being moved to support a campaign into the neighbouring region of Opuntan Locris. Orchomenus had been heavily fortified with two full *morai*, at least 1,200 Spartan hoplites. The Spartan plan was for most of those soldiers to march north to Locris, and they were to be relieved subsequently by a smaller contingent assigned to defend the city. This would leave a little precious time before the arrival of the reinforcements, when the city was compromised – and that was when Pelopidas and his Sacred Band would strike.

Orchomenus was a prize for Pelopidas. It was one of the most ancient cities of Boeotia and of fabled prosperity. Homer wrote of 'the wealth of Orchomenus',[1] comparing it to Egyptian Thebes, the wealthiest city of the day. It was also one of the greatest Mycenaean citadels, and likely was that Bronze Age civilization's capital for the entirety of central Greece. The tomb of the prominent poet Hesiod was there, as well as an ancient treasury so beautiful that the geographer Pausanias called it 'a wonder second to none either in Greece itself or elsewhere.'[2] Orchomenus features prominently in Greek mythology, too – Heracles was said to have fought the Orchomenian king to the death and diverted the Cephisus river to flow into the city. Early Orchomenians established colonies across the region and founded the port city of Iolcus, from where Jason and the Argonauts set sail on their legendary voyage.[3]

Orchomenus was strategically located near the western shore of Lake Copais and controlled access to the road systems of northwest Boeotia. Thebes controlled the east of the critical lake, but it was Orchomenus that controlled the west. Its fertile lowlands, fed by Lake Copais, made it wealthy from grain. The towering Mount Akontion protected it from the west, and the many rocky ridges and hills combined with marshes near the lake were a daunting prospect for any would-be invader.

The prestige and mythological origin of Orchomenus was also precisely why they hated the Thebans. It had only been a century or so since Thebes eclipsed Orchomenus in strength and relevance, and the Orchomenians had not yet come to terms with that reality. They had been a reluctant member of the Boeotian Confederacy during the Peloponnesian War, but there had been rising tension with Thebes over the direction of the symmachy. They finally saw their chance for rebellion during the Corinthian War, and seceded from the Boeotian Confederacy to join the Spartan side after Lysander had cultivated a relationship with the Orchomenian leaders. Following the King's Peace of 387, Orchomenus had been left independent as a reward. They competed with Thebes for dominance in Boeotia and willingly permitted Spartan forces to establish garrisons in their city, which became the main base for Spartan operations in the region.

In short, conquering Orchomenus would be a feather in the cap for Pelopidas and a turning point in the Boeotian War. With Sparta having not yet proven it could mount an invasion of Boeotia, the loss of Orchomenus would substantially weaken their capacity to conduct any activities in the territory. It would also ensure that the minor cities still under Spartan control would return to the Boeotian Confederacy. So when Pelopidas learned that the city would be temporarily vulnerable, he ordered his Sacred Band and a contingent of cavalry to march. In all, Pelopidas took at least 500 men with him, as Diodorus Siculus reports.[4]

Pelopidas and his army journeyed to Orchomenus along the south side of Lake Copais, hugging the coastline to avoid having to climb the steep mountains. After passing the city of Haliartus – home to the first great battle of the Corinthian War – they turned north and arrived at Orchomenus. But upon their arrival they found the city had already been reinforced by an additional, unexpected Spartan regiment. A last-minute change of plans for the Spartans had resulted in a brand new crop of reinforcements arriving from the Peloponnese, while the Spartan soldiers who were rotating back from Locris were still on their way. Dismayed at the shoddy information he had received and eager to avoid the full Spartan army that was advancing his way, Pelopidas ordered a retreat. He turned his army north and began the long, indirect road back to Thebes. Floods from the Meleas river blocked much of the route as it turned the fertile plains into swamps, and this route was the only one Pelopidas could take without climbing the high mountains. But before he had cleared the craggy foothills of the northern shore of Lake Copais, disaster struck. The Thebans marched right into the path of the returning Spartan *morai*.

The two armies intersected near the city of Tegyra. A small village just three miles northeast of Orchomenus, Tegyra was home to a respected temple of Apollo and up until the last century had also hosted a well known oracle of Apollo. Since the Persian Wars, both had largely fallen into disuse and the village had lost most of its former glory. Nevertheless, Tegyra boldly claimed itself the birthplace of Apollo, no doubt frustrating their neighbours in Delphi with their far more famous oracle.

The Spartans were equally caught off guard by the encounter, not expecting an assault by the Thebans. As the two armies unknowingly marched towards each other through a narrow pass, the sudden appearance of their opponents sent shock waves through Theban and Spartan alike. One panicking Theban shouted, 'We have fallen into our enemies' hands!'[5] The courageous Pelopidas shot back, 'And why haven't they fallen into ours?' Like all the most celebrated Greek generals, Pelopidas had a gift for striking remarks that captured the moment perfectly. Pelopidas' clever turn of phrase also revealed his decisive strategy for the surprise battle – he would go on the offensive. This was no easy task as the Thebans were vastly outnumbered. The Spartans had two full *morai*, at least 1,200 soldiers, which more than doubled the 500 Thebans. In their many centuries of hoplite warfare, the Spartans had never lost a battle when they outmanned their opponents. The outlook was grim and the logistics were certainly not of his design, but at that moment Pelopidas knew this engagement could be the inflection point of the Boeotian War. It would be the conflict's first pitched battle between the Thebans and the Spartans, and perhaps more importantly the first true test of the Sacred Band of Thebes. Pelopidas did not intend to waste the opportunity that the gods had given him.

He ordered his 200 cavalry to hold the front lines of the Theban ranks and skirmish with the Spartans, who were arranging themselves in standard phalanx formation. This in itself was an unusual command, as cavalry typically followed the hoplites. His options were limited, however, as Pelopidas had only brought soldiers intended for a surprise attack on an undermanned city. He had not planned on a full, pitched battle. While the Spartans had two full battle regiments, the Thebans had to make the best of their skeleton crew. Pelopidas next ordered the Sacred Band to align behind the cavalry in tight formation. This was a marked departure from his preference of placing them on a single wing, but the narrow pass at Tegyra limited his options. Pelopidas did not intend for his cavalry to charge; they were merely to harass the Spartan lines, buying time for the Sacred Band.

The Spartan commanders, Gorgoleon and Theopompus, were overconfident. Apart from the restrictive battlefield geography, the Spartans held every advantage. Each ordered their *mora* to advance. Their strategy appeared to be a standard Spartan phalanx, and once they were done skirmishing with the cavalry they would advance on the Theban hoplites. But to the shock of the Spartans, the Sacred Band suddenly stormed forward and smashed into the shields of the Spartan hoplites, breaking through the ranks quickly and efficiently. Their training and experience as stormtroopers had prepared them well for this and the Spartans had not expected such concentrated aggression. The blitzkrieg assault worked and the Sacred Band broke the front lines of the Spartans in a matter of moments.

Following the unexpected assault and the Sacred Band's rapid success, Pelopidas met the two Spartan polemarchs in battle himself shortly after the battle commenced. This is curious since Gorgoleon and Theopompus must therefore have been quite close together, an unusual arrangement given they each led their own *mora*. The military historian Murray Dahm suggests that this positioning may have been to 'represent their equal status.'[6] No matter the reason, Pelopidas recognized their unique formation and made sure to place himself so he could meet both Spartan leaders in combat. Pelopidas personally slew both the polemarchs.

In the heat of battle and now without their commanders, the Spartan tactics at Tegyra wound up mirroring the last battle in which the Spartans and Thebans had fought in the Corinthian War. At the battle of Coronea, the Thebans had been positioned on the right wing of the allied force and first shattered the Orchomenian formation, believing they had penetrated the Spartan lines and divided them. The Spartans, though, had cunningly allowed their middle to break so they could pivot back and attack the rear of the Theban hoplites. It proved devastatingly successful at Coronea, where the Thebans witnessed their victory dissolve into defeat within moments. The Spartans at Tegyra tried the same movement, intentionally splitting into two columns and allowing the Sacred Band to push through the middle. Plutarch suggests that this was less to attack the rear flank of the Thebans and more to allow them to pass by, hoping that they would continue on to a retreat. He also prefaces his description of the formation by noting how the 'whole [Spartan] army was seized with fear'[7] after the loss of their two polemarchs. Whether part of a grand strategy or not, a large tunnel now formed in the Spartan ranks.

But before the Spartans could decide on their counterattack, Pelopidas sprang another surprise on them. Instead of passing through the invitingly open lane, the Sacred Band entered it, then turned their assault on the centre of both Spartan columns (see Figure 8.1). The Thebans won the engagement overwhelmingly. In violation of all their sacred vows, the Spartans retreated. The Thebans intended to pursue, but were concerned about their proximity

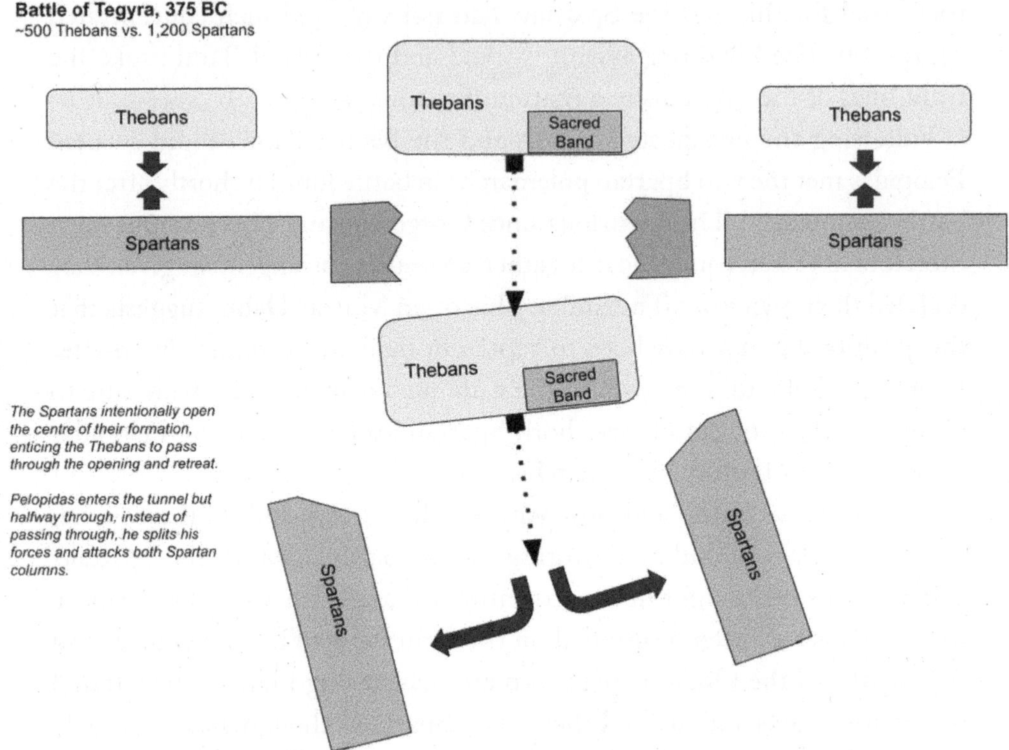

The Spartans intentionally open the centre of their formation, enticing the Thebans to pass through the opening and retreat.

Pelopidas enters the tunnel but halfway through, instead of passing through, he splits his forces and attacks both Spartan columns.

to Orchomenus and the possible arrival of Spartan reinforcements. Pelopidas constructed a trophy quickly and returned triumphantly to Thebes.

The battle of Tegyra ended more quickly and decisively than either side had envisioned. No specific numbers for casualties are given, but the real damage to Sparta lay in the blow to their reputation and mystique. Sparta had set multiple precedents in the battle, and none were welcome. It was the first occasion in historical record in which a Spartan force had been defeated by a numerically inferior enemy in a set battle. Moreover, it was the 'first time they were overpowered by the Thebans in a pitched battle',[8] as Plutarch remarks in his *Life of Agesilaus*. Continuing the precedents, it was one of the few times that Spartan hoplites retreated from battle in a panicked defeat. But the most important thing about Tegyra was that the engagement marked the combat debut of Thebes' Sacred Band, whose performance exceeded all expectations. The elite unit's maiden battle saw them crush a larger Spartan contingent and demolish the enemy's confidence.

Ancient historians wax lyrical over the battle of Tegyra. Diodorus Siculus and Plutarch both frame this as the pivotal battle that pulled back the curtain on Spartan military supremacy. It revealed what had never before been so clearly demonstrated: that Spartan warriors were not the only Greeks capable of achieving military excellence and rigorous discipline. Plutarch explains the Tegyra's legacy:

> But this battle first taught the other Greeks also that it was not [people of Sparta and its territories who] alone produced warlike fighting men, but that wheresoever young men are prone to be ashamed of baseness and courageous in a noble cause, shunning disgrace more than danger, these are most formidable to their foes.[9]

Perhaps most revealing is Xenophon's glaring omission of the battle of Tegyra from his many books. While his Spartan benefactors undoubtedly welcomed the exclusion of such a humiliating defeat from his chronicles of Greek and Spartan affairs, the deliberate silence ironically demonstrates to contemporary scholars just how profoundly the engagement affected Sparta.[10]

Meanwhile, Thebes was exuberant. They were confident that they were now entering the endgame of the Boeotian War and that Sparta was nearing defeat. Diodorus Siculus summarizes the jubilation in Thebes:

> The result was that the Thebans swelled with pride, became more and more renowned for their valour, and had manifestly put themselves in a position to compete for the supremacy of Greece.[11]

With all the momentum, the Thebans were ready to end the war with another decisive battle or two. Their hopes were to shortly re-establish the Boeotian Confederacy and cement it as Greece's new superpower, fuelled by the might of the Sacred Band. The Spartans, though, were dispirited by their lacklustre performances at Naxos, Alyzeia, and Tegyra – not to mention their repeated failures to invade Boeotia – and of the absence of their great king Agesilaus. They were ready to sue for peace. In early 374, both sides convened for a peace conference to explore updating the King's Peace and ending the Boeotian War.

The Peace Conference of 374

A summit was arranged to be held in Sparta to discuss a *koine eirene*, or 'common peace,' that would bring an end to the war. Although both sides were interested in ending the conflict, Diodorus tells us that it was Artaxerxes, King of Persia who arranged the negotiations. He had been eager to invade Egypt and add its riches to the Persian Empire, and if the Greeks were busy with civil wars they could not be hired as Persian mercenaries. Artaxerxes had created the first *koine eirene* in Greece, through the King's Peace twelve years earlier, and now endeavoured to do it again. Multiple scholars also argue that the Spartan diplomat Antalcidas, the broker of the King's Peace, had approached Artaxerxes to arrange these negotiations, which would surely illustrate the escalating pressures confronting Sparta in the conflict.

Despite their recent string of victories, the Athenian-Theban alliance was beginning to sour. In the weeks after Tegyra, Thebes was emboldened by shattering the Spartan mirage of military supremacy and was systematically adding cities across central Greece into the Boeotian Confederacy. The most consequential addition was Plataea. This was no pure-hearted liberation from Spartan oppression, however. Plataea had remained firmly pro-Athenian, despite its geographic location in Boeotia, and was growing concerned about losing autonomy with the swift return of the Boeotian Confederacy. Accordingly, Plataea sent emissaries to discuss a formal alliance with Athens.

Concerned about other cities defecting from the restored Boeotian Confederacy, the boeotarchs now ordered an attack on Plataea. They quickly took the city and razed the surrounding farmland as punishment. The Thebans expelled all the Plataean aristocrats who were too cosy with Athens and banished them from ever returning to Boeotian soil. To show the other cities they meant business, the Thebans also conquered nearby Thespiae which by now had been the Spartan forward base into Boeotia for years. The exiled Plataean leaders naturally emigrated to Athens. To make matters worse, they were granted full citizenship rights by the sympathetic Athenian government. This was an exceptionally rare move by the Athenians, and probably motivated by Plataea having been their sole ally against Persia at the historic battle of Marathon. Crucially, this enfranchisement allowed the Plataeans an influential voice in the Athenian assembly and even a vote. The embittered Plataeans used their voice to stir up controversy around

Athens' alliance with Thebes, arguing that the rising tide of the Boeotian Confederacy was already showing signs of the same corruption that had infected the Athenian and Spartan hegemonies.

The Plataeans' speech is recreated by the orator Isocrates. Although its accuracy is dubious at best, it reveals the depth of Plataean desperation over the loss of their city. Dripping with anti-Theban sentiment, that the speech survived in some form and was included in Isocrates' compiled speeches illustrates the influence it had over the sympathetic Athenians. The *Plataicus* climaxes with a stunning criticism of Thebes:

> And these men of Thebes, who have recently shown who they truly are to your city and in ancient times proven to be traitors to all of Greece, considered themselves to be worthy of a pardon despite their wicked deeds. But as for the rest of us, despite being forced to act under threat, they think we ought to be guilty and without excuse. Because they are proper and true Thebans, they dare to reproach others with the accusation of supporting Sparta – yet they themselves were men who, we all know, happily served the Spartans for decades and fought more eagerly for Sparta's empire than for their own safety.[12]

Athens, therefore, entered the peace discussions of 374 in a downright foul mood, distrusting the Spartan adversary and Theban ally alike.[13]

Leading the Theban ambassadors at the conference in Sparta was none other than Epaminondas. Although he had played a central role in the Theban army, he was still relatively unknown outside of Boeotia. Plutarch makes sure to emphasize this and describes him as 'a man of repute for culture and philosophy, although he had not yet given proof of capacity as a general.'[14] In fact, his relative absence from the battlefield had earned him a poor reputation among certain Thebans and Greeks thus far in the war. Plutarch points out how some allies felt that 'by reason of his schooling he is superior in virtue to all other Boeotians, [and was] not keen or eager to help the men who are braving danger for their country.'[15] The peace conference of 374 was his first real foray into the Boeotian War and he was facing a man who was equally adept in combat and diplomacy.

Agesilaus led the Spartan delegation. Although this was Agesilaus' heralded return from his devastating leg injury, it was nevertheless a concerning situation for some Spartans to have him at the helm of the diplomatic table. Agesilaus could hardly be impartial given his longstanding hatred of Thebes. Ever since the incident at Aulos before his invasion of the Persian Empire, Agesilaus simply could not think clearly when it came to the Thebans, and he would seize any opportunity he had to inflict pain on the Boeotian Confederacy.

Lastly, the Athenians were led by the orator and statesman Callistratus of Aphidnae. Callistratus was serving as a strategos alongside Timotheus and Chabrias, and like his colleagues was one of the most popular and influential men in Athens. Motivated by the recent Theban acquisition of Plataea, Callistratus brought with him the new Athenian agenda of limiting Theban growth. While Athens would never align herself with Sparta, it is safe to say that the Thebans and Athenians were no longer true allies in the Boeotian War. Instead of the planned two-way debate between Sparta and the alliance of Thebes and Athens, the Peace Conference of 374 was now a negotiation among the three great Greek powers.

After a pair of introductory speeches, Callistratus began the conference in earnest when he delivered a speech laced with rhetorical skills. He appealed to Sparta by declaring all parties could end the war immediately and thus avoid a prolonged struggle that exhausted everyone's resources and finances. It would be far wiser, he argued, to reach an agreement now than to fight further and let 'irremediable mischief'[16] destroy their countries further. They should all make peace while they were relatively strong. His speech was met with acclaim. The Spartans, no doubt, were increasingly concerned about their population decline and *oliganthropia*, so this would have been a sensible argument.

It was Epaminondas, though, who delivered the truly memorable oration. While it has not survived, both Plutarch and Diodorus extol its impact on the conference and those who heard it. Clearly, Epaminondas' philosophical training in Pythagoreanism had prepared him well for this critical moment. We do know that Epaminondas was keenly aware of how the rest of the conference was 'cringing before Agesilaus,'[17] and he must have felt pressure to splinter support away from the Spartan king. However, Epaminondas did not speak on behalf of the Thebans but instead for all of Greece, demanding that the summit recognize that Sparta had become great on the basis of war and oppression, in violation of the grand promises of autonomy in the King's Peace of 387. Despite explicit assurances that each state's independence would be respected, Sparta had behaved purely as a hegemon. Lasting peace, said Epaminondas, would be possible only if that autonomy was steadfastly upheld. The pursuit of *koine eirene* at this conference must be based on equality and justice among all three city-states, and with no special favouritism to any of their symmachies.

It was this appeal to equality and justice that incensed Agesilaus. The Spartan king openly questioned Epaminondas, asking, 'Is it just, then, that the cities of Boeotia be subject to Thebes? Shouldn't they be independent?'[18] To which Epaminondas coolly replied with his own question: 'Are the cities of Laconia and the Peloponnesian League also free and equal? Would you allow the helots to be independent and autonomous?'

This reply further enraged Agesilaus, who immediately leapt from his seat and demanded Epaminondas say whether the Thebans would release all city-states from the Boeotian Confederacy if they agreed on a common peace at the conference. It was a legitimate question given recent events at Plataea, but it rang hollow coming from the man who had sanctioned violations of agreements in the cases of Phoebidas and Sphodrias. Epaminondas again made the obvious retort: would Sparta agree to release all members of the Peloponnesian League and liberate all her helots? His response provoked Agesilaus to a fury reminiscent of Achilles' wrath, yet it resonated with the other diplomats. Peace would be agreed upon at last.

Several rounds of negotiation followed, and led to a detailed agreement that all Greek cities would see the withdrawal of foreign harmosts and governors, the disbanding of all garrisons, and the guarantee of autonomy for every state.[19] Athens and Sparta agreed that the contract would be signed city by city. Just when all seemed to be ending well, Thebes dissented on this point – Epaminondas and the Thebans scoffed at the idea that the treaty could be signed city by city. He demanded that Thebes should sign for all of Boeotia, as head of the Boeotian Confederacy. While this ultimatum no doubt had an imperial ring, its true motivation was likely founded in the dissolution of the Boeotian Confederacy by Agesilaus and Sparta during the King's Peace. At that *koine eirene*, Agesilaus had intervened to specially guarantee that Thebes could not speak for the Boeotians. It was a deep insult, but Thebes held no power at the time and could not effectively fight the matter. Now, however, the tables had turned. Thebes refused to sign the agreement.

While Epaminondas gave a convincing speech about Thebes' position on the matter, he was not willing to abandon peace talks over it however. His message was sufficiently heard, and Thebes had improved her diplomatic position with both Athens and Sparta. Thebes signed the treaty without their requested amendment, but departed confident that the treaty would not last for long. The treaty of 374 was the second *koine eirene* in Greek history. In addition to enshrining the terms of the King's Peace of 387 and the autonomy of all cities, this new agreement also guaranteed collective security measures and established penalties for states that violated the autonomy principle. Spartan garrisons across Greece were now being evacuated, and the survival of the Boeotian Confederacy was assured – even if Thebes could not sign the document on their behalf.

Critically, the Peace Conference of 374 forced Sparta to officially recognize several new symmachies – something that they had been reluctant to do before. First was the Boeotian Confederacy, which had been deliberately excluded from the King's Peace of 387 but was now legally ratified in the new treaty. Next was the Second Athenian League and the formal acknowledgement of the return of Athens' naval empire. Having to recognize these entities was a bitter concession for Sparta and Agesilaus, but their weakened military and diplomatic standing no longer permitted them to resist. After their string of military losses, the mounting problem of *oliganthropia* and the decline of Spartan citizen-soldiers, and Thebes' new tactic of fomenting helot rebellion, Sparta opted to act conservatively and avoid escalating the conflict.

Perhaps the most enduring impact of the Peace Conference of 374 was the improved diplomatic relations between Athens and Sparta. The two rivals were by no means friends, of course, but they considered themselves the only superpowers in Greece and were growing impatient of Thebes' relentless rise to power. The Greeks had enough trouble surviving two powerful symmachies fighting for control – adding a third power to the mix could be devastating. As part of the peace of 374, Athens formally recognized Sparta's land supremacy in Greece, while Sparta did the same for Athenian naval supremacy. Diodorus aptly summarizes their sentiments:

They were consequently annoyed by the claims to leadership advanced by a third contender and sought to sever the Boeotian cities from the Theban confederation.[20]

Siege at Corcyra

Despite the formal signing of the *koine eirene*, no one expected the treaty to last very long. However, with the power dynamic diffused among three leagues instead of just the Spartans, the Peace of 374 appears to have been more successful than the King's Peace at actually honouring the independence of Greek states. Diodorus Siculus devotes an entire chapter to explaining how multiple cities gained unprecedented liberty through the withdrawal of garrisons and occupying forces throughout Greece.

It was not a time of flourishing, however. What was rather unexpected was the civil disintegration of many Greek city-states as they wrestled with autonomy for the first time. Diodorus' chapter is a litany of corruption and partisanship as states abruptly transitioned from oligarchy to a crude form of democracy. Civil strife erupted in cities where Spartan oligarchy abruptly vanished and a power vacuum had to be filled. In most cities, the sudden access to power led to the middle and lower classes 'taking foolish advantage of the liberties which democracy allows itself,'[21] as Diodorus terms it. Those unlucky aristocrats who had been loyal to Sparta were left without an ally, and many were arrested or exiled, their properties seized for the state.

Rebellions occurred across Greece. In Phialeia, a massacre in the theatre highlighted a violent resistance against Spartan-aligned oligarchs. In Corinth, the remnants of the Corinth-Argos union disintegrated into factional conflict and the execution of many aristocrats. In Megara and Sicyon, oligarchs and democrats fought openly in the streets. Phlius, the site of Spartan oppression in the years before the Boeotian War, saw the worst carnage in this wave of violence: over 900 men were killed in the escalating conflict between oligarchs and democrats.

Plato once wrote about the 'five regimes' of a just government and the gradual devolution of states. In what he called the *kyklos* (cycle), Plato outlined a degenerative sequence of five government types, each less just than the last: aristocracy, timocracy, oligarchy, democracy, and tyranny. He argued that aristocracy regressed into a timocracy when the elite chose weak, selfish successors, who eventually become oligarchs grabbing for power. When the general population has enough of the corruption, they overthrow the oligarchy and replace it with a chaotic, poorly organized 'democracy' that rules for self interest. Eventually, a tyrant would bring a despotic order to the mayhem by taking over the state. The years after the Peace of 374 were, in a nutshell, a hyper-accelerated Platonic *kyklos*. And Plato, writing *The Republic* during this time period, may have even drawn inspiration from this civil anarchy.

One such state stricken by this factional infighting was Corcyra in the west of Greece. Last seen being added to the Second Athenian League by Timotheus, the Athenian garrisons were abdicated according to the peace terms and Timotheus and the Athenian fleet sailed home. The city immediately descended into conflict and pro-Spartan forces quickly took control. When Timotheus departed in 373, however, he ferried home exiles from the island of Zakynthos who had sought refuge in the Athenian colonies further north. Zakynthos was substantially closer to Sparta's homeland and just 20 miles off the shore of the Peloponnese. A key location as a stopover in naval trade routes, Zakynthos was also essential for its supply of bitumen. Timotheus hoped the infusion of pro-Athenian dissenters would encourage yet another civil rebellion in Greece, and bring Zakynthos back into the Athenian naval empire.

Sparta saw through the facade, and was enraged at what it considered a blatant act of war. From the Spartan perspective, Timotheus' actions had functionally shattered the peace terms that had just been agreed upon. Meanwhile, Corcyra's civil strife had seen the island returned to the hands of democrats loyal to Athens. Then the Spartan loyalists sent word to the ephors that if Sparta would sent triremes to assist them, the Corcyrans would retake the island for Sparta. The Zakynthians sent a parallel request to fight the democrats who had just arrived with Athenian support. The Spartans immediately agreed.

Sparta sent a fleet of 60 triremes under the command of the admiral Mnasippus. Little is known of him prior to this campaign, but he must have been held in the highest esteem since the ephors gave him command of the expedition that formally broke the Peace of 374. His fleet included ships from a staggering ten city-states across the Peloponnesian League, including the historic naval power of Corinth, and at least 1,500 soldiers. They sailed for the west of Greece, and even invited the Syracusans to join the campaign. The Boeotian War was back on.

Mnasippus was immediately successful in the assault on Corcyra. Upon arrival, he secured the countryside, destroyed four enemy ships and forced the Corcyrans to beach or burn the rest of their ships to avoid capture. He closed off all trade to the capital city and took bounty in the rich land of Corcyra. The pro-Athenian Corcyrans put up rather a lacklustre fight. Their army was blocked from exiting the city and when some Corcyran hoplites were caught unawares outside the city walls, Mnasippus' men cut down a substantial number of them. Despite this early success, the walls were formidable and the Corcyrans had prepared well, so the Spartans were forced to settle in for a siege.

Unwilling to cede territory to Sparta, the Athenians voted to send a fleet of their own to Corcyra led by Timotheus, and another to Zakynthos led by the admiral Ctesicles. Timotheus launched his fleet of 60 ships bound for northwestern Greece. Already underway to Zakynthos, Ctesicles was ahead of the larger fleet and was able to deliver 600 light-armoured peltasts to Corcyra in the dead of night. They stole silently into the city, providing ample infantry for an extended siege. Regrettably, the Athenian reinforcements did not bring food with them and 600 more mouths quickly became a burden on the Corcyrans' dwindling supplies. The siege continued into 373, and Corcyra began to starve.

Timotheus, meanwhile, was taking a leisurely route – in fact he had not even rounded the cape at Malea yet, but was heading in the opposite direction into the Aegean islands. His 'cruise' around the Aegean was ostensibly due to a shortage of finance and crew for his 60 triremes, and he claimed to be raising funds and recruiting oarsmen. There may be some truth to this, as Timotheus had personally loaned his own money to man the triremes in his last campaign – something that had helped him to win the goodwill of the Athenian middle- and lower-class rowers. It is also likely that Athens was simply running out of funds due to the constitutionally-mandated low tributes of the Second Athenian League. Furthermore, the *liturgy* tax system was unlikely to have been systematically followed, and if some Athenian aristocrats were not paying their share then funding multiple naval expeditions at once would have pushed Athenian finances into arrears.

But while Timotheus' self-funding efforts had endeared him to the Athenians in his previous command, this time it was seen as unnecessary delay. This was probably because, despite having departed in late April at the advent of the sailing season, he had made no progress by late July and indeed had still not set a course in the general direction of Corcyra when the season's conclusion was in sight. The Athenians found this to be entirely unacceptable and recalled him to Athens. On his return Timotheus was put on trial and although the eventual verdict was not guilty, the Athenians revoked his command. As his replacement, they appointed the hero of the Corinthian War, Iphicrates. The architect of the Athenian move to light-armoured peltast fighting and lightning-fast ranged tactics, Iphicrates had established himself as the most respected Athenian general of his generation. During the past few years, he had been one of the few Greeks to take up the offer of King Artaxerxes of Persia to serve as a mercenary in the Persian war against Egypt.

Iphicrates immediately set about improving the financial situation. He forced the Athenian aristocrats to honour the *liturgy* and pay the necessary taxes to fund the triremes and rowers. He seized for the state any seaworthy vessel near Athens, even taking the famous *Paralus* which had been the ship that delivered the news of the end of the Peloponnesian War, and he succeeded in increasing the fleet to about 70.[22] His new fleet now sailed for Corcyra, and this time they were heading in the proper direction.

Back in Corcyra, Mnasippus held all the cards. With the Corcyrans and Athenian troops starving and bottled up behind the city walls, he was feeling very confident of his chances. Overly confident as it happened. Still short of funds, Mnasippus began to fall behind in paying his soldiers, many of whom were mercenaries hired by the Spartan government. When he defaulted on two months' salary, soldiers began to resign and head home. Mnasippus responded by lowering the pay of the men who remained. The Corcyrans took notice of the lax defence from the suddenly undermanned Spartan forces, and steeled themselves for an offensive move they had never planned to make.

The peltasts that Ctesicles had smuggled into Corcyra began with an attack on the Spartans, the first open combat of the siege. The demoralized Spartans were slow in putting on their armour, and when Mnasippus snapped orders at them one lieutenant responded that it was difficult to obey promptly when the army lacked basic provisions. Mnasippus responded by hitting him with his staff. Xenophon, who was especially critical of Mnasippus and his arrogance, recounts the response of the dwindling mercenary army: 'Without spirit and full of resentment against their general, the men mustered – a condition very unfavourable to success in battle.'[23] Given these circumstances, the battle went as one might imagine. The Athenian peltasts and the Corcyrans were able to kill 200 Spartans in the initial assault, having charged out from the walls. With that quick success, they returned behind the walls to regroup, throwing spears and chunks of gravestones at the Spartans to ensure they did not reach the city walls.

The Spartans now arranged themselves for a more conventional attack, forming a phalanx eight ranks deep. That was the standard depth of a phalanx, but Mnasippus judged this one to be of a poor standard due to the defections of the unpaid mercenaries. Sure enough, when the Corcyrans and Athenians smashed into the shield-wall on the Spartans' right flank, it began to buckle. A better trained and commanded phalanx would have been able to weather such a challenge, but the Spartan army under Mnasippus' leadership was verging on mutiny. Mnasippus now ordered a movement called a 'wheel-around,' or *anastrophe* in the Greek, where hoplites from the neighbouring column execute a quarter-turn and reform behind the embattled column to provide reinforcement.[24] If they can file in behind the weaker column, the phalanx is strengthened and battle-ready once more. The move was known to be a successful one, and Agesilaus had used it multiple times even during the Boeotian War.

But Mnasippus was no Agesilaus, and this time all the wheel-around managed to accomplish was the fortification of the right wing at the cost of collapsing the left. When the Spartan soldiers executed their 90-degree turn, the Athenians and Corcyrans misinterpreted the move as a retreat and, emboldened by the thought of imminent victory, pushed further into the Spartan lines. It was the decisive moment of the battle and the rest was merely a formality. Mnasippus fought his hardest, but was targeted by the Corcyrans and Athenians. They overcame his bodyguard and killed him in the centre of the formation. No Spartan mourned his death. The Corcyran-Athenian army then encircled the Spartan hoplites and began the battle's endgame. The surviving Spartans fled back to their camp.

The Spartan camp, which had for months enjoyed lax security, was suddenly in chaos. The sight of the advancing Corcyrans, together with rumours of the imminent arrival of Iphicrates' ships and the added spectacle of the Corcyrans launching their own triremes, after months of leaving them beached, amalgamated into a despairing situation for the surviving Spartans. They quickly retreated, leaving behind almost all their provisions, booty, and even the sick and injured. The siege of Corcyra was a catastrophic failure for the Spartans, and it all unravelled before the Athenian ships even arrived.

Iphicrates did eventually arrive with his fleet, whom he had been arduously training for the entire voyage – much to the delight of Xenophon, who ranks him among the greatest of Spartan leaders. The Athenian fleet, now expertly disciplined, found no Spartan ships to fight, however. The Athenians did intercept some Sicilian triremes that were only just arriving – they had been summoned by the Spartans early in the siege but arrived now to find only catastrophe. Nine vessels were captured and incorporated into the Athenian fleet, while their crews were sold into slavery, providing welcome revenue that temporarily eased Athens' financial pressures.[25]

Having accomplished all their goals in western Greece by the end of 372, the Athenians were in an increasingly strong position. Iphicrates intended to keep it that way, and never let his men rest. He constantly put them to work farming, rowing, building, and training for war. He exacted tribute from all the Spartan-allied islands on Greece's west coast, securing the long-term funding for his campaign – but also revealing the continuing financial problems of the Second Athenian League. Instead of returning to Athens, Iphicrates now sailed his army to the mainland and disembarked into Acarnania. He intended to raid all the Spartan cities he could, working to the Theban plan of sowing discord between Sparta and the Peloponnesian League and the helots.

The siege at Corcyra was virtually the end of Sparta's naval interests. While their relatively brief foray into naval warfare had seen great heights, particularly with their key victory at Aegospotami that won the Peloponnesian War, and then later with Lysander's attempt to create an Athenian-style naval supremacy, it fizzled out after the failure at Corcyra. Athens, meanwhile, inaugurated the return of an unchallenged naval empire in Greece. To put it mildly, Sparta was beginning to feel the burden of its deteriorating position in the Boeotian War. The Spartans' solution was to call a second peace conference in early 371. Swallowing their pride, they forced themselves to make an offer to Athens to declare a renewal of the King's Peace – again – and focus their joint efforts on ridding Greece of the growing problem that was Thebes.[26] The Athenians were tempted, especially since they were still livid over the conquest of Plataea, but peace was not meant to be. While the conference technically resulted in another *koine eirene*, it was indistinguishable from the Peace of 374 in every way except for being even shorter. Peace barely lasted a few weeks before the Spartan king Cleombrotus invaded Boeotia.

With this action, Cleombrotus and the ephors unwittingly sealed Sparta's fate. It sparked a chain of events that would culminate in the battle of Leuctra later in 371. Sparta's relentless expansion had finally overextended her reach. It had taken generations, but the Fates were at long last about to catch up with the Spartans. What Diodorus Siculus would later observe about humanity's hubris would soon come true for Sparta with devastating clarity:

> For fortune has a knack, when men vaunt themselves too highly, of laying them unexpectedly low and so teaching them to hope for nothing in excess.[27]

Chapter 9

The Gathering Storm at Leuctra

Trouble in the North: Jason of Pherae

In addition to their mounting losses and failed invasions, Sparta had another motivation for pursuing the renewal of the *koine eirene* that had led to the Peace of 374 and its paltry sequel in early 371. His name was Jason and he was a tyrant whose aim was to unify Thessaly under his own rule. His rise to power was sudden and unexpected, made possible by his hiring of thousands of mercenaries in campaigns that illustrated his vast wealth. After inheriting the rule of his hometown of Pherae from his father, he moved rapidly to become a chief magistrate, known as *tagos*, in Thessaly. The Thessalian *tagos* was akin to the Theban boeotarch and oversaw one of the four Thessalian districts – Jason was on his way.

A man who never shied away from voicing his opinion, Jason is quoted by Aristotle as saying, 'one should sometimes commit injustice, in order to be able also to do justice often.'[1] Such a statement certainly represents his administrative style. He demanded nothing but the best from his mercenaries and soldiers, requiring them to have the highest discipline and endurance. But Jason led from the front, and prioritized modelling that same discipline and endurance to his troops. He offered generous rewards to high-performing soldiers, while weeding out the weak.

Xenophon details Jason of Pherae's magnetic leadership and how he earned not only the respect of his soldiers, but also attracted many mercenaries to his service:

This Jason is a man stout of limb and robust of body, with an insatiable appetite for toil. Equally true is it that he tests the mettle of those with him day by day. He is always at their head, whether on a field-day under arms, or in the gymnasium, or on some military expedition. The weak members of the corps he weeds out, but those whom he sees bear themselves stout-heartedly in the face of war, like true lovers of danger and of toil, he honours with double, treble, and quadruple pay, or with other gifts. On the bed of sickness they will not lack attendance, nor honour in their graves. Thus every foreigner in his service knows that his valour in war may obtain for him a livelihood – a life replete at once with honour and abundance.[2]

It was just Sparta's luck that yet another challenger to their hegemony had emerged. They were having difficulty enough dispatching the Theban and Athenian threats. Now Jason was giving signs he intended to challenge Sparta for supremacy over Greece.

Jason had conquered nearly all of Thessaly and secured the role of *tagos* when he sent a message to the ruler of the last region not under his control, Polydamas of Pharsalus. It was a timeless message: join my empire or we will destroy you. Polydamas took the third option and appealed to Sparta for help in 375. He travelled to Laconia himself to give an impassioned speech to the Spartan ephors. The exact nature of his request clearly showed he felt mortally threatened; he audaciously asked for a king to lead the army and specifically rejected aid from *neodamodes* or *perioeci*.[3]

The ephors genuinely considered sending aid, but by this point in the Boeotian War they could hardly afford to stretch themselves further. It had now been years since they had had a real victory over the Thebans or Athenians. Worse, Jason claimed the Boeotians supported his ascendancy to *tagos* of Thessaly – and this was probably the case, but only so that Sparta could open a war on another front. Thessaly was far enough north that the Thebans had not yet felt threatened, but as the Boeotian Confederacy began to target Phocis to their west it was only a matter of time before Boeotia would be at odds with their ancestral home, Thessaly.

In his speech, Polydamas had recounted how Jason had made subtle threats about toppling Sparta himself once he had united all of Thessaly. He had even claimed that with their army 'there is not a nation or tribe of men to which Thessalians would deign to yield submission.'[4] Pointing to the fact that Macedon and the north of Greece were the source of the timber that built Athenian triremes, Jason had ominously implied that Thessaly could even build their own navy to rival the Second Athenian League if they so chose.

Still, with all this in mind, the Spartans rejected offering aid to Polydamas. They did eventually send a large army to Phocis under Cleombrotus to fend off Boeotian expansion, and make their presence known to the Thessalians in 371. Further, Spartan armies had also passed through Thessaly many times in their long war against Olynthus. That was sufficient to demonstrate that they could mobilize to fight Jason any time they chose, even with the Boeotian War raging on. But they did not wish to open another front in the wars and refused to send aid to Polydamas. Jason would inevitably become *tagos* of Thessaly.

While Jason kept quiet for some time after this adventure, the Spartans were by no means rid of him. After consolidating power in Thessaly, Jason did venture into the south of Greece with imperial goals. He would even arrive at the upcoming battle of Leuctra and attempt to broker peace. However, his ambition of conquering Greece was never to come to fruition. What Jason of Pherae primarily accomplished, apart from a helpful distraction of Sparta that Thebes certainly appreciated, was to push Macedon towards Athens.

The Macedonian king Amyntas III, father of Philip II and grandfather of Alexander the Great, had been a steadfast supporter of Sparta. He had allied with the Spartans against the Olynthians at great personal cost, and had been a diligent and consistent ally to Agesilaus and the ephors. Holding the Macedonian throne was a notoriously difficult endeavour, and Amyntas had been their sixth king in a decade when he took the throne in 391. He knew there was no wiggle room for showing weakness, as his tribal rivals in Macedon would not hesitate to assassinate him if they scented blood in the water. Sparta's rejection of aid to Polydamas was interpreted by Amyntas as an ungrateful move, in the wake of Macedon's unwavering support for Spartan campaigns. So Amyntas and the Macedonians now sought more reliable allies in Athens.

Though this was a relatively small diplomatic shift at this point in the chaotic fourth century, the long-term consequences would be substantial. Sparta was haemorrhaging allies at a time when she desperately needed them. Losing Macedon not only destroyed a bulwark against Thessaly's rise to power, it also provided Athens with a strong new ally who could offer ship materials and capable soldiers. More importantly, it represented Sparta's waning influence and the ephors' unwillingness to invest resources in maintaining their diplomatic network. For now, though, the Spartans chose to prioritize the short term and not send their soldiers to the north of Greece. Since 375, Jason had only accumulated more power. By 371 his army of more than 20,000 Thessalian hoplites and 8,000 cavalry was a wildcard, ready to tip the balance of the Boeotian War to whichever side Jason of Pherae might decide to align with.

Prelude to Leuctra

Strictly from a military perspective, Thebes and the Boeotian Confederacy continued to be highly successful in 371, systematically adding cities to the confederacy. After the conquest of Plataea and Thespiae, Tanagra was subdued and joined the symmachy. By late 371 Thebes was in direct control of almost every major Boeotian city, while Sparta was almost completely devoid of fortresses in the region. Orchomenus remained allied with Sparta, but Orchemenian influence in Boeotia was a shadow of its former self.

By now, Thebes' imperial ambitions lay beyond just Boeotia. Pelopidas and the Sacred Band began a targeted campaign in Phocis, expanding the footprint of the Boeotian Confederacy. Ever since Timotheus' imperial additions in the west of Greece, prior to the battle of Alyzeia, the region had been slowly slipping from Spartan control, creating a power vacuum that Thebes now sought to fill. The trouble was that a pro-Athenian bloc had emerged in the region, and several western Greek states, having observed Sparta's reluctance to intervene against rising powers like Jason of Pherae, increasingly viewed Athens as their most reliable southern ally.

When the short-lived Peace of 371 was declared, Sparta and Athens agreed to withdraw all their armies, navies, and garrisons once more. Unlike the Peace of 374, however, there was no uniform compliance with the terms of the agreement. Occupied cities were not fully liberated and armies were not often recalled. Only a portion of the Athenian navy was summoned back to the harbour at Piraeus, though Iphicrates and his fleet were. Sparta withdrew enough harmosts to look respectable, but simply left their army out on campaign. Greece had learned from the chaos following the last treaty.

Thebes, in particular, did not participate at all. As with the previous common peace, Thebes' primary motivation was to act on behalf of the entirety of Boeotia. In what was by now their most consistent diplomatic position, they again rejected the notion that Boeotian cities could sign for themselves, saying Thebes would act for all of Boeotia, or no treaties would be observed. In this way, Theban leaders remained as occupiers in Boeotian cities. The Boeotian Confederacy would not shrink one inch because of a *koine eirene*. Despite her military gains, however, Thebes was becoming increasingly isolated diplomatically. By 371, Sparta had made tenuous peace with Athens and the Boeotian War was a direct conflict between Sparta and Thebes alone.

In the increasingly relevant west of Greece, Thebes now committed a striking error by endorsing Jason of Pherae. Theban support, despite Jason's unpopularity across Thessaly and the neighbouring regions, alienated cities such as Larissa, Pharsalus, and other major Thessalian *poleis*, as well as potential allies in Phocis and Locris, who viewed Jason's tyrannical ambitions with suspicion, and feared Theban expansion into their traditional spheres of influence. Sorely needing allies against Sparta, Thebes was hardly intending to embrace Jason's policies, but the Thebans' myopic statecraft limited their ability to find friends when they most needed them.

Cleombrotus and a massive Spartan army of four *morai* was currently in Phocis to defend primarily against the Boeotian Confederacy but also, to a lesser extent, against Jason of Pherae's army of mercenaries. The size of this army cannot be overstated – Sparta had a total of six *morai* in all, and Cleombrotus had taken a full two-thirds of them to Phocis. This invasion force was made up of at least 2,400 hoplites in the *morai*, several thousand other hoplites from the helot and *perioeci* classes, 1,000 cavalry, another 1,000 skirmishers, plus assorted allied forces. The total number was likely 10,000 soldiers.[5] Sources differ in the exact numbers given, but it is clear that there were only 400–700 full Spartiates. Even with the strategic move of appointing additional citizens from the *perioeci*, the *neodamodes*, the *perioeci* still doubled the number of Spartiates on this campaign.[6] Despite this radical proportion and the fact that the *mora* had been dramatically diminished in quality due to the decline of Spartiates over the years, this was the most centralized a Spartan army had been for a long time. The Spartans clearly expected to decisively engage the Thebans during the Phocian campaign – whether in Phocis or through a subsequent invasion of Boeotia.

Upon receiving word of the peace of 371, Cleombrotus sent messengers to Sparta inquiring as to his next orders. Should he and his army return to Sparta? Should the Spartans honour the autonomy of the other Greek states? Should they take other cities? Or should Sparta march to war against Thebes? Cleombrotus clearly was concerned that Spartan factionalism might splinter the ephors' vision for the critical next steps in the war.

The ephors took several days to give a response, but there was no true deliberation. Xenophon writes that Sparta was motivated by a divine will: 'an unseen power, it would seem, was already driving them onwards.'[7] The Greek word used for this 'unseen power' was the famed *daemon*, the divine spirit that mediates between the gods and humanity, that had blessed Socrates. That Xenophon, a fiercely religious man, included such an emphasis on the daemon illustrates his belief that it was divinely appointed fate that the Spartans would invade Thebes and meet them in battle at Leuctra. This was no ordinary battle for Xenophon, and he sets the scene for an engagement so consequential it would reshape the entire Greek world.

Inevitably, whether driven by divine intervention or by obedience to the ephors, Cleombrotus turned his army of Spartan hoplites towards Boeotia. With this the Peace of 371, so recently signed, was officially broken. The stated reason for Sparta breaking the common peace was Thebes' steadfast refusal to honour the independence of Boeotian city-states. Sparta's claim was a continuation of Agesilaus' longstanding criticism of Thebes: the Thebans treated the Boeotians as vassals and did not respect their constitutional autonomy. Like the King's Peace of 387, the two *koinai eirenai* of the Boeotian War had explicitly promised the autonomy of all Greek city-states. Of course, Sparta had never bothered to honour the independence of client states during their hegemony, but these details mattered little.

The true reason for Sparta's invasion of Boeotia was the simple matter of the survival of her empire. Since the return of the Boeotian Confederacy, Sparta had been increasingly envious of Thebes and increasingly desperate to cling to power. As Diodorus Siculus phrased it, Sparta 'cast an extremely jealous eye upon their increase of power, fearing lest with the leadership of all Boeotia they might break up the Spartan supremacy.'[8] For Agesilaus, this was a deeply personal grudge. A burning hatred for Thebes had festered in him since their insult at Aulis decades before, when they had spoiled his grand, Homeric-style departure for the Persian campaign and – in his view – brought a divine curse upon the expedition that sealed its doom. Though Agesilaus was not leading the campaign, his hand still guided Spartan diplomacy as it always had.

The question arises: why did Cleombrotus command this colossal invasion force rather than the far more seasoned and esteemed king Agesilaus? Though Agesilaus had eventually recovered from his leg injury in 375, he had only managed to return to Spartan diplomacy in a limited context, and we see proof of his lively presence at the peace conferences. But those conferences took place in Sparta and did not require him to travel – clearly his health remained poor in 371 and he was not fit enough to lead the decisive campaign to destroy Sparta's greatest rival. Cleombrotus, meanwhile, was capable enough physically, but the lingering concerns about his suspicious habit of avoiding battle were never far from the minds of the Spartans.

When Cleombrotus invaded Boeotia in the summer of 371, it was the first Spartan invasion from the west, their previous failed invasions having come from the south. Because his army was on campaign in Phocis, immediately west of Boeotia, Cleombrotus was expected to pass into Boeotia via a narrow mountain pass near Coronea. The primary road into Boeotia would go through the valley between Orchomenus to the north and Coronea to the south, where it would form a natural corridor along Lake Copais that led straight to Thebes. The mountain range of Mount Akontion near Orchomenus, named after the 'javelin' as it pierced the skyline, forced travellers southward, while the formidable peaks of Mount Helicon south of Coronea were so dense and impassable they were written about in ancient mythology. With this topography, the Thebans quite logically focused all fortifications near Coronea to halt the Spartan advance. No man in his right mind would lead an army over the mountain passes of Mount Helicon.

Unfortunately for the Thebans, King Cleombrotus was not in his right mind, and he promptly headed for an obscure pass over Mount Helicon. The route led to Thisbe, a small coastal village equidistant from Coronea and Thespiae. It was a narrow and difficult pass that nobody expected Cleombrotus' massive army to attempt. Mount Helicon rises to nearly 1,650 metres and while they would only have ascended part of that, it was a difficult path made just slightly easier by the drier conditions of the summer.

The season was unrelenting in terms of wind, however, and it is likely that taking this pass cost the Spartans not only time but also personnel, supplies, and pack animals.

Ironically, Cleombrotus' years of avoiding direct confrontation served him well. The brilliant and unexpected tactical move to take the Thisbe path flustered the Thebans. Having arrived in Thisbe, Cleombrotus plotted a route that hugged the southern coast and aimed for Creusis, the port city of Thespiae and a key trading post for the export of Boeotian wheat and the import of food and other goods. Creusis also had a modest navy of 12 Theban triremes, which the Spartans quickly appropriated and added to their own fleet – a most welcome addition after years of naval losses. From Creusis, Cleombrotus' army had an open pathway to any city in the rolling hills of Boeotia. To the north was Thespiae, which sat at the crossroads where they would have arrived if they had taken the main road through Coronea and fought through the Theban fortifications and embankments. Their circuitous route through Thisbe had outflanked the Theban forces and enabled the Spartans to establish a forward position at Thespiae, effectively severing that detachment from the rest of Thebes' army. Cleombrotus naturally ordered his army on to take Thespiae, from where the Spartans would plan the long-awaited direct assault on Thebes.

While there was a direct route to Thebes from Creusis, the Thebans had not yet figured out the Spartan strategy. From their perspective, the Spartans seemed to be on a long, winding course across all of Boeotia. Rumours would have spread of the Spartan army appearing here and there, and the Boeotians had no idea where the massive army was heading. They had assumed it would be straight to Thebes, or maybe to liberate Plataea, but nobody had foreseen them arriving at the port city of Creusis on the southern shores. Cleombrotus had kept the Boeotians guessing and dread quickly overtook the population. Despite the many failed invasions by Sparta and Cleombrotus' own reputation for underachievement, panic set in and 'an unprecedented fear reigned in Boeotia'.[9]

The Boeotians well knew their homeland's reputation as 'the dancing floor of Ares'[10] and this Spartan army was the largest invasion force they had seen in decades. The battles of Plataea, Delium, and Coronea had all been enormous in size, but Thebes had not been the primary target of the enemy army. And, when they were participating in those battles, they had the advantage of multiple allies. Thebes now faced complete isolation, bereft of allies while the city bore the full brunt of enemy attention. Pelopidas' own family was not spared from the national anxiety. When he was departing to lead the Sacred Band off to eventually face the Spartans, his tearful wife desperately begged him to stay behind and not risk his own life. Pelopidas replied with the stoic eloquence of the great commanders, 'This advice, my wife, should be given to private men; but men in authority should be told not to lose the lives of others.'[11]

The Boeotian Confederacy convened a meeting of the boeotarchs to vote on the best course of action. They clearly knew they would soon meet the Spartans in battle, but confusion over their opponents' route sparked heated discussion about where to march. A strong argument could be made for remaining in Thebes, fortifying the city and its walls, and not to risk sending the Theban army and the Sacred Band in the wrong direction. Pelopidas arrived at the council later than his colleagues and found the boeotarchs in a voting deadlock. We do not have a complete list of all the boeotarchs of 371, but we do know that Epaminondas was serving that year and Pelopidas was not.[12] The boeotarchs were in a 3:3 vote before Pelopidas arrived. It is also possible, or even likely, that the vote split along geographical lines, with the three present Theban boeotarchs supporting war while their non-Theban colleagues favoured waiting.

Pelopidas' tardy arrival, though, seemed to bring divine agency to the vote. The council knew he would favour aggressive action, and his mere presence may have been enough to persuade the locked council. The last Theban boeotarch changed his position, so that four Theban boeotarchs quickly outvoted the non-Thebans: Thebes would march to Thespiae to intercept the Spartan army. The council gave the high command to Epaminondas, his first major military command, and Pelopidas would of course continue to lead his Sacred Band.

Topography and Geography of Leuctra

On the journey north to Thespiae, Cleombrotus' army made camp at Leuctra, a small village four miles south of Thespiae, home to the Leuctrides, the murdered girls whose narrative we covered in the introduction of this book. These two maidens had been assaulted by Spartan men and, unable to bear the shame, sadly ended their own lives. Their devastated father Scedasus had sought justice, travelling all the way to Sparta to petition the ephors when Sparta was at the pinnacle of her empire. But the arrogant Spartan leadership dismissed him. In Sparta's hegemony, no justice would be offered for the marginalized. Legend told that Scedasus returned home and built a beautiful tomb for his daughters, that stood as a memorial to the brutality of life under Spartan oppression. The tomb, if it existed, was also a foreboding sign to Sparta that vengeance would one day come. So well-known was this myth to the local population that Plutarch made sure to emphasize the 'prophecies and oracles [which] kept warning the Spartans to be on watchful guard against the Leuctrian wrath.'[13] Pious Spartans would surely have felt uneasy if Leuctra was to become the battlefield, and no doubt they hoped to make it closer to Thespiae before engaging the enemy.

In most respects, Leuctra was merely an obscure village in ancient times – so obscure, in fact, that we cannot locate its precise location. Today Leuctra is associated with the existing village of Lefktra, but this modern town of fewer than 1,000 citizens, though named after the ancient one and very close to it, was not built directly on top of the old village. Modern Lefktra is situated in the grassy foothills of Mount Cithaeron, about nine miles southeast of Thebes.

Cleombrotus' army encamped on a prominent peak in the foothills of Mount Cithaeron, overlooking the Boeotian plains to the north. On their journey north from Creusis, the Spartans had crossed a moderately high range rising up to 450 metres. Cleombrotus would have selected a large hill that could not only fit his army, but also give them a line of sight north to the plains. It would also have needed to overlook the village of Leuctra, which had an elevation of approximately 350 metres. There are several hills in this area that would fit the description, all of around 400 metres. This guaranteed the Spartans had the high ground, at least 50 metres worth, and also provided a quick escape route back to Creusis should that become necessary. Given Thebes and Thespiae were both to the north, and the Spartans had their backs to a sizeable mountain range, the army was safe from any surprise attacks.

The plains that the Spartan army would have seen at Leuctra were typical of the Boeotian countryside. Sun-drenched, gently rolling hills led into open valleys that stretched on almost endlessly, until they reached mountains far in the distance. That summer of 371 would have looked similar to summers in the region today, coloured by warm earth tones from the wheat fields and a beautiful mixture of amber, dark gold, and patches of green brush on the hillsides. There was no water visible; while the Asopos river was near to Leuctra, it was not close enough to be seen with the naked eye. In the summer, Leuctra typically sees only two days of rain a month, less than half an inch of rainfall in total. Consequently, the battleground would have been dry and cracked, the earth baked under the strong summer sun. Modern weather reports for Leuctra give an average of 29–30 days of sun during July, with hardly any cloud cover – temperatures soar to an average of 31°C (88°F). In such conditions, the sweat and blood of the soldiers would not be absorbed quickly into the soil, but would pool on the surface as if signalling the price of victory.

Apart from the absence of the sea, the area was a characteristically Mediterranean sight: a beautiful picture of golden, agrarian countryside with a bright blue sky and the rare white cloud. The vegetation was sparse, and almost anything vertical was either a hill or manmade. Sunsoaked and dry grass varieties would have been the dominant greenery, though there would have been little green in them. Left untended, the scratchy grasses would rise up to a man's knees. Apart from a rogue olive or two, there were hardly any trees in sight for miles around. Dry, hardy shrubs were the only foliage that thrived, providing splotches of dusty green here and there.

Such countryside not only allowed for a wide array of infantry manoeuvres for the commanders Cleombrotus and Epaminondas, but it was also ideal for cavalry. The wide, flat plains consisted of firm and dry ground without obstacles to slow down the horses' hooves. This was no marshy Marathon, where the Persian cavalry had been bogged down and rendered useless against the Athenian hoplites. The cavalry-friendly terrain was awful news for King Cleombrotus, however, as even though he had 1,000 horsemen with him, all of Greece knew that Theban cavalry were superior. Sparta's position on the higher ground, Cleombrotus hoped, would give him tactical flexibility to reduce the impact of the Theban horsemen.

The Thebans had spent some time discerning where the Spartans actually were amidst all the confusion of the unlikely invasion route, and it delayed their arrival. By the time the army of Epaminondas arrived, the Spartans had already secured the most favourable hill and Epaminondas had to settled for a hill opposite the Spartans, with a valley in between. Given the topography of the area, it could have been no higher than 350 metres, at least 50 metres lower than the Spartan hill. Between them was a wide and open plain where, no doubt, the two armies would meet. The Theban army at Leuctra was clearly outnumbered, but not so much that all was forsaken. They had around 6,000 infantry and another 2,000 cavalry. It was a respectable army, though dwarfed by the opposition's 10,000 men. Thebes' sole statistical advantage was a cavalry twice the size of the Spartans' cavalry.

Considering the scale of these forces, the battlefield of Leuctra most probably aligns with a wide plain located approximately 1.5 miles west-southwest of the modern village of Lefktra. This location, today still very rural with only farmland in sight, contains the largest and most prominent hills while still offering an adequately large valley below them for a battle of this size.[14] From their respective hilltop positions, both the Spartans and the Thebans enjoyed a sweeping view of the entire battlefield, maintained visual contact with their opponents, and held elevated terrain that had both adequate space for their troops and sufficient height for them to hold their ground in an attack.

Divine Omens

On this hot summer day in June 371, the Thebans sorely needed good omens and divine favour. Unfortunately, the bad omens were not in short supply. When Epaminondas was organizing his army and preparing to depart from Thebes, the rising tide of panic in Boeotia hit a boiling point. A blind old man challenged him at the city gates, proclaiming that he must not lead the army or the gods would not favour the Thebans in the upcoming battle. According to Diodorus, there was a visceral public reaction. The older generations were immediately gripped with fear and took this to be a curse on the army, while the younger generations steeled themselves to avoid showing their trepidation. Hoping to calm the distressed Thebans,

Epaminondas had a response already prepared: 'One only omen is best, to fight for the land that is ours.'[15]

As all Greeks would immediately recognize, this is a quote from the Trojan hero Hector who spoke to encourage his own soldiers in the Trojan War. It was a wise choice of words. The Thebans saw themselves as modern Trojans, suffering an unrighteous invasion from a totalitarian regime. And their leaders Epaminondas and Pelopidas were, of course, heroes in the vein of Achilles and Hector. Nevertheless, for Epaminondas it had limited success. He was too clinical and philosophical a man for most Thebans, and though he continued marching on towards battle he realized he had become widely unpopular.

Epaminondas clearly understood that an ancient quote was not quite the same as the Thebans' own divine omens, so he and Pelopidas now sought to create their own good auguries. They saw a great opportunity in the Leuctrides. The two maidens had become demi-goddesses in death, and a small but well-known cult of worship honoured them in Leuctra. This worship of the Leuctrides was probably the only thing most of the soldiers in the battle knew about Leuctra. To win their favour – or, for the Spartans, their forgiveness – would be the most important divine blessing before this pivotal battle.

Pelopidas, meanwhile, had seen ghosts. In his tent that evening, he was awakened by a vision of the Leuctrides spitting curses on the Spartans. He was then visited by Scedasus whom he spoke to at some length. Even in the afterlife, Scedasus still mourned the loss of his daughters and his rage against the Spartans had not abated. He encouraged Pelopidas to seek out the tomb of the Leuctrides and make ritual sacrifices there to the gods, so that the Spartans would be guaranteed the crippling defeat they had so long deserved. Encouraged by the vision though deeply sceptical, Pelopidas sent his scouts to find the tomb which they quickly identified. Losing no time, Pelopidas and Epaminondas then made the ritual sacrifices at the tomb of the Leuctrides.

In his talk with Pelopidas, Scedasus had also made a second, more gruesome request. He asked that the Thebans sacrifice a young virgin to the gods to ensure victory in the looming battle. Such human sacrifice was rare but not unknown in Greek history, and was most common on the eve of a major battle or campaign. Famously, Agamemnon had sacrificed his own daughter at Aulis, before departing for the war against Troy which he would eventually win. Themistocles had sacrificed several Persian captives before the battle of Salamis, where he saved Greece. On the other hand, Agesilaus had refused to sacrifice his own daughter when aiming to replicate Agamemnon's actions at Aulis, and he consequently failed in his great Persian invasion. The Theban council now debated whether they should follow the ruthless path of Agamemnon and Themistocles or follow Agesilaus in not offering a human sacrifice – and risk a grave loss.

While they were arguing over this murderous matter, a young female horse burst onto the scene. The filly had broken free of her restraints among the cavalry's horses and was now running wildly through the Theban camp. The animal had a striking red coat and a beautiful mane, and instead of being annoyed the Theban army was enraptured. Sensing divine intervention at hand, Pelopidas caught the horse and brought her to the tomb of the Leuctrides. After showering her with prayers and garlands, the Thebans sacrificed the young virgin horse – sparing the humans – to fulfil Scadesus' request. A human price at Leuctra had already been paid years ago when Scadesus' two daughters were so tragically killed, and soon their sacrifice would at last guarantee a Spartan loss.

While Epaminondas had made the requisite sacrifices at the tomb of the Leuctrides, he did not truly feel that this would be sufficient to boost the flagging morale of the Boeotian army. When they arrived at Leuctra, the sheer size of the Spartan forces frightened even the most hardened soldiers. Ever since the regrettable experience with the blind man as he left Thebes, Epaminondas had been bitterly aware of the multitude of poor omens for the Thebans. Thankfully, he was not above manufacturing his own divine portents. To alleviate the camp's general dismay, Epaminondas ordered several soldiers who had just arrived from Thebes to share encouraging news from the city. Apparently, the weapons on the statue of Heracles in his temple at Thebes had vanished. The statue itself was even visibly sweating.[16] The citizens of Thebes reported that 'the heroes of old had taken [the weapons] up and set off to help the Boeotians.'[17] Not only would Thebes have divine blessing, but the great mythological heroes of Thebes such as Heracles and Cadmus might be showing up for the battle!

Of course, Epaminondas knew this was false. But the story had the desired impact, and the encouraging words spread like wildfire through the Boeotian camp. Not satisfied with just this one ruse, Epaminondas also arranged for another man to claim that he had just returned from the dreaded cave of Trophonius. Home to the primary Boeotian oracle and prophet, this was perhaps the most respected and culturally significant religious site in Boeotia. But it was also a dreadful experience to receive a prophecy. Reaching the oracle meant descending into a dark, terrifying cave and having a nerve-racking conversation directly with the oracle that also involved participating in a series of mysterious rituals. There was no beautiful priestess to give a prophecy here. All that was known was that people left the cave of Trophonius traumatized and never wishing to speak of it. So bad was its reputation that the phrase 'descending into the cave of Trophonius' became a saying for experiencing a horrible and scarring event. (Kierkegaard and Nietzsche would later adopt this expression when articulating the gloomier aspects of their philosophies.)

Epaminondas ensured that this man explained in detail how he had survived the encounter and that the oracle at Trophonius had assured him the Boeotians would win the day and change Greece forever. They also reported that all of the roosters in the village nearest the oracle had begun crowing in unison at the exact moment the man received his prophecy.[18] Again, the Boeotian camp was overjoyed to hear this news. Epaminondas was a man of his word and surely followed through on his bribes to all the men involved in these ruses. Apparently orthodox Pythagorean philosophy could only take Epaminondas so far, and even he had to occasionally resort to the Greek tradition of trickery.

Over on the opposing hill, the Spartans were also receiving bad omens from the gods. They had brought a flock of sheep with them to make their own sacrifices before the battle. This flock was complemented by a small number of female goats, which had been specially chosen by the priests to be the main sacrifice to Sparta's patron deity Artemis. Theirs was an intricately organized system, and for all Spartan military campaigns the sacrificial animals were a symbolic part of a grand send-off, which included everything from musical celebrations to elaborate processions of warriors, priests conducting ritual purifications, and even a flamekeeper who tended an eternal fire.

However, the divine portents continued to get worse for the Spartans. First, a crown of thorns and bramble appeared on the head of Lysander, the great commander and conqueror who had died during the Corinthian War. This was no victory crown. The Spartan seers proclaimed that the thorns were a sign of Zeus' rage. Even more ominous, a group of golden stars plummeted like meteors from their perch atop a temple in Delphi.[19] These had been installed in honour of Lysander's conquest of Athens, but now the Spartans saw that the name of Lysander must be cursed. Lysander had famously sacked the city of Lebadeia in Boeotia, near the Cave of Trophonius – so perhaps this was divine retribution. Worst of all, the Spartans witnessed a sacrilegious destruction of a prophet's sacred tools. They had sent an envoy to Epirus to make a sacrifice at Dodona, one of the foremost oracles in all of Greece after Delphi. But much to their disgust the oracle consultation was disrupted when a local king's pet monkey burst into the temple and unleashed chaos, smashing whatever it could get its hands on. The animal scattered the sacred lots of the oracle in all directions and the exasperated priestess warned the Spartans they should think of safety rather than victory.[20] It was a spectacle fit for the comic stage at the Theatre of Dionysius, but the monkey would soon prove to be the truest prophet of the coming disaster at Leuctra.

Then, in the last hours before the battle, tragedy struck when a pair of wolves charged into the Spartan camp, ran past the defenceless sheep, and grabbed the goats. The wolves killed and ate the army's principal offerings, and Artemis was left without her sacrifice. The symbolism harked back yet again to Aulis before the Trojan War, when Agamemnon had offended Artemis. The goddess sent relentless winds and delayed the entire Greek invasion for weeks until Agamemnon's daughter had been offered as a sacrifice to calm the waters.

Despite their numerical advantage, the Spartans were now almost as terrified of the coming battle as the Thebans were. Cleombrotus, unfortunately, was in no position to help raise morale. He had received word that the ephors were still concerned about his history of avoiding direct battle. Now leading the largest Spartan invading force in a generation, and commanding almost all of the remaining Spartiates, Cleombrotus truly held the fate of Sparta in his hands. The ephors would not accept anything but a full pitched battle and a clear victory. To deliver less would almost certainly mean a death sentence or exile for Cleombrotus.

As if that were not sufficient cause for concern, there were swirling rumours that Cleombrotus' habit of evading hostilities was due to corruption, not cowardice. Certain political opponents, perhaps influenced by Agesilaus, were suggesting that Cleombrotus was sympathetic to Thebes. Several friends of Cleombrotus came to deliver this news and speak honestly about the gravity of the situation. They said that some Spartan leaders believed that Cleombrotus' previous two failed invasions of Boeotia were fraudulent. These expeditions had, of course, resulted in no seized territory and suspiciously quick retreats. Worse, Cleombrotus had also been the driving force behind Sparta's pivot away from the land war with Thebes and towards the naval war with Athens – and that war ended disastrously with two lost battles and countless lost territory. As his friends left Cleombrotus' tent, they are said to have exchanged dark thoughts to each other: 'Now our fine friend will show whether he really is so concerned on behalf of the Thebans as he is said to be.'[21] Wracked with anxiety and a determination to prove himself a worthy Spartan commander, Cleombrotus resolved that he would go on the offensive. The very next day, the Spartans would descend from their hill and meet the Thebans in the direct battle that Cleombrotus had avoided for so long. The coming conflict at Leuctra would determine the destiny of all Greece and become one of antiquity's most renowned battles.

Chapter 10

The Battle of Leuctra

Historical Accounts of the Battle

Before beginning a narrative of the battle, it is important to understand the body of ancient sources available, as well as their strengths and limitations. In the surviving literature, we have four detailed accounts of the battle of Leuctra. The first, and only contemporary source is Xenophon in his *Hellenica*. In theory, the existence of Xenophon's record should thrill modern historians; it is a primary source account with meticulous detail and access to eyewitnesses. The trouble with Xenophon, however, is precisely his access to first-hand accounts because he was so biased towards Sparta. Despite his Athenian background and rigorous education under Socrates, Xenophon was a clumsy historian who gave inconsistent details and added a creative flair to his interpretation of key events. Although he is reliable for the basic facts of historical events, his interpretation of those facts and arguments about their causation and impact were heavily influenced by a fierce allegiance to his adopted home of Sparta. For this reason, Xenophon gives a clinical analysis of the battle of Leuctra that accurately explains the process of the conflict, but avoids anything that might seem to favour the Thebans or insult the Spartans. He makes no mention at all of Pelopidas, Epaminondas, or the Sacred Band.

Xenophon's account is most helpful then, when partnered with the later historians Plutarch, Diodorus Siculus, and Pausanias. The Boeotian Plutarch, who was born up the road in Chaeronea, provides the most details on Leuctra in his *Life of Pelopidas* and the tragically lost *Life of Epaminondas*. Had his *Epaminondas* survived, it would undoubtedly be the best source for the battle of Leuctra given the titular character's leading role, though Plutarch was writing four centuries after the event and is therefore bound to be inaccurate in some respects. On the other hand, Plutarch had access to dozens of historical writings and records that are now lost but would have provided him with substantial details and extra information.

Writing in the first century BCE, Diodorus Siculus came before Plutarch but the massive scope of his project *The Library of History* held him back, and he struggled with accuracy and contradictions with other accounts. Significant errors in the chronology of the Boeotian War and the battle of Leuctra cause many historians to rank Diodorus at the bottom of the primary source record for this particular topic.[1] Lastly, Pausanias' helpful geographical and historical survey, *Description of Greece*, gives a limited account of Leuctra though one which ties in well with the existing corpus. Pausanias' narrative is ultimately too brief to serve as a major historical source about the battle.

Hoplite Warfare and Equipment

When the Sacred Band of Thebes marched into battle at Leuctra, they donned the traditional arms and armour of a Greek hoplite. The hoplite was a heavy infantry soldier of ancient Greece who served his city-state in battle, equipped with a long spear, large bronze shield, and a sword for close combat. These citizen-soldiers formed the backbone of Greek armies, fighting in tight formations called phalanxes ('fingers'). The origins of the hoplite system lie in the rising middle class of fledgling city-states, where farmers worked the ground for half the year and campaigned in defence of their city for the other half. Citizen-soldiers often earned their place in the *polis* by their service. They tended to be of the middle class because most had to pay for their own equipment, which was often passed down through the generations as a result.

The hoplite's equipment was centred around his iconic shield. The *hoplon* (from which we get the name hoplite) was a circular shield with a diameter of one metre. The shields were made of wood, overlaid with bronze, and had a convex form curving slightly back in towards the bearer. The inside of the shield had an armband and a hand grip, affording comfort and dexterity when it was held in interlocking formation. The shield was held in the left hand, protecting the left side of its holder and the right half of his neighbour. Because hoplites on the rightmost line of the phalanx had their right side unshielded, they were considered the boldest and bravest.

On its front, the *hoplon* was colourfully decorated with a symbol of a city-state or a family. Spartan hoplites bore the infamous red lambda, which stood for their home region of Lacedaemon. Other Greeks were more imaginative, their city emblems coming from mythology or other culturally significant art. Athenian shields bore the owl of Athena, representing wisdom. Cretans had the minotaur of Knossos. Corinth used a trident to show their naval history and worship of Poseidon. The Thebans used the club of Heracles, their great ancestor, to illustrate their rich mythological history and the strength of their army.

In battle, the hoplite used a 6–8 foot spear called a *dory*. Modern fascination tends to focus on the sword, but ancient Greeks primarily used spears in combat. They trained with their spears all year round, and could wield it with excellent precision when called upon. In the phalanx, spears had to be used with the right hand even if the soldier was lefthanded. At its tip, the *dory* had a leaf-shaped spearhead. On the butt was a *sarouter* ('lizard-killer'), which was still sharp but designed to serve as a counterweight for the tip. Though it could be used as an emergency weapon if necessary, hoplites would typically use the *sarouter* to stick the spear in the ground when not in use. The name suggests these warriors may have amused themselves by skewering small creatures when planting the spears in the earth.

The hoplite did also have a short sword, a *xiphos*, fastened on his waist as a back-up weapon. They were used in the event a spear was broken or the fighting was in such tight quarters that the spear was rendered useless. The sword would be on their left hip, underneath the shield and quickly accessible in the event they had to drop a spear. The blade would be up to two feet long, though Spartan swords were famously shorter.

For armour, hoplites traditionally wore a bronze-covered cuirass, often with the musculature moulded into it. But these cuirasses were unbearably heavy and substantially limited the agility and endurance of the wearer over the course of battle. At the height of the Bronze Age, a hoplite could be carrying 90 pounds of armour. By the fourth century, most Greek hoplites were wearing a *linothorax* which consisted of crosswoven layers of fabric and dramatically reduced the weight. Up to thirty layers could be used in its construction, making it decently protective against a glancing blow from a spear especially when bronze pieces were sewn in. Though labour-intensive, the *linothorax* was much easier to produce and repair in mass quantities.

Ancient hoplites would have worn a traditional, heavy Corinthian helmet. With a prominent nose guard and full facial coverage, these bronze helmets were burdensome but provided maximum protection. It was so ubiquitous that the vast majority of popular images of hoplites show them wearing Corinthian helmets. But as hoplite armour evolved to be lighter and more flexible, the Chalcidian style grew in popularity and became the dominant helmet of the late fifth century. The Chalcidian retained a good degree of protection but opened up the face much more, with just a small noseguard and coverage only down to the eyebrows. The bottom of a soldier's face would be fully visible.

The next generation of military prized speed and agility, and designed a new helmet that consisted of a conical cap covering only the top of the head, with no nose or cheek guards. This was called a *pilos*, and was modelled directly after fashionable felt caps of the day. The only difference was the material, as the *pilos* helmet was made out of bronze. The year 371 was at the height of the transition to faster, lighter armour and so the hoplites at Leuctra would have worn a mixture of either Chalcidian helmets, as the Spartans likely did, or *pilos* helmets.

The hoplites had been the primary infantry in Greek warfare for centuries by this point, but times were changing. Significant reforms had been instituted by Athens' great general Iphicrates, about fifteen years earlier after his spendid victory at the battle of Lechaeum. Instead of hoplites he had used peltasts, the light infantry and skirmishers who threw javelins, and had routed a full Spartan *mora* in the process. This sparked a move towards the style of armour and equipment of peltasts. Hoplites increasingly were using longer spears and lighter armour, with a premium on speed above all else. Never ones to jump on the latest fashions, however, the Spartans clung to a more traditional version of hoplite armour and tactics. The Thebans had not been as quick as their Athenian brethren to implement Iphicrates' reforms, but they were further down the path than the Spartans.

By 371, hoplites were truly in decline and on the verge of being phased out in favour of the lightning-fast peltasts. Hoplite warfare had peaked during the Persian Wars, and had not changed sufficiently over the past century. The battle of Leuctra was their final moment in the spotlight, and they were sure to make it a memorable and impactful one.

Pelopidas leading the Sacred Band at the Battle of Leuctra. *Attribution:* (*Public Domain*)

Arranging the Battle Lines

On this early July day in 371, Cleombrotus had breakfast with his generals and advisors to formalize the decision to go into battle and to discuss tactics in detail. Their conference lasted until midday, when both the Thebans and the Spartans began to organize for battle in the plain between their hilltop camps. Cleombrotus was steadfast in his commitment to the battle, and hell-bent on proving his worth as a Spartan and a commander. He could not, however, escape the rumour mill.

Xenophon implies that the Spartans were sluggish by this time in the day, and that the summer heat was taking its toll. Among some Spartans, whispers were spreading that Cleombrotus and his commanders had overindulged in wine during their notably long council meeting, and they were now about to lead the combat while slightly intoxicated. Xenophon quips, 'in the heat of noon a little goes a long way,'[2] a double entendre that could apply either to the intense heat or the overconsumption of wine. Either way, it was another sign that the Spartans were not favoured by the gods as they went out to the 'dancing floor of Ares'.

Over on the Boeotian side of the battlefield, Epaminondas faced two final hurdles before going into combat. First, a regiment from Thespiae – a reluctant member of the Boeotian Confederacy – was showing alarming signs both of fear and disobedience while putting on their armour. For a man of Epaminondas' gravitas, in these hallowed moments before battle the disciplined warrior should focus solely on the coming engagement and the sacrifice it would demand. He was infuriated that the Thespians were so brazenly showing their dissatisfaction but also knew that if he ordered them to depart then it would destroy the already compromised morale of his army.

Still, Epaminondas could not risk the Thespians fleeing once the battle began, and endangering his soldiers. He therefore announced to the entire Boeotian army that if any soldier wished to depart in the moments before battle, they would be permitted to do so. Those who left, he knew, would reveal their own cowardice and face shame when they returned home. The Thespians, however, appeared not to care about this and promptly retreated in full view of the rest of the army. Worse yet, Pausanias adds that the Thespians were joined by 'any other Boeotians who felt annoyed with the

Thebans.'[3] This was surely a healthy number of soldiers, and the Boeotian forces, already at a severe numerical disadvantage, now had to face even greater odds.

The second issue the Thebans had to consider was the personnel from their supply chain. Typically, Greek armies were accompanied by an entourage of merchants, slaves, craftsmen, priests, musicians, and animal handlers, all of which could bring the numbers up by hundreds or even thousands of people, meaning more mouths to feed and a slower pace. Right before a battle, though, it was usual for these companions to retreat from the battlefield. Epaminondas' offer to the Thespian soldiers to go home likely came at this very moment. The Theban attendants began their journey away from the battlefield as normal, but were surprised to find a small group of Spartan cavalry and Phocian peltasts attacking from their rear. Despite the clear vistas, this strike force was too small to have been clearly seen, and they may have been reinforcements arriving to link up with the main Spartan army. The Spartans surrounded the Boeotian entourage, who had almost no fighters with them, and caused them to turn back towards the battlefield. The Spartan squad was too small to engage the full Boeotian army, and abandoned their chase, whereupon the returning Boeotioan civilians had no choice but to filter into the back of their army, seeking protection.

The visual impact of this, however, unexpectedly demoralized the Spartan army. They believed this was the arrival of hundreds or even thousands of reinforcements who were now adding depth to the Theban phalanxes. The Theban army appeared to swell in numbers just as both sides marched onto the battlefield. Astonishingly, Xenophon even claims that the members of the entourage fought in the shield-wall during the battle, which would have been impossible.[4]

With both sides now on the field, Cleombrotus and Epaminondas set about organizing their battle formations. A traditional Greek phalanx of the fifth and early fourth centuries would be arranged 8 hoplites deep, their interlocking shields and 8-foot spears creating an impenetrable shield-wall. Precise placement of soldiers and weapons within the phalanx was essential. The first row, or the frontage, would have the primary task of keeping their shields firmly vertical and blocking any penetration. While their spears were pointed directly forward and at a 90-degree angle, their mission was far more defensive and focused on maintaining the integrity of the wall during the 'push' (*othismos* in Greek), when the ranks behind them would push forward to meet the enemies' shields. Instead of shouting and screaming, the moments during the push were said to be eerily silent.

The hoplites in the second line would point their spears forwards as well, usually raised over their shoulder and aiming for the openings between the frontage's shields. They delivered quick, repetitive strikes to the enemy between the heads and shields of their own countrymen. The second row's task was the most offensive, and it was this row that aimed to break the enemy shield-wall. The third row, and the ones behind, would raise their spears at a 45-degree angle or higher and assist with the push as much as possible, supporting the men in front of them. When a hoplite fell in battle, the man directly behind him in the column would move forward and take his place directly. Hypothetically, in a long battle with many losses, a hoplite in the back row could work their way forward to the front lines.

While for many years the depth of a Greek phalanx was relatively consistent at eight men, the width of the phalanx was where the true strategy lay in fourth-century Greek warfare. There was no standard here, and commanders exercised their autonomy in determining the size of the frontage. To keep it organized and versatile, Greek armies would break their units down into building blocks of a set number wide and deep. These sub-units would be arranged tactically at the commander's discretion, given the opponent's size, the composition of the enemy army, the battlefield terrain, and the opposing commander's tactics. In a Spartan army, such a sub-unit was called a *lochos* and was composed of up to 144 men, though it would also be used to refer to a single file or column that ranged from several dozen to as few as 8–16 men. Ironically, as mentioned earlier, it is the same Greek word used to refer to the Sacred Band of Thebes: the *Hieros Lochos*.

Cleombrotus arranged the Spartans in 'sections three files abreast'[5] with a depth of 12 men for the phalanx. This meant that at Leuctra, Cleombrotus divided the Spartan army into multiple sub-units of three hoplites across and 12 hoplites deep. With these rectangles of 36 men, he had a collection of hundreds of building blocks to arrange his forces. The ancient historians almost never clarify the width of a phalanx frontage, but focus exclusively on the depth of the phalanx instead. Depending on the width of the field and how he arranged his other units such as cavalry and skirmishers, Cleombrotus likely had at least 200 Spartan hoplites as the frontage of his phalanxes at Leuctra.

Despite a comfortable, if pedestrian, organization of the hoplites, Cleombrotus would have tried to hide his cavalry at all costs. The Spartan cavalry was already at a severe disadvantage because of their numbers, which were half those of the Boeotian cavalry. But the main issue was the quality of the Spartan cavalry. They were, to put it mildly, not up to standard. Xenophon calls them 'the least able-bodied of the men: raw recruits set simply astride their horses, and devoid of soldierly ambition.'[6] Worse yet, the Theban cavalry had far more experience. They had been in repeated actions against Orchomenus and Thespiae, while the Spartan cavalry had not fought in direct confrontation for years. Undoubtedly, Cleombrotus would have hidden these horsemen on the far sides of his ranks.

The significance of Epaminondas' tactical arrangement of the Boeotian phalanxes and infantry cannot be overstated. He settled on an unorthodox tactic of stacking his phalanxes to a stunning 50 men deep. Even if this is an exaggeration on the part of Xenophon, from whom we get the number, a phalanx of this size was without question the deepest known in any Greek battle. The standard had been eight deep since the Persian Wars, and while it had ticked up over the years this would still be double the size of any phalanx in recorded history. The Thebans had been experimenting with this formation at major battles over the years. Most recently, at the battle of Nemea in 394 during the Corinthian War, the Thebans had been placed on the right wing and had stacked their phalanxes 25 men deep, much more than the other members of the anti-Spartan league, who had agreed on a phalanx 16 deep. The Thebans saw success with it, however, forcing the Spartan allies they fought to retreat, while the Spartiates on the other wing swiftly penetrated the Athenian phalanx, which was arranged in standard formation.

Even more critically, Epaminondas placed his monstrous phalanx not on his right flank, in the Greek tradition, but on his left wing. Apart from simply surprising the Spartans, there were several reasons for this positioning. Firstly, it was so the Sacred Band of Thebes could be situated in the frontage of the phalanx and lead the initial attack with the full support of a deep phalanx behind them. If they were not on the very front line, the Sacred Band was assuredly in the first half dozen lines. The Sacred Band's practice of lightning-quick assaults aimed to break through the enemy lines immediately, causing confusion and dismay. Pelopidas would command his Sacred Band on the front lines. Secondly, it meant that the Thebans could directly confront the Spartan king Cleombrotus. The Spartans had gone with the traditional positioning of commanders leading each wing. Diodorus notes that 'the descendants of Heracles were stationed as commanders of the wings,'[7] with Cleombrotus taking the right and Agesilaus' son Archidamus taking the left wing. If the Thebans could capture or kill Cleombrotus quickly, the day would be over.

Thirdly, and most importantly, Epaminondas aimed to test a new arrangement of troops that would come to be called the 'oblique order'. Epaminondas was keenly aware of the significant size advantage that the Spartans held, and had been looking for a tactic that would benefit an outnumbered army. For centuries, phalanxes had met head-on, each army marching straight at the other, and arranged in a balanced formation, where the depth of each phalanx was consistent across the entire army. As this resulted in parallel formations across both armies, the better-trained and more experienced soldiers held the advantage. Under these conditions, the Spartan hoplites had long established their supremacy with unmatched expertise.

But in the oblique order, a commander intentionally concentrates fighters on one wing of his army with double or triple the strength of its centre or opposite wing. That stronger flank then advances towards the enemy, while the weaker sections move at a slower pace. When the armies meet, the stronger wing first delivers a smashing blow to the opposition that ruptures the front lines. As the lines begin to crack, undisciplined soldiers are then forced to defend their front, from the still-advancing weaker lines, at the same time as their side, under assault from the stronger wing. Once the stronger wing has taken sufficient ground, they rotate at right angles and attack the enemy's side with their full force.

This technique had first appeared at the battle of Tegyra a few years earlier, though the surprise nature of that battle certainly disallowed any intentional strategizing and the tactic materialized organically. Clearly, the Thebans had debriefed on the order of that battle and tinkered with the formations to try to replicate it. The oblique order was a revolutionary development, and

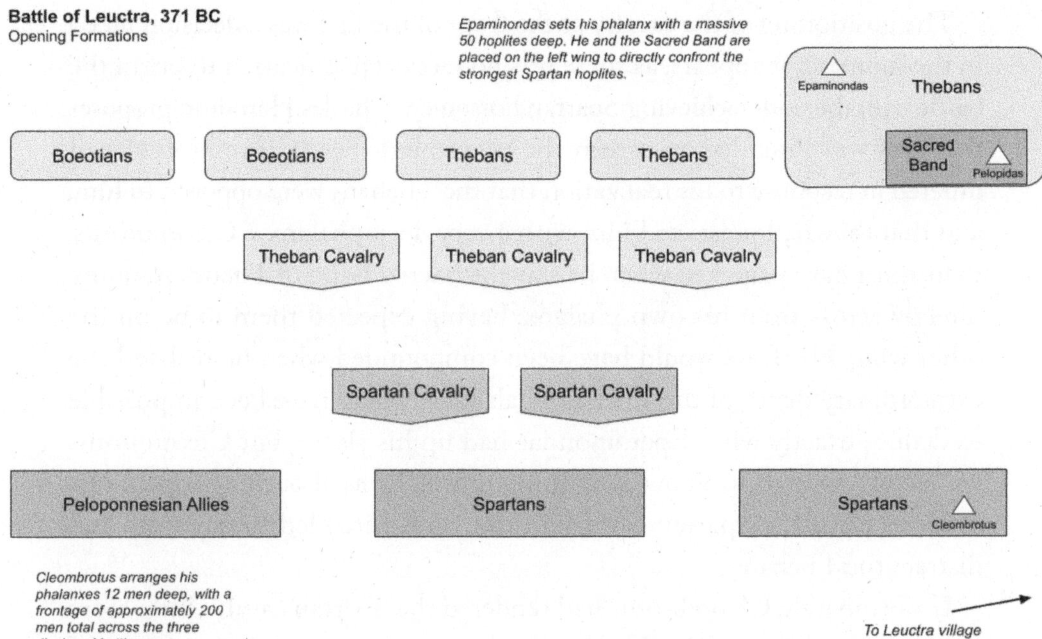

was adopted by other armies for centuries even into the modern era. Still taught in military colleges today, it is one of the standard tactics used by a smaller army to assault a larger force and break through at the critical point.

With the help of their unique strategy and their clever use of Greece's greatest fighting force, the Sacred Band, the Boeotians were well positioned for success despite their inferior numbers.

Opening Movements

With both the Spartans and the Thebans now arranged in battle formation, the action began in the heat of the day at approximately 1:00 in the afternoon. The opening engagement of the battle of Leuctra was unexpected – it took place between the two sides' cavalry and did not involve the Sacred Band as everyone had anticipated. In classical Greek warfare, cavalry were more commonly used as scouts, they only dabbled in skirmishes and flanking manoeuvres. In the field their main task was to support the hoplites and phalanxes, serving as distractions and chasing down fleeing opponents or attacking enemy archers. It is curious, then, that the cavalry were the first to draw blood in this decisive battle.

The positioning of the cavalry at the front of the line was a decision taken in the moment, it appears, as there was no tactical justification to begin the battle with the underachieving Spartan horsemen. Charles Hamilton proposes that this was intended 'to screen the movement that [Cleombrotus] had ordered in response to his realization that the Thebans were opposed to him, and that they had presented him with a very deep phalanx.'[8] Cleombrotus, then, must have panicked when he saw the Sacred Band of Thebes standing directly across from his own phalanx, having expected them to be on the other wing. His fears would have been compounded when he realized the extraordinary depth of the Theban phalanx. It would have been impossible to deduce exactly what Epaminondas had up his sleeve, but Cleombrotus was astute enough to know something unusual was about to happen. His order to place the Spartan cavalry in front was intended to buy time and distract the Thebans.

Unfortunately, Cleombrotus had rendered the Spartan cavalry little more than sacrificial lambs. The Theban cavalry swept in to attack their Spartan counterparts, and the result was never in doubt. With twice the men and at least twice the skill, the Thebans quickly dispensed with the Spartan

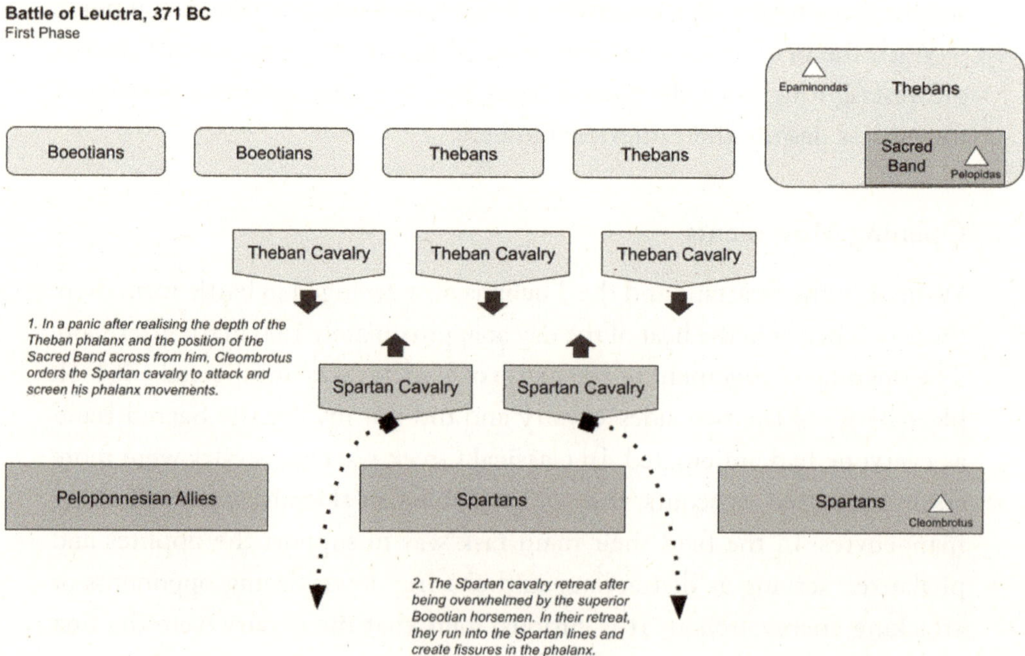

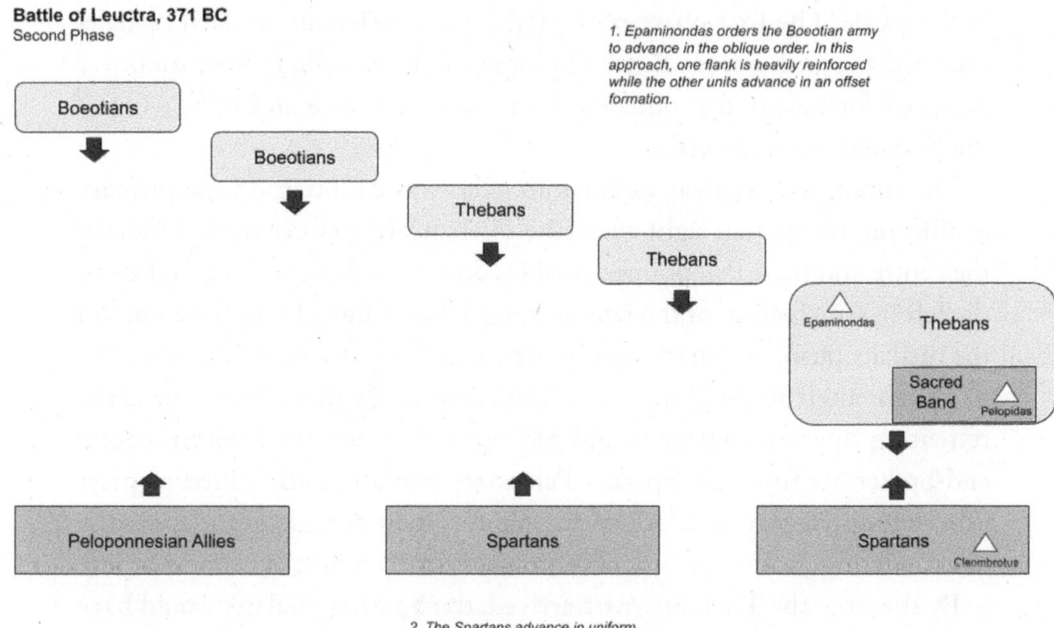

1. Epaminondas orders the Boeotian army to advance in the oblique order. In this approach, one flank is heavily reinforced while the other units advance in an offset formation.

2. The Spartans advance in uniform fashion. Cleombrotus's phalanx engages the Thebans and the Sacred Band directly.

horsemen. The Spartan cavalry began retreating towards their own lines, but in their disorder they accidentally collided with Spartan hoplites preparing for their own assault. Cavalrymen and hoplites shouted angrily, each blaming the other for their situation. The battle could not have got off to a worse start for King Cleombrotus and the Spartans.

And at that point, the Thebans attacked. Epaminondas seized the moment and ordered his assault during this unusual breakdown of Spartan discipline. This development is particularly notable as every other pitched battle between the Thebans and Spartans had seen the Spartans deliver the first charge. Given the dry conditions obtaining, the air of the battlefield was surely thick with dust that had been kicked up by the cavalry. This would have bought the charging Thebans a few precious moments to catch the Spartan phalanx by surprise.

Epaminondas attacked in his oblique order. The first Thebans to make contact with the enemy were the front lines of the left wing. The Sacred Band of Thebes was among them, striking hard at the Spartan lines. The ancient sources give frustratingly few details about the Band's actions at Leuctra, but given their position at the front they must have been in the heat of the battle. The first phase of the fight was a stalemate, as each phalanx executed the push evenly. But Epaminondas' clever oblique formation was designed for exactly this outcome, and soon the centre and right wing of the Boeotian army arrived.

The timing was critical, as Epaminondas was counting on the primary conflict on the Spartan right wing (the Theban left) to force the Spartans in the centre and their Peloponnesian allies on the far flank to drift slightly to the left in anticipation of the late-arriving Theban lines. Over the course of the phalanx push, the Spartan right wing may have also worked themselves to a slight angle towards the battlefield's centre. Making things worse, the retreating Spartan cavalry would have slowed down the Spartan centre and broken its frontage. Sparta's Peloponnesian allies also failed to meet expectations, displaying a lack of discipline as they struggled to adapt to the disorientating timing and unconventional formation of the oblique order.

By the time the Theban centre arrived, the Spartan phalanx would have been awkwardly angled and with unexpected gaps. Cleombrotus quickly

Battle of Leuctra, 371 BC
Third Phase

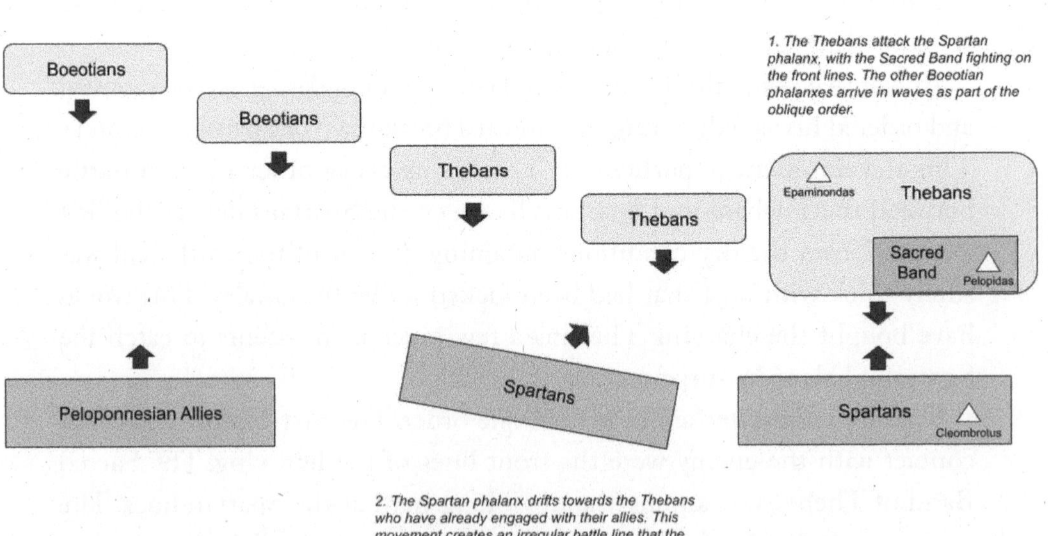

1. The Thebans attack the Spartan phalanx, with the Sacred Band fighting on the front lines. The other Boeotian phalanxes arrive in waves as part of the oblique order.

2. The Spartan phalanx drifts towards the Thebans who have already engaged with their allies. This movement creates an irregular battle line that the remaining Theban hoplites will exploit upon their arrival. Creating this opening is the intent of the oblique order.

assessed this issue and, realizing the catastrophe it might cause, ordered his phalanx to execute a version of the 'wheel-around,' or *anastrophe*. This was the movement that Agesilaus had perfected in past battles, but it was also the one that Mnasippus had failed to properly accomplish at the siege at Corcyra. In the *anastrophe*, the hoplites from the neighbouring column turn at a 90-degree angle and line up at the rear of the most vulnerable column.

Plutarch describes how the Spartans 'were opening up their right wing and making an encircling movement, in order to surround Epaminondas and envelop him with their numbers.'[9] Instead of an effective *anastrophe*, the disarray of the crowded battlefield stunted the formation and instead a paltry crescent formation resulted. Diodorus claims the Spartans used this formation from the battle's onset, but it is more likely that it happened during the abortive *anastrophe* attempt after Cleombrotus' tactical change.[10]

The moment had come for the heroic action of the Sacred Band of Thebes. At the very point the Spartans moved towards the rear to reorganize at the back of the neighbouring column, a large gap opened up in the Spartan phalanx. Pelopidas and the Sacred Band rushed into the breach. This critical strike triggered a domino effect that rippled across the Spartan ranks, leading to multiple breakdowns as hoplites from across the formation's depth and breadth swivelled to meet the Sacred Band. Plutarch says the Spartans were caught completely by surprise and were 'moving confusedly.'[11] They were wholly unprepared for the speed and precision of the Sacred Band's assault. Chaos reigned in the Spartan phalanx after Pelopidas' decisive action. Occupied solely with the Sacred Band who were now in their midst, the Spartan hoplites completely forgot about the much larger phalanx that Epaminondas was commanding. He now ordered his phalanx forward at double-speed, to capitalize on the carnage that the Sacred Band had started.

With Epaminondas taking care of the larger phalanx, the Sacred Band of Thebes began work on their secondary mission: to kill King Cleombrotus. Despite his poor reputation and questionable sobriety, Cleombrotus was first and foremost a king of Sparta and therefore, as all Spartan monarchs were, a direct descendant of Heracles. His presence bolstered not just the people's morale but gave them purpose and direction. Diodorus argues that as long as Cleombrotus was alive, 'it was uncertain which way the scales of victory inclined.'[12] But the Thebans were themselves also descendants of Heracles – and Heracles himself was Boeotian.

Pelopidas and his strike force found Cleombrotus surrounded by his royal guard of 300 horseguards or *hippeis*. The Spartan royal guard was a collection of full Spartiates, but they had not yet reached thirty years of age. With the vanishing number of Spartiates, this group of 300 young men with their whole careers still ahead of them were the best and brightest of Sparta's next generation. The 300 *hippeis* were nearly half of all the Spartiates at Leuctra, as there were no more than 400 others among the ranks of the phalanx. But they proved to be no match for the 300 warriors of the Sacred Band of Thebes. The Thebans sliced through the *hippeis* and Cleombrotus was left unguarded. The king fought valiantly but soon fell at the hands of the Sacred Band. And with the death of their king, the Spartans began to break. First, there was a fierce fight over the body of Cleombrotus. As in the Trojan War, the body of a fallen hero required a proper burial, but was also a target for the opposition, who would attempt to take the corpse. Quickly, a 'great mound of corpses'[13] amassed in the scrum for Cleombrotus' body.

Battle of Leuctra, 371 BC
Fourth Phase & Decisive Action

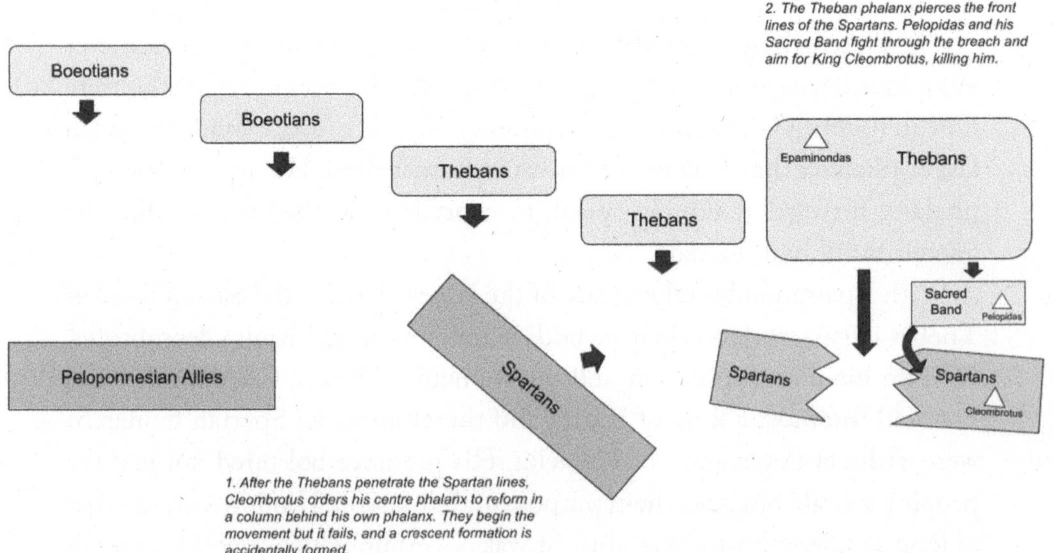

2. The Theban phalanx pierces the front lines of the Spartans. Pelopidas and his Sacred Band fight through the breach and aim for King Cleombrotus, killing him.

1. After the Thebans penetrate the Spartan lines, Cleombrotus orders his centre phalanx to reform in a column behind his own phalanx. They begin the movement but it fails, and a crescent formation is accidentally formed.

The gears of battle do not slow for anybody, though, and Epaminondas' phalanx did not relent. The Spartans were slowly being crushed by the weight of the deepest phalanx Greece had ever seen. No help was coming for the Spartans, not even from their Peloponnesian allies. Perhaps sensing the changing tide, Sparta's allies on the far flank apparently gave up and ceded ground 'wherever the enemy attacked them.'[14]

Desperate to find some positives for the Spartans in his narrative of Leuctra, Xenophon claims that the Spartan hoplites actually won the early phase of the battle. His evidence, though, is suspect at best. He cites the fact that the Spartans were able to successfully recover the body of their fallen king Cleombrotus and take it back to their camp for proper burial and honours. The straw he grasps at is the claim that such a recovery would have been impossible 'unless his vanguard had been masters of the situation for the moment.'[15] He offers no further details or evidence. His Spartan benefactors must have appreciated this rosy view.

Even if true it was the only silver lining the Spartans would find that day. With increasing rapidity, the battle of Leuctra began to slip away from them. Spartan commanders died in rapid succession. The ignominious Sphodrias was killed, along with multiple polemarchs and chief advisors. Xenophon names a half dozen commanders or units that suffered heavy losses. Plutarch writes:

> Their courage and skill were so confounded that there was a flight and slaughter
> of the Spartans such as had never before been seen.[16]

The Spartan retreat began slowly but soon spread to the rest of the army. At first, their left flank had been content to make light engagement with the Boeotian right flank. This part of the battlefield had seen much less intense fighting, as all the units here were discontented Peloponnesian allies of Sparta or Boeotian allies of Thebes. But as the lines began to break up on the Spartan right flank, a full retreat began. The Spartans tried to flee back to their hilltop camp, but a small ditch at the hill's base tripped many men, who were summarily cut down. The Thebans could have pursued them and destroyed the entire army, but Epaminondas called a halt and ordered his forces to regroup. The battle was won.

The surviving Spartan polemarchs reassembled in their camp and debated their next step. While some pushed for re-engaging the Thebans, primarily to take back the bodies of their dead, most said that was folly. They did debate attacking just to stop a trophy from being erected, but as this was Boeotia they knew it was only a matter of time before a trophy signalling this major Theban victory was standing tall over the golden plains of Leuctra.

Xenophon records the Spartan losses at 1,000 soldiers, but Diodorus, the only other historian to give an exact number, puts it at a staggering 4,000. Importantly, both historians agree that 400 Spartiates died at Leuctra. With there being perhaps fewer than 1,000 total Spartiates in 371, it is possible that around half of them were now dead, representing the greatest single loss of Spartiates in any known battle. Since it took at least thirty years to become a Spartiate, this was a crippling blow to the very existence of Sparta's empire.

The Thebans suffered far fewer losses. Xenophon reports that just 300 men died at Leuctra and Pausanias gives a much lower figure still, saying only 47 Thebans died. While the Spartans came to the field the next day to gather their dead, the Thebans had little need to and instead spent the day building their trophy, or *tropaion*, at the field.

A version of this trophy still stands in the empty fields of Leuctra today. The Thebans would not have had time or resources to build a permanent monument immediately following the battle, and what is there today is a reconstruction dating from later times. The large, cylindrical stone monument is decorated with relief sculptures of shields and other religious imagery. It once bore a domed top that is thought to have supported a sculpture of a triumphant Theban hoplite in full armour. This image of a victorious hoplite became a symbol of Leuctra and, accordingly, the Boeotian Confederacy's new place at the head of Greece. It was printed on coins across Boeotia. Survivors of Leuctra – that is almost the entire Boeotian army considering their minuscule losses – embraced the trophy as a personal insignia commemorating their heroism. Epaminondas' friend and lover Asopichus even put the crest on his *hoplon* shield, and ensured it was commemorated on a portico at the Temple of Apollo in Delphi.[17]

Towering ten feet above the flat field at Leuctra, the commemorative trophy still celebrates the remarkable victory that the Thebans won on that hot July day in 371. The oblique order and innovative tactics of Epaminondas and

The remains of the Leuctra trophy in 1904 (Underwood & Underwood (1904) *Leuctra – remains of trophy set up by the Thebans after the battle of Leuctra [371 B.C.] – looking N.W., Greece* [Stereograph]. New York: Underwood & Underwood, Publishers. Library of Congress Prints and Photographs Division, Washington, D.C.)

Pelopidas had saved Boeotia and badly rattled the Spartan empire. Thebes had achieved an historic victory at Leuctra, and though they did not yet know it, Greece would be forever transformed.

Chapter 11

The Inauguration of the Theban Hegemony

The Aftermath of Leuctra for the Spartans

The statistics from the battle at Leuctra give only a taste of the depth of Sparta's losses. She had lost at least 400 Spartiates, which amounted to almost half of the total number. To remedy this the Spartans could accelerate the next class of the *agoge*, but to do so would break centuries of precedent and result in an inferior and unproven phalanx. They could appoint more *neodamodes*, but this would be little more than a sticking plaster. They could call up more men from their Peloponnesian allies or their subjugated helots, but after Leuctra the Spartan grip on their vassals was loosening by the day.

The only real solution to the depopulation crisis was to create more Spartiates through the traditional *agoge*. But this would involve time and a massive financial investment – two resources the Spartan hegemony no longer had in plenty. In addition to the crippling loss of their soldiers, Sparta had to grapple with the precedents set by Leuctra. As with the impasse over numbers, there was no escape from the relentless loss of reputation for the Spartans.

First, Leuctra was the most decisive defeat ever chronicled between Greek city-states – never before had one *polis* so completely dominated another in battle. Pausanias called the battle at Leuctra 'the most famous ever won by Greeks over Greeks.'[1] Sparta had won plenty of battles by a wide margin, but none of their victories matched the scale or totality of Thebes' success at Leuctra.

Second, over their hundreds of years of warfare, this was the first time the Spartans had ever lost to a smaller army. It was rare that Sparta was ever defeated in fact, especially on land and in a pitched battle. Their few losses are difficult to list, as most were down to extenuating circumstances. They had certainly lost at Thermopylae, but that was an intentional sacrifice to stall for time and in the end became a moral victory for Greece. At Sphacteria in 425, the Spartans had surrendered after a long siege, but it was not a true pitched battle. Spartan mercenaries had not completed the 401 campaign in Persia to overthrow the king, but still won glory for the manner of their return home in the March of the Ten Thousand. Agesilaus had also failed in his invasion of Persia, but that was mainly due to his being recalled to Greece at the outbreak of the Corinthian War. And in that war the battle of Haliartus was the only true Spartan loss – yet even that was not nearly as decisive as Leuctra, and Sparta wound up winning the war overall.

Perhaps worst of all, the Theban victory had proved for the first time that Sparta could not only be defeated in a pitched battle, but could lose to an outnumbered enemy with fewer resources. For both Sparta and for Greece at large, the psychological impact of this revelation cannot be overstated. Spartan hegemony was built on the image – perceived or real – of an invincible military machine. That myth was now irreparably shattered. From now on, Sparta's allies started questioning their loyalty, or simply seeing their opportunity for rebellion. It began even before the battle of Leuctra concluded: Xenophon reports that the Peloponnesian allies at Leuctra were not only unhelpful in the conflict, but were even showing signs of satisfaction at the Spartan defeat.

Internally, the Spartan people now had to wrestle with the destruction of their cultural identity. If their army could be defeated in such overwhelming fashion, why did Sparta still organize her society on military lines? Why did Spartans commit to the authoritarianism and brutality of the Lycurgan reforms? Why did they wall themselves off from the outside world, never trading or travelling? Why did they abolish private property? Why did they replace all money with iron coins, ensuring the Spartans could never leave their homeland? And why did they give up their children to the state – sometimes even infants to a harsh death on a mountainside? All of these were sacrifices that the Spartans had made for centuries, but only in exchange for the protection of the state. If that was a security that Sparta's army could no longer guarantee, why preserve their culture?

Spartan foreign policy became reactive and defensive. They had never truly settled on a cogent strategic plan for diplomacy before, except for the unifying theme of securing Sparta's supremacy, but now they struggled simply to survive at the negotiating table. Allies took notice. Defections from the Peloponnesian League started with a trickle but turned into a flood. Without the ruthless efficiency of Spartan hoplites, the Greek city-states questioned Sparta's place in the power structure of Greece. Elis broke away instantly. Mantinea attempted the same, fortifying their city for war and rejecting Agesilaus himself. Tegea, one of the most ancient Spartan allies, erupted into civil war. Astonishingly, the entirety of the central Peloponnesian region of Arcadia – long a stronghold for Sparta – broke away and began to form their own symmachy called the Arcadian League. For the first time in three decades, the Spartans were not the unrivalled hegemon of Greece: Thebes did not immediately supplant Sparta, but for the next decade the two would jockey for supremacy.

When Spartan messengers arrived home to announce the defeat at Leuctra, a choral performance was being held in the theatre to celebrate a religious festival. The ephors decided not to interrupt the performance, but instead to announce the bad news and give a list of the fallen warriors after the chorus had finished. The women were instructed not to cry, but to react in the stoic, Spartan fashion. In a remarkable account of the day after the battle, Xenophon illustrates Sparta's warrior ethos by describing how the families of dead soldiers rejoiced while the families of survivors mourned their disgrace.

Though they could never show it, the Spartans were in a panic the like of which they had never felt before. They knew that not only was Sparta's empire in freefall, but also that the Thebans were not finished. Epaminondas was now certain to lead an invasion into the heartland of Laconia – something no other city-state had ever dared attempt. Plutarch vividly captures the mood in Sparta in the days after Leuctra:

> The greater number, however, when their allies were falling away from them and it was expected that Epaminondas, in all the pride of a conqueror, would invade Peloponnesus, fell to thinking of the oracles, in view of the lameness of Agesilaus, and were full of dejection and consternation in respect to the divine powers, believing that their city was in an evil plight because they had dethroned the sound-footed king and chosen instead a lame and halting one, — the very thing which the deity was trying to teach them carefully to avoid.[2]

For the Spartans in the days after Leuctra, the only possible way forward was to give Agesilaus the sort of absolute authority that no individual citizen had ever before wielded. The entire Spartan government was designed to share power and prevent potential tyrants through an intricate system of checks and balances. One need look no further than their uncommon practice of having two monarchs. All of these checks on power were thrown out of the window in 371, though, so that Agesilaus would have absolute authority. In addition to his role as king, which oversaw both the military and the state religion, Agesilaus was given temporary jurisdiction over the legislature and the judiciary. This was an unprecedented move, especially if one remembers that Agesilaus was still recovering from his leg injury and had been in poor health for years by this point. With his emergency powers he held now a unique role that was something akin to a Roman dictatorship, having been given temporary but unlimited authority in order to solve an existential crisis for the state. In fact, Agesilaus proved to be nearly as worthy of the position as Cincinnatus, and he 'did not venture to weaken the constitution by establishing any new laws.'[3] Instead, in order to bolster morale and to ensure the army maintained its numbers, he actually refrained for a while from enforcing the harsher laws of the Spartan constitution.

Agesilaus used this humane approach to address a problem Sparta had never faced before: deserters. At Leuctra, the Peloponnesian allies had apparently not been the only soldiers to stop fighting when they realized the Thebans were winning. Hundreds of native Spartans had also abandoned their posts and fled the battlefield. Under Spartan law, these men should have met a fate considered worse than death. They were to be essentially excommunicated from Spartan society, never allowed a home, employment or a spouse. They were legally allowed to be beaten by any Spartan at any time. They were also forced to shave half their beard, leaving the other half as a visible sign of their cowardice.

If Agesilaus had enforced this punishment for all the Spartan deserters, then not only would he have massively accelerated the depopulation of the militia, but he would have created a new social class – one that was disaffected and naturally inclined to rebel. And with Spartan blood in the water, that was an entirely unwelcome prospect; the helots had surely begun planning their next revolution the moment they heard of Leuctra's outcome. Considering these factors, Agesilaus opted not to prosecute the deserters. Though his softly-softly approach worked much better, over the next decade Sparta's problem of deserters only increased as the war dragged on and the Spartans continued to be on the defensive. Agesilaus became adept at mitigating the issue as much as possible, but the fact that soldiers defected on a regular basis only added fuel to the fire: Sparta was in a rapid, unprecedented decline.

The Theban Hegemony

Life was far rosier on the Theban side of Leuctra. What had begun as the Boeotian Confederacy soon expanded rapidly far beyond the borders of Boeotia. Thebes quickly reforged the historic alliance with Persia, securing a long-term military and trading partner. Multiple city-states across Greece submitted to the Boeotian Confederacy, including several who dared to defy Sparta for the first time ever. Athens retreated into Attica, disgusted with Theban arrogance after the conquest of Thespiae. Athens and Sparta would continue their tepid coalition, but Athens avoided direct confrontations with Thebes and focused instead on the operations of the Second Athenian League. While Sparta was reeling and Athens content with her seafaring, Thebes quickly became the emerging superpower of Greece. Allies leaving Sparta flocked to Thebes for protection.

Opportunities for Theban influence arose in the north as well. In 370, Jason of Pherae choked on his own imperial ambitions. After arriving at Leuctra late and taking credit for the peace negotiations, Jason had counselled Thebes to not attack Sparta immediately but rather to allow the victory to be heralded across Greece first. Jason quickly turned his attention to the north of Greece, and conquered large territories in Phocis on his route back home to Thessaly. He was soon assassinated by his own countrymen after he revealed plans to seize the Oracle of Delphi and her temple complex. The perpetrators were celebrated as heroes. More importantly, his death opened the door for Thebes to expand northwards and make a bid for supremacy over northern Greece.

The historical accounts show that Leuctra very quickly became an important dividing line for the chronology of ancient Greece. The ancient historians and orators consistently refer to Greek history in terms of 'before

Leuctra' and 'after Leuctra'. Even following the Macedonian conquest of Greece in the fourth century's final decades, later Greeks and Romans still arrange history into the periods pre- and post-Leuctra. Given Sparta's central role in defining the classical era, their defeat at Leuctra is frequently regarded as that period's final momentous event. Ancient and mediaeval writers referenced Leuctra as marking the sunset of this extraordinary period for Western civilization. Rather than citing Macedonia's conquest of Greece or Alexander's campaigns as the transition point to the Hellenistic era, most thinkers point to Leuctra as the watershed.

The Roman orator Cicero exemplifies this in his *De Officiis*, his most important philosophical work, when he considers questions of moral virtue and civic responsibility. He argues that a civilization champions courage above all else, and references the great battles of the Greek world to demonstrate his point. Needless to say, his list concludes at Leuctra and leaves out all the Hellenistic battles:

> When…we wish to pay a compliment, we somehow or other praise in more eloquent strain the brave and noble work of some great soul. Hence there is an open field for orators on the subjects of Marathon, Salamis, Plataea, Thermopylae, and Leuctra…[4]

Accordingly, Epaminondas became known as the greatest Theban commander ever. With his victory at Leuctra, he had earned his place among the most accomplished commanders in all Greece. Yet not since the days of myth, of Heracles and Cadmus, had the pre-eminent Greek hero of the day hailed from Boeotia. Agesilaus was bumped from his position as the undisputed military strategist of the early fourth century in Greece.

Cornelius Nepos summarizes the contributions of Epaminondas and how his fate was inextricably tied to the fate of Thebes:

> Before the birth of Epaminondas, and after his death, Thebes was subject constantly to the hegemony of others; but, on the contrary, so long as he was at the head of the state, she was the leading city of all Greece. This fact shows that one man was worth more than the entire body of citizens.[5]

The Theban Hegemony, then, could not fail as long as Epaminondas led its armies and Pelopidas led the Sacred Band. Following the victory at Leuctra, both would be voted as boeotarchs almost annually for the rest of their lives. Epaminondas worked quickly to secure the rise of the Theban military machine, instituting a series of reforms to ensure their victory over Sparta was not an aberration.

Epaminondas drilled his Theban soldiers at an intensity that only Sparta and its *agoge* could match. The Boeotian army rapidly became a professional, full-time army just like Sparta's. Epaminondas trained his men in multiple tactics, eschewing the rigidity of the classical phalanx and always keen to innovate. If it worked in battle, Epaminondas would adapt it into his playbook. The oblique order was, of course, now a standard tactic in Thebes. So also was a deeper, weighted phalanx that could stretch dozens of rows deep, just as at Leuctra. The Theban army prioritized flexibility, adapting their formations and tactics to their enemy and the context of the battle. No opposing commander could predict how the Thebans would line up for battle, where the Sacred Band would attack, or how deep a phalanx might be.

Epaminondas also designed longer spears, stretching a couple of feet further than the eight-foot spears of the Spartans. Though it took more training, the Theban hoplites were thus able to attack effectively from a longer distance – and any strategic advantage mattered in combat. This change bucked the recent trend in Greek warfare that Iphicrates had started with his own reforms in Athens, preferring peltasts and ranged, light infantry fighters. But it was Epaminondas' ideas that caught on and would be continued by the Macedonians, who would eventually have spears up to 20 feet long.

Epaminondas did find great value in the Iphicratean-style peltasts, however. In fact, he embraced them and many other types of soldier, diversifying the Boeotian army and increasing the number of peltasts, cavalry, skirmishers, and archers. As he had done at Leuctra, Epaminondas would use them to shield his phalanxes and distract the enemy, never letting the opposition discern the size or formation of the Theban forces. No longer was the heavy-infantry hoplite and the phalanx the exclusive model for Greek warfare. The Theban emphasis on combined arms tactics was radical in Greece for the early fourth century, but would soon become the standard.

Of course, the most important unit in the Theban army was the Sacred Band. The elite strike force remained the most feared fighting force in Greece. With Pelopidas at the helm, the Sacred Band would pivot to running their own special missions, such as invasions in the north of Greece, but would remain true to their original mission. Though they suffered losses, they had yet to lose a single engagement.

The result of Epaminondas' many military reforms was an army that not only rivalled Sparta's, but exceeded it. Increasingly, the Greek city-states not in close proximity to Sparta, and not historic rivals of Thebes, submitted to the Boeotian Confederacy. As Athens had been with the Delian League and Sparta with the Peloponnesian League, Thebes was now the authoritative power in Greece. If they did not outright force a city-state to join the Boeotian Confederacy, they threatened or cajoled it into a tacit submission.

Sparta was by no means destroyed, but her grip over Greece had never been looser. The rivalry between Athens and Sparta for Greek dominance created natural fault lines, as their opposing capabilities – Athens' navy versus Sparta's army – allowed Greek city-states to organically join one side, if they were given the choice. But the Theban hegemony was something new entirely. Both Sparta and Thebes were land-based powers, and both now had excellently trained and highly effective armies. The only thing separating their empires was policy and geography.

The battle of Leuctra and its aftermath marked the end of the Boeotian War. What had begun with the Theban revolution in 379 had now been crowned with a convincing victory for Thebes. The next phase of the Theban-Spartan Wars would prove to be more challenging, but Thebes would no longer be on the defensive. Post Leuctra, Epaminondas and the Thebans plotted to seize the opportunity and entirely take out the weakened Spartans. And just one year after Leuctra, Thebes would aim to do what no other Greek city-state had ever dared attempt: invade Sparta itself.

Theban Invasions of the Peloponnese

The audacity of Thebes' plan cannot be overstated. Though it was not terribly far as the crow flies, nobody had attempted an invasion of Sparta in over six centuries. It had been so long that the ancient writers could not even accurately name the last time an invading army had marched through the Peloponnese. Plutarch claims that it was in the Dorian invasion, though that event is considered mythological by modern scholars. It is likely that Sparta and Laconia had not been attacked since the era of the Mycenaeans or perhaps the Greek Dark Ages.

To get to Sparta, an invading army had to traverse hundreds of miles of rugged, mountainous countryside and overcome the thousands of helots, *perioeci*, and Spartan loyalists who had only ever known life under the Spartan banner. The land was agrarian and the infrastructure underdeveloped after centuries of fiercely isolationist policies. The cost would undoubtedly be high, but then again the Peloponnesian allies were increasingly breaking away from their Spartan overlords, while the helots were always eager to revolt.

Epaminondas and the Thebans were counting on that spirit of rebellion, both from the helots and from former members of the Peloponnesian League. A plan quickly emerged: Epaminondas' army would sweep into the Peloponnese after crossing the Isthmus of Corinth. They would ravage the countryside of city-states still loyal to Sparta, while also supporting the formation of the new Arcadian League. The Arcadians would then become his new allies, and together they would march to Sparta. Critically, they would also encourage helots across the Peloponnese to rebel against their Spartan masters. This plan was proposed not by Epaminondas, but by the Elians and Mantineans, though the Thebans quickly approved it.

All was looking well for Thebes, except for one major factor: the Athenians would not be joining them. Right after the victory at Leuctra, the Thebans had sent messengers to Athens to deliver the triumphant news of Sparta's defeat. They expected sonorous applause. Instead, they received a stunned and awkward silence. Xenophon describes the uncomfortable moment when the Athenian senate first heard the news of Theban victory: 'The annoyance caused by its announcement was unmistakable.'[6] Athens refused to join Epaminondas' invasion, and increasingly detached herself from any involvement in the Boeotian Confederacy. For now, the Athenians would not actively oppose the Thebans, but were steadfast in refusing to support them. Thebes had gained new territories such as Locris, Phocis, Euboea, Acarnania, and more regions that had recently been grafted into the Boeotian

Confederacy, but they would not benefit from the excellent fighting skills of Greece's most historic city.

It was the winter of 370, when the Thebans set out on the first invasion of Sparta in centuries. The expedition force was massive with nearly 40,000 Boeotian soldiers. Moreover, Plutarch says that 30,000 additional light-armoured troops and even unarmed soldiers joined the invasion force 'for the sake of plunder'.[7] And, once the Arcadians and – hopefully – the helots joined the army, it would be even more impressive. Epaminondas quickly accomplished his initial goals and was soon following the Eurotas river towards Sparta herself.

Before reaching Sparta, Epaminondas took the time to found one of the greatest cities of the latter days of classical Greek history. Realizing that the small villages of agrarian Arcadia were strong fighters when banded together, but had little ability to defend their individual hamlets, he recommended that the Arcadian League construct a new capital city, developing up to four dozen small villages into a single urban centre – this way they would stand a much better chance in any attack from Sparta. Also, they would become a true Greek *polis*, which had never existed in Arcadia, since Sparta had conquered them before the advent of this unique form of Greek city-state. Epaminondas even gave the new capital a name: Megalopolis, or the 'great city'. The vision was soon realized beyond his wildest dreams and Megalopolis thrived for the next three centuries, serving as the headquarters of Greek resistance to Roman conquest in the second century and as the main cultural centre of southern Greece for generations.

Meanwhile in Sparta, Agesilaus had done his best to prepare for the looming assault on the city, but his efforts were limited by the chaos that consumed Laconia. Never before had an army so quickly come within striking distance of Sparta. The city itself famously had no outer walls, since the Spartan hoplites themselves were said to be its walls. However, looking out at the vast advancing Theban army, the Spartans surely regretted this laconic quip and would have gladly had real walls for their protection.

Inside the city, traditional Spartan stoicism and military culture was tested as never before. The women could no longer hide their fear as they had after Leuctra, and mourned openly. Old men lamented that Sparta's soldiers had fallen so far so fast, blaming anyone and anything they could.

Agesilaus faced more defections from the army than one would have ever thought possible for the greatest Spartan king of all time. Antalcidas, the great Spartan diplomat, sent his entire family away, convinced that the city was doomed. Plutarch captures the drama and tension of the moments before the Thebans arrived at the city:

> But now [the Thebans] burst into an unravaged and inviolate land, and burned and plundered as far as the river and the city, and no one came out against them. For Agesilaus would not suffer the [Spartans] to fight against such a 'billowy torrent of war,' to use the words of Theopompus, but surrounded the central and most commanding parts of the city with his men-at-arms, while he endured the boastful threats of the Thebans, who called upon him by name and bade him come out and fight for his country, since he had caused her misfortunes by lighting up the flames of war.[8]

Despite it being a radical break from conventional Spartan tactics, Agesilaus' defensive strategy now proved devastatingly successful. The Spartans simply holed up in the city and refused to meet the Thebans in battle. Also it was winter – an unusual time for invasions given the unpredictable weather – and snowstorms delayed the invaders for almost three months. Soon, the Thebans began to face defections from their new Arcadian allies. Epaminondas, sensing the conquest of Sparta was receding fast out of reach, may have even accepted a bribe of ten talents from Agesilaus to leave.[9]

The sting of the failed conquest of Sparta was not yet over for Epaminondas, however. The Athenians now voted to send an army to the Peloponnese – but in support of Sparta, not Thebes. The great Athenian general Iphicrates marshalled an army and marched it to Sparta to confront the Thebans. In lieu of either meeting the Athenians or returning home to Thebes, however, Epaminondas opted to break Sparta's remaining allies and to this end he now ventured deeper into the Peloponnese. He led the Thebans south as far as the coastal city of Gythium, freeing more helots and *perioeci* from Spartan tyranny as they went. Then they turned west and travelled to the southwest corner of the Peloponnesian Peninsula to Messenia, whose people had been the first helots. For three centuries now, their lives had been nothing but brutality. The Spartans had enslaved and subjugated the Messenians and forced them to become the economic and agricultural foundation of the Spartan empire. Spartan citizens were the only professional, full-time soldiers in Greece and Sparta's entire infrastructure was predicated on keeping the Messenians demoralized enough not to consider active rebellion. If Epaminondas could empower the Messenians and give them a sustained independence, then the Spartans would starve.

Epaminondas now endeavoured to do exactly that, spreading the word far and wide that all helots across the Peloponnese should return to Messenia, which would henceforth be its own sovereign state. In 369, he founded another city to be the beacon for this reborn country. Named Messene, it was built on the ruins of the city of Ithome, which had been the capital of Messenia in the days of its fight for survival against Sparta, centuries earlier. The Messenians had lost that war, and the city had lain destroyed and abandoned ever since. The rebuilt city proved a great success, with thousands of helots taking up the Theban invitation to reside there. Within a few years, Messene was a major city-state in the region and flourished for centuries after.

The Spartans were increasingly infuriated with Agesilaus, particularly after the newfound freedom of their all-important slave force. Once again, their very identity had been rattled to the core – and it was Agesilaus who had overseen yet another shocking precedent. Plutarch explains the growing Spartan discontent:

> But when Messene was built by Epaminondas, and its former citizens flocked into it from all quarters, the Spartans had not the courage to contest the issue nor the ability to hinder it, but cherished the deepest resentment against Agesilaüs, because a country which was not of less extent than their own, which stood first among Hellenic lands for its fertility, the possession and fruits of which they had enjoyed for so long a time, had been lost by them during his reign.[10]

While he had not conquered Sparta, Epaminondas' invasion of the Peloponnese had been a smashing success. Sparta had not only faced an existential threat, but they now had no allies and no helots. Their entire economic and political structure had collapsed. Two new symmachies in Arcadia and Messenia now threatened their existence. Epaminondas returned to Thebes, with the Boeotian Confederacy more powerful than ever before.

Three more invasions of the Peloponnese followed in the 360s, but each was less effective than the last. In 368, Epaminondas led a campaign that was thwarted by Sparta's new 'allies' from Athens and Corinth. Both the Athenians and Corinthians preferred a weakened Sparta to a triumphant Thebes, and assisted in the fortifications at the Isthmus of Corinth. While the Thebans broke through the barriers and had limited success in the northern Peloponnese, they were not strong enough in their fight against the alliance of Athenians, Spartans, Corinthians, and failed to march on Sparta.

The following year in 367, after facing increasing scrutiny at home – where he was placed on trial and then removed from his position as boeotarch – Epaminondas led an even less successful invasion. While he easily marched into the Peloponnese this time, he succeeded only in agitating local political factions. A brewing conflict between the Arcadians and their neighbours in Achaea boiled over, and Epaminondas made the short-sighted decision to accept aid from the Achaeans and their oligarchic governments, which frustrated the democratic Arcadians and the Thebans back home. To allow an ally to maintain such oligarchies might have been pragmatic diplomacy, but risked the ire of allies and, worse, the rise of pro-Spartan oligarchs.

In fact, both of these things happened in due course, and pro-Spartan oligarchs soon returned to power in Achaea. They promptly withdrew their support for the Thebans, so when the Thebans returned in 362, the Achaeans were allied with the Spartans and Athenians. Epaminondas' attempts at effective pragmatism in negotiating with oligarchs would prove to be a fatal error.

Despite the diminishing returns on invasions of the Peloponnese, Thebes was nevertheless successful at diminishing Spartan influence. After three invasions, Sparta was confined to their smallest territory in centuries. Thebes was the undisputed hegemon of Greece, and while they had not vanquished Sparta or Athens they held the allegiance of nearly all of central and northern Greece and large swathes of the Peloponnese. As always, the Aegean islands were partial to Athens, but Thebes gained allies in Byzantium, Cyzicus, and several other territories in Asia Minor. Ever since Leuctra, Thebes had kept her grip on Greek supremacy, while Sparta's fortunes had weakened considerably.

Philip II of Macedonia and the Theban Influence on Alexander the Great's Empire

When Jason of Pherae was assassinated in 370, his son Alexander eventually became *tagos* of Thessaly. But the cut-throat politics of northern Greece did not bode well for his independence, and he lacked the martial skills of his father. Pelopidas himself was sent to Thessaly to ensure their compliance, and though it took several campaigns he was eventually successful, though he died in combat there. Thessaly and the other regions of northern Greece were forced to join the Boeotian Confederacy by the mid 360s.

More critically, Thebes' acquisition of Thessaly opened the door to bringing their northern neighbour Macedonia into the fledgling empire as well. In an ill-advised move, the Macedonians had interfered in Thessaly and had angered Pelopidas and the Thebans, who marched north and subdued Macedonia. As part of the peace terms, the Thebans demanded a ward from Macedonia, a young member of the royal house who would be held hostage in Thebes in order to discourage rebellion. The ward would be treated well, given a quality education and would never want for privilege or luxury – but he would nevertheless be a prisoner, not free to return home.

By chance, the Thebans selected a young prince named Philip II to be the ward. Philip II was the younger brother of the king, but as we have seen the Macedonian throne was plagued by ongoing civil strife and turnover. Philip lived in Thebes from 368 to 365, at the height of the Theban hegemony and the military glory of Epaminondas. He was accommodated in the home of Pammenes, the Theban general who had advocated strongly for the unique design of the Sacred Band, and it was from him and from Epaminondas, that Philip learned the art of war and, more critically, the art of cultivating virtue. Philip was said to be much taken with Epaminondas and his Pythagorean ways. It was a far cry from the leadership he had seen while he was growing up in Macedonia, and Epaminondas was the wisest and most strategic leader he had encountered in his young life. Philip desired to emulate him. Plutarch summarises Epaminondas' influence on the young Macedonian prince, while also insulting Philip for failing to fully absorb the Theban leader's lessons:

Hence he was believed to have become a zealous follower of Epaminondas, perhaps because he comprehended his efficiency in wars and campaigns, which was only a small part of the man's high excellence; but in restraint, justice, magnanimity, and gentleness, wherein Epaminondas was truly great, Philip had no share, either naturally or as a result of imitation.[11]

While Philip might not copy Epaminondas in virtue, he could certainly copy in military tactics. When he seized the Macedonian throne in 359, he instituted major reforms that – when combined with his son Alexander's brilliance in combat – would lay the foundation for the greatest empire the world had yet seen. Many of these reforms were Theban in origin and directly adapted from Epaminondas and the Sacred Band. The Macedonians dramatically increased the size of a phalanx to an average of 16 hoplites deep, much larger than the common phalanx before Leuctra. As the Thebans had begun to do, the Macedonians also extended the spears of the hoplites. Their new *sarissas* stretched up to 21 feet long, and took specialized training and discipline to wield. This training regimen was directly influenced by Epaminondas' sophisticated drilling of the Theban hoplites.

The Theban emphasis on combined arms was also a stalwart of the Macedonian army, which incorporated hoplites, skirmishers, light infantry, cavalry, archers, and strike forces in equal measure. Alexander would eventually include new fighters from the many lands he conquered and brought into his empire, creating one of the most diverse armies in history. The Macedonian emphasis on cavalry was especially significant. While Epaminondas had toyed with using cavalry first at Leuctra, this became a standard in Hellenistic warfare. Further, the Macedonian use of the Companions as an elite strike force was in many respects in emulation of the Sacred Band of Thebes. This heavy cavalry unit operated similarly to the Sacred Band as the primary means of breaking through the enemy lines, and would be strategically situated in the battle formations as a result.

Perhaps most important was the Macedonian adaptation of the oblique order. Epaminondas' signature tactic not only became a favourite ploy of the Macedonian army but would be used consistently by Alexander the Great. Alexander's version was known as the 'hammer and anvil' technique, wherein the Companions on the right flank smashed through the enemy frontage and then wrapped around to trap the enemy between the slower-moving Macedonian left wing. Alexander used this tactic at nearly every one of his major battles, and never lost a single fight.

Alexander the Great and the Macedonians may very well have found the same success without this Theban influence, but it would have looked quite different. Nearly all of the major military reforms of the Macedonians had some roots in innovations of the Boeotian Confederacy under Epaminondas and Pelopidas. In this way, the legacy of Leuctra was woven into the tapestry of the Hellenistic world and its great political, cultural, and economic accomplishments.

Death of Pelopidas

Epaminondas was not the only star of the Theban hegemony's rapid rise over Greece. Pelopidas may have taken a less glamorous role while Epaminondas was leading the army, but his leadership of the Sacred Band of Thebes remained a key component in the Boeotian Confederacy's military and diplomatic strength. Pelopidas was often elected a boeotarch himself, and remained in the inner circle of Theban politics.

In 367, Pelopidas led a diplomatic mission to Persia to reaffirm peace with the Great King and legitimize the Boeotian Confederacy as the new power in Greece. While no other Greek could be as revered by the Persians as Antalcidas of Sparta was, Pelopidas found great acclaim. The Persians were well aware of the battle of Leuctra and the prestige of the Sacred Band of Thebes, and Pelopidas had secured their respect. He guaranteed Persian support for Messene, which was enormously important as a direct challenge to Sparta, and which Persia would not have dared do even a few short years earlier. While the Persians still demanded Thebes abide by the rules of the King's Peace of 387 and its strictures about the autonomy of all Greek city-states, they also did not push the point. By the time Pelopidas left Persian territory a few months later, it was said that for the Persians 'the fame of Pelopidas was more potent than any number of rhetorical discourses with a man who ever paid deference to those who were mighty in arms.'[12]

While Epaminondas spent the 360s attempting to vanquish Sparta, Pelopidas was tasked with expanding the Confederacy's influence in the north of Greece. Pelopidas had been sent to Thessaly to address the turmoil following the death of Jason of Pherae. His son Alexander of Pherae had ascended to the throne, and proved a capable successor. Pelopidas was unable to defeat him in several campaigns, and was even taken hostage for several years until Epaminondas led his only northern campaign to rescue Pelopidas.

When he was at last freed, Pelopidas sought retribution for his imprisonment and the audacious challenge to Theban supremacy. He got his chance in 364 when the last free Thessalians appealed to him once more, terrified that Alexander of Pherae was growing strong enough to conquer all of Thessaly. Pelopidas and the Sacred Band marched on Thessaly for the final time, determined to end the bloodline of Jason of Pherae once and for all. Pelopidas was substantially outnumbered by the Thessalians, who again had their ranks bolstered by mercenaries as they had in the days of Jason. Despite his small force, about half the size of the Thessalians, Pelopidas remained full of confidence, boasting, 'All the better…for there will be more for us to conquer.'[13]

The battle took place in the hills near Cynoscephalae in Thessaly. The two armies began the engagement in two separate valleys separated by a rugged hill, which became the focal point of the fighting. Alexander's forces won the hill, but Pelopidas cleverly took the entire base of the hill and began a flanking manoeuvre that forced the Thessalians back down, giving up the high ground. Pelopidas single-handedly led this assault, causing both Thebans and Thessalians to be inspired by his courage and conviction as he fought from the back of the Theban lines all the way to the front, just so he could personally lead the assault up the hill.

Just as the Thebans were on the verge of triumph, Pelopidas caught sight of Alexander of Pherae on the opposite side of the field. The normally stoic Pelopidas was unable to contain his rage and entered a frenzy of bloodlust that would have made Achilles proud. He fought his way through towards Alexander's position, leaving his Sacred Band behind and fighting virtually on his own. The cowardly Alexander retreated, sending his mercenary bodyguards forward to deal with Pelopidas.

Pelopidas fought very bravely, but without his Sacred Band at his side he was overwhelmed by the mercenaries and killed. Thirsty for vengeance for the death of their beloved leader, the Thebans' counterattack was devastatingly effective and they shattered the Thessalian phalanx, killing 3,000 men. The Thebans went on to win the battle quickly and with minimal losses, but the death of Pelopidas was a crushing blow for Thebes that soured any single tactical victory. Alexander of Pherae lost all his territorial holdings outside his homeland, and was forced to join the Boeotian Confederacy as a vassal state. He would linger on for several more years before he was assassinated by dissidents, just like his father Jason.

In a funeral service following the battle, the Thebans gave Pelopidas honours worthy of the greatest heroes of the Trojan War. Upon learning of his death, his men did not immediately take off their armour and weapons but instead went to pay homage to his body, leaving the spoils of war at his feet. They then cut their own hair and their horses' manes as a symbol of mourning. A dark silence fell over the camp that evening, and hardly a fire was lit. Instead of a celebration for the long awaited victory over Alexander of Pherae, the Thebans were drowning in profound and inconsolable grief.

The Thessalians were no less in despair. Though Pelopidas had been an enemy to many of them, the cities of Thessaly brought down their banners and hung laurels and wreaths as if their own national hero had passed. They even asked to bury Pelopidas in the local tradition, essentially adopting him as their own. Plutarch describes the funeral scene and national lament over the fallen champion:

> Now, that the Thebans who were present at the death of Pelopidas should be disconsolate, calling him their father and saviour and teacher of the greatest and fairest blessings, was not so much to be wondered at; but the Thessalians and allies also, after exceeding in their decrees every honour that can fitly be paid to human excellence, showed still more by their grief how grateful they were to him.[14]

We do not have a record of Epaminondas' reaction to the death of his great friend Pelopidas, but he would have doubtless been in mourning for weeks. Epaminondas' mission to avenge the personal and national loss took the shape of one last, grand invasion of Sparta. This time, the fate of the Theban hegemony would be decided at the very site where Pelopidas' and Epaminondas' relationship had begun: Mantinea. At the siege of Mantinea in 386, when both were serving their Spartan tyrants, Epaminondas had saved

Pelopidas in combat and so began their great mutual friendship, or *philoi*. Now, that deep bond would culminate on the same plains outside Mantinea.

Battle of Mantinea, 362

The fourth and final Theban invasion of the Peloponnese occurred in 362, two years after the death of Pelopidas. While Pelopidas had secured Theban interests in the north of Greece, the situation in the south was more complicated. A failed attempt at a common peace in 366 had added fuel to the rising resentment of Thebes who, like many city-states before them, were now suffering the backlash that came with being undisputed hegemon of Greece. Multiple cities in Arcadia had now turned back to Sparta, and Thebes had to endure a lacklustre naval campaign in 364 that resulted in no serious territorial gain. While the Thebans still had a firm grip on most of central and northern Greece, their only major holdings in the Peloponnese were in Messenia, where the former helots were fiercely loyal to their liberators.

Mantinea was the primary Arcadian city-state to have rejected Theban rule. The Mantineans had then led a successful publicity campaign to persuade other Peloponnesian cities, claiming that Thebes was no better than Sparta and that the Theban goal was to see the Peloponnese 'reduced to such an extremity of weakness that it might fall an easy prey into their hands who were minded to enslave it.'[15] The Mantineans had appealed to Athens, Achaea, Elis, several other Arcadian cities and even Sparta for aid. All answered the call. Agesilaus himself led the Spartan army and marched to Mantinea, expecting to meet Epaminondas and his army of Boeotians, northern Greeks such as the Thessalians, and former Spartan allies from Sicyon, Tegea, and Messenia. This broad coalition of forces made the battle of Mantinea the most comprehensive military engagement in Greek history, with representation from virtually every corner of the Greek world. Only the mythologized Trojan War involves a more diverse collection of Greek city-states.

Agesilaus and the Spartans had expected Epaminondas to march straight to Mantinea, as the Theban army was encamped in nearby Tegea. Epaminondas had a vast army of nearly 30,000 men, and was not outnumbered as he had been at the battle of Leuctra. The Spartans and their allies had only about 20,000 soldiers, but this time were being led by their legendary commander. Agesilaus thought Epaminondas would press his numerical advantage and march north to Mantinea, where the Spartans were busy setting up fortifications.

However Epaminondas, as ever, refused to be predictable and in the middle of the night marched due south to Sparta. He reasoned that since Agesilaus had taken the Spartan army with him, the city would be left unguarded. Xenophon was so impressed with Epaminondas' tactical decisions before Mantinea that he lauded him with praise – almost unheard of from the pro-Spartan historian. Xenophon had written most of his *Hellenica* avoiding the very name of Epaminondas, and when he wrote such praise of a Theban, he was risking his very life with his Spartan editors. Xenophon actually wrote, 'in the particular combination of prudence and daring which stamps these exploits, I look upon him as consummate.'[16]

By a twist of fate, a Cretan ally of the Spartans had seen the Thebans march off to Sparta and was able to send a warning to the city, where Agesilaus' son Archidamus organized a panicked fortification. Due to this piece of bad luck, Epaminondas arrived to a well-defended city and, despite a wise tactical approach into the city from the high ground, suffered a quick loss to the desperate Spartan defenders. Worse, a Spartan regiment was arriving from Mantinea to reinforce the city. Undaunted, Epaminondas simply abandoned that fight and ordered a countermarch straight back to Mantinea. His forces were able to outpace his Spartan rivals and make camp safely back inside the walls of Tegea, sending his cavalry forward to the battlefield at Mantinea. The cavalry would keep the enemy occupied while the main army gathered themselves to begin the main assault.

Xenophon recounts how, before the battle began, Epaminondas reflected on the future of his campaign and the fact that, should he fail to conquer Sparta for a fourth time, it was likely both his career and reputation would be destroyed. The dramatic setting for this last, climactic battle was bittersweet: a final invasion of Sparta, against the greatest Spartan king ever, and in pursuit of vengeance for his beloved friend Pelopidas. If Epaminondas could not achieve victory here – or die trying – then he did not deserve to rule over the Theban hegemony. And he knew it. Xenophon continues his rare praise of Epaminondas in the moments before the battle of Mantinea begins:

> That such thoughts should pass through his brain strikes me as by no means wonderful, as these are thoughts distinctive to all men of high ambition. Far more wonderful to my mind was the pitch of perfection to which he had brought his army. There was no labour which his troops would shrink from, either by night or by day; there was no danger they would flinch from; and, with the scantiest provisions, their discipline never failed them.[17]

Epaminondas and the Thebans soon made themselves ready for battle, following the cavalry's skirmishes with a late-arriving Athenian cavalry. As they prepared, the Arcadian hoplites painted the club of Heracles on their shields, as if they were Thebans themselves. This showed the passionate support that many Greeks still had for the Thebans who had shattered Sparta's tyranny. No matter how difficult things would be under Thebes, it would pale in comparison to life under the Spartan boot.

Epaminondas ordered battle formations akin to Leuctra, perhaps in an attempt at psychological warfare. Once again his left wing was very deep and he would employ the oblique order. Xenophon gives us a poetic image of the left wing of Epaminondas' army like the battering ram of a trireme: 'Wherever he brought his solid wedge to bear, he meant to cleave through the opposing mass, and crumble his adversary's host to pieces.'[18] It is not clear where the Sacred Band of Thebes was situated in the formation, but if the theme of recreating Leuctra held true then they would again be fighting in the frontage of the Theban left wing. This time however, in yet another military innovation, Epaminondas arranged his cavalry in a wedge formation as well. Though Philip II of Macedonia was no longer his ward, this model was directly adopted by the Macedonian cavalry under Philip and Alexander the Great. The Macedonians copied the move because it evidently worked very well, combining the shock tactics of the Sacred Band with new levels of speed and armour.

Agesilaus had countered with an unusually deep phalanx, a rare sight indeed and indicative of the desperation the Spartans felt. They had not meaningfully changed tactics in centuries, but Agesilaus knew that the moment demanded something new. This larger phalanx was able to absorb the initial attack from the Thebans, and the fighting soon came to a gridlock as Greece's two greatest armies fought in a battle of the titans. Diodorus Siculus describes the heroic struggle between Thebans and Spartans:

And although their bodies were all locked with one another and they were inflicting all manner of wounds, yet they did not leave off; and for a long time as they persisted in their terrible work, because of the superlative courage displayed on each side, the battle hung poised. For each man, disregarding the risk of personal hurt, but desirous rather of performing some brilliant deed, would nobly accept death as the price of glory.[19]

Seeking to break the stalemate, Epaminondas gathered a small group of his best fighters – likely members of the Sacred Band – and led them in a strike aimed at the Spartan commander. His group of several dozen men smashed through the Spartan lines at long last, and fought their way to the Spartan polemarch.

Epaminondas' courage here was undeniable, but tactically the move forward created a brief opening in the Theban frontage that the cunning Agesilaus immediately identified and exploited. He ordered his men forward into the breach, cutting off Epaminondas' strike force from reinforcements. This proved deadly for Epaminondas and his men. The Spartans pelted them with spears and javelins, and at last a hoplite spear struck Epaminondas in the chest. He fell, but his fellow Thebans rallied around him and pushed back the Spartan lines. While he lay wounded, his army charged the Spartans and forced them to retreat. They were not defeated, however and were able to push back on the opposite Boeotian flank. Both armies subsequently made credible claims of victory, and erected trophies.

Epaminondas held on to life long enough to hear that his men had successfully pushed the Spartan flank back. When he heard the news, he uttered his final words, 'I have lived long enough, since I die unconquered.'[20] He spoke true: Epaminondas had never lost a major engagement and the Theban hegemony, despite not winning outright at Mantinea, retained its position at the head of all Greece. The Sacred Band of Thebes remained undefeated.

When Epaminondas died, as with Pelopidas, both armies mourned his death. And, since the two armies were composed of nearly all mainland Greek city-states, it was perhaps the first national funeral in Greek history. Though they respected Epaminondas' accomplishments, the Spartans so celebrated his death that they awarded the hoplite who killed him tax-exempt status for the remainder of his life and his descendants were given a special title based on the weapon used to slay Epaminondas.

Diodorus Siculus devoted an entire paragraph to a funeral lamentation for Epaminondas, devoting more words to him than perhaps any other individual in his tome of history that covers the entire ancient world. He compares Epaminondas to a list of the great Greek champions, naming such luminaries as Agesilaus, Leonidas, Solon, Themistocles, Gelon, Miltiades, Cimon, and Pericles. Without reservation or qualification, he claims Epaminondas is greater than them all:

All the same, if you should compare the qualities of these [men] with the generalship and reputation of Epaminondas, you would find the qualities possessed by Epaminondas far superior. For in each of the others you would discover but one particular superiority as a claim to fame; in him, however, all qualities combined. For in strength of body and eloquence of speech, furthermore in elevation of mind, contempt of lucre, fairness, and, most of all, in courage and shrewdness in the art of war, he far surpassed them all. So it was that in his lifetime his native country acquired the primacy of Hellas, but when he died lost it and constantly suffered change for the worse and finally, because of the folly of its leaders, experienced slavery and devastation.[21]

Even in death, Epaminondas had earned a victory for the Boeotian Confederacy and a strong standing for Thebes. While Thebes would never again reach the heights the city saw under him, he left a strong enough foundation for the Theban hegemony to survive for several more decades. His death in battle saved his reputation, for that final invasion of Sparta was not an outright failure – it brought enough success to secure Thebes' survival. Sparta was sequestered to the southern Peloponnese, and their ageing king Agesilaus was not healthy enough to campaign into Boeotia, even if he had had enough soldiers. The battle of Mantinea saved Thebes' supremacy in Greece and it was made possible by the earlier victory at Leuctra, and the expert leadership of Pelopidas and Epaminondas. Though both had died before conquering all of Greece, they had achieved their shared lifelong vision to liberate Thebes and make it the greatest city in the land. Through sheer grit and determination, and a ceaseless talent for innovation, they had earned their position among the greatest of Greek leaders.

Conclusion

The Demise of Thebes

On an August day in 338, Philip II of Macedonia walked through the piles of dead bodies on the Boeotian plains outside the city of Chaeronea. The battle at Chaeronea had been the last stand not just for the Thebans, but for most of Greece. Philip had spent decades successfully employing Epaminondas' strategies and innovations in Macedonia, growing the former frontier country into the pre-eminent power in Greece. As usual, the country had descended into another civil war after the Theban-Spartan Wars and each state fought the other to a bloody stalemate – so that all the city-states were thoroughly weakened before a lightning-fast Macedonian army swept south. Thebes was no longer the dominant power, but maintained a strong position with the Boeotian Confederacy.

The Sacred Band of Thebes had been Greece's last hope. While not as formidable as they were under Pelopidas, they had still never lost a battle since their formation. But the mighty Macedonians had developed an entirely new brand of warfare that turned the Thebans' strengths against them. The Sacred Band fought as bravely as ever at Chaeronea, but all 300 men died when the Macedonian phalanxes overwhelmed them. It was the first and only loss for the Sacred Band. Their history ends at Chaeronea. Having lived so long in Thebes as a teenager, Philip held the Sacred Band in the highest regard, and mourned their loss as much as any Theban. Plutarch gives the event special attention:

After the battle, Philip was surveying the dead, and stopped at the place where the three hundred were lying, all where they had faced the long spears of his phalanx, with their armour, and mingled one with another, he was amazed, and on learning that this was the band of lovers and beloved, burst into tears and said: 'Perish miserably they who think that these men did or suffered aught disgraceful.'[1]

It had taken the greatest army that history had yet seen to overcome the Sacred Band of Thebes, and they put up an excellent fight. It also took the greatest commander in all of history, Alexander the Great, to defeat them. Chaeronea was Alexander's first major command, and he led the wing opposing the Sacred Band. It would be his first victory of many. Thebes, and the rest of Greece except for an obstinate Sparta, was now part of the Macedonian Empire.

Just a few years after Chaeronea in 335 the Thebans revolted, following Philip II's untimely death. The Macedonian throne was claimed by his young son Alexander, but the Thebans supposed that the inexperienced prince would not be up to the task. They could not have been more wrong. When Thebes refused to negotiate, Alexander used the opportunity to give an example of what the Macedonians would do to cities that refused to submit to them. He razed the city and sold the Thebans into slavery. The Cadmea itself was destroyed and Greece's oldest city-state was wiped off the earth. Thebes, the great city of myth and the most recent hegemon of Greece, would never again be a major power. The city itself was eventually rebuilt, but for nearly two decades it was either empty or little more than a village.

Greece came together to rebuild Thebes in 315, after Alexander's death. Megalopolis and Messene sent the most support, in honour of Epaminondas. Despite its rebirth, the narrative of Thebes essentially concludes with Alexander the Great's conquest of the city. In 371, Leuctra had made the Thebans the champions of Greece, but less than forty years later the Macedonians completely obliterated their seat of power. In antiquity, perhaps only Carthage and Nineveh experienced such a dramatic collapse from imperial dominance to complete destruction in so brief a span.

Historical Significance of Leuctra

Thebes suffered a catastrophic fall at Chaeronea, but it was an oddly fitting end to their historical arc. Thebes had spent centuries as a significant but not dominant Greek city-state, always opposing the leading power of the time. In the Persian Wars they had opted to side with Persia, in part to settle their grudge against the other Greeks. In the Peloponnesian Wars, they fought against the ascendant Athenians. At Aulis, they ruined Agesilaus' invasion of Persia out of spite. In the Corinthian War, they joined the anti-Spartan alliance and hoped to liberate Greece from Spartan tyranny. Never once did the Thebans ally themselves with the dominant power in Greece. They were recalcitrant and headstrong, and always eager to humble Greece's leader.

But something had changed when the Spartans unceremoniously conquered the city in 382. Phoebidas' self-interested actions awoke the Thebans to the reality of their historical position, and transformed many of the citizens from those who accepted mediocrity to those who craved greatness. Thebes had surely had men of excellent military and civic virtue before, but the city's conquest by Sparta awoke the greatness in Pelopidas and Epaminondas. These two led Thebes to heights it had never seen before.

Under their joint leadership, the Thebans rapidly turned a regional power into an undisputed superpower. In just a few years, Pelopidas and Epaminondas built a world-class army, created a new breed of shock troops that dominated Greece, and pushed tactical innovation further than it had progressed in decades. All of this was forged from an enslaved city that had been subjugated by the mightiest military state in Greek history.

And it was the battle at Leuctra that had been the pivotal moment. While the Theban revolution of 379 began the trajectory of Thebes' rise, it was this battle that permanently reconfigured the Greek world. Leuctra remains the most important event in the late classical era, demarcating it from the Hellenistic world. Leuctra distilled all the main elements of classical warfare: the primacy of the phalanx, the Spartan military machine, an emphasis on hoplites, and civil war between fellow Greeks. And yet this engagement also showed Greece the future by including, for the first time, innovations such as the oblique order, combined arms tactics, and strategic use of cavalry.

The battle of Leuctra also witnessed the final appearance of Sparta at the height of her imperial power. For centuries now, the Spartans had maintained military supremacy and no Greek army could defeat Spartan hoplites in direct engagement. But over the years their famous superiority had become a veneer: Sparta's army had deteriorated. When Epaminondas and Pelopidas defeated the Spartans at Leuctra, they did not just gain a victory over the enemy, they also revealed the 'Spartan mirage', showing the rest of Greece that Sparta was now a mere shell of her former glory. Her Peloponnesian allies and the helots soon realized the truth, and Sparta's empire crumbled. While the Spartans had not been destroyed outright after Leuctra or Mantinea, they were successfully confined to the Peloponnese. They lacked the citizens and helots to rebuild their empire. In the centuries that followed, they were still strong enough to defend themselves, but too weak to travel outside the borders of Laconia. Within a few centuries, Sparta was to become little more than a tourist attraction for wealthy Romans.

The Theban-Spartan wars and the battle of Leuctra represent the last era of purely Greek warfare, before foreign interventions first from the Macedonians and then the Romans broke Greece's longstanding isolationism. The world was changing rapidly, and Leuctra was the final internecine conflict that singularly changed Greek history. The next generation of Greece's battles would be with outsiders.

Historians often focus on contingencies, or the notion that chance and interconnectedness play decisive roles in shaping history as we know it. In nearly every consequential historical event, small changes in the conditions that determine outcomes could have led to vastly different results. History is, therefore, contingent and not predetermined. The battle of Leuctra is one of these lynchpin events that alters the flow of history forever. Had the events leading up to the battle gone in any number of different directions, Leuctra might not have become the seminal moment that it was. But since that battle did result in a great Theban victory, Thebes became the foremost Greek city-state for nearly four decades, while Sparta spiralled downward towards her inevitable demise, Macedonia received all the tools and techniques needed to build one of the greatest empires ever, and arguably the most influential period in western human history – the classical Greek world – came to a conclusion. Truly, Leuctra belongs amongst the most consequential and important battles in recorded history.

Shortly before his death, Epaminondas was criticized for never marrying or having children. As things stood, his family line would die out and he would leave no legacy. In response, he declared Leuctra would be his true legacy. He famously said,

> I cannot lack offspring; for I leave as my daughter the battle of Leuctra, which is certain, not merely to survive me, but even to be immortal.[2]

Glossary

agoge The Spartan system of rearing warrior-citizens. From a young age, boys were rigorously educated in military tactics, fighting skills, and Spartan virtues. Graduates became the Spartan hoplites and full citizens, the Spartiates.

battle of Leuctra The decisive battle of the Boeotian War between Thebes and Sparta, it ended Sparta's long dominance of Greece and inaugurated Thebes' ascendancy.

boeotarch An elected magistrate in the Boeotian Confederacy. Epaminondas and Pelopidas often served terms as boeotarchs.

Boeotian Confederacy An alliance of Boeotian city-states that ensured mutual protection for each state that contributed soldiers and finances. It was broken into eleven districts that each elected a magistrate, or *boeotarch*.

damos The ruling assembly in Boeotia.

ephor A ruling oligarch in Sparta, elected by the assembly. Only five ephors served at any one time and their primary duties involved foreign affairs, military strategy and checking the power of the two monarchs.

gerousia The council of elders in ancient Sparta, composed of two kings and 28 men over the age of 60, who were elected for life.

harmost A military commander appointed governor of a garrison or city-state. Lysander appointed many of these, personally loyal to him, across Asia Minor.

helot The enslaved population of Sparta and her home territories, mainly Messenia. They massively outnumbered the Spartan citizenship and Sparta brutally oppressed them in turn, leading to many helot rebellions.

homoioi Meaning 'the equals' or 'peers', these were the elite, full-citizen men of ancient Sparta, a small but powerful minority of the population who were devoted to military service and governance.

hoplite Heavy infantry soldiers of classical Greece. Armed with an 8–10 foot-long spear, 40–50 pounds of heavy armour, a short sword, and a shield, they were a unique development in Greece and were highly successful against the faster and lighter Persian infantry.

King's Peace of 387 The peace treaty that concluded the Corinthian War, it promised autonomy for all Greek city-states under Sparta. Sparta's violation of these terms caused Thebes to rebel.

lochos A 'war band' of soldiers, this was the Greek word for the 'band' in the Sacred Band of Thebes. A *lochos* is also a unit of 144 men in the Spartan army.

mora A full Spartan regiment of approximately 600 hoplites.

neodamodes The 'new citizens' of Sparta, composed of freed helots who served in the Spartan army.

oliganthropia The descriptive term for critical population decline of Spartan citizens. Since Spartiates could only be replaced every thirty years as young men graduates of the *agoge*, Sparta was slowly losing its citizen-soldiers and was forced to elevate helots or *perioeci* to form the majority of the army.

oligarchy Rule by a few elite individuals. Oligarchy was a common form of government in ancient Greece, and Athenian democracy emerged from a long struggle in Athens against tyranny and oligarchy.

peltast A light infantry fighter of Greece. Armed with javelins and focusing on mobility and flexibility in lieu of close combat, the peltast became the primary fighter in the fourth century in Greece, supplanting the heavy infantry hoplite.

perioeci Free non-citizens of the Spartan state.

phalanx A military formation of hoplites in closely arrangement with interlocking shields to guard your allies. The phalanx formed a shied wall and could attack an opponent with its 8-10-foot-long spears strategically arranged to complement the shields.

polemarch A military commander or war leader.

proxenoi Citizens appointed as hosts to foreign ambassadors.

Sacred Band of Thebes The elite fighting force of 300 warriors, famously composed of pairs of romantic partners. Each member of the 150 couples fought to protect his beloved, and they quickly became the greatest military unit in Greece, never losing a battle for nearly forty years.

Second Athenian League The reforged Athenian naval empire founded in 378, marking the revitalization of Athens after its near destruction in the Peloponnesian War

Spartiate A full citizen of Sparta with legal and political rights, earned by birth, graduation from the *agoge* and service as a hoplite.

stasis Meaning a 'standing still', but in political history describing faction or discord, *stasis* was a term for the constant political struggle between the pro-democracy forces (often aligned with Athens) and the pro-oligarchical factions (often aligned with Sparta).

symmachy An alliance of Greek city-states banded together to fight against a common enemy.

Theban hegemony The period of Greek history when Thebes exercised dominance over the entirety of the Greek world. After their great victory at Leuctra in 371, they ruled Greece for decades until the rise of Macedon.

trireme A three-storied warship of the ancient world built for fast travel and ramming opponents. Triremes had about 180 rowers and were the gold standard for naval warfare during the Persian Wars, on both sides.

Notes

Introduction

1. Ps-Plutarch, *Love Stories* III.
2. *Ibid.*
3. Diodorus Siculus, *The Library of History* 15.53.1–3.
4. Thucydides, *History of the Peloponnesian War* 1.44.1.
5. Xenophon, *Hellenica* 2.2.20.
6. *Ibid.*

Chapter 1

1. Strabo, *The Geography* 9.2.32.
2. Pliny the Elder, *Naturalis Historia* 18.12
3. Cartledge, P., 2020. *Thebes: The Forgotten City of Ancient Greece*. Abrams Press. p. 6.
4. Aristotle, *Rhetoric* 1407a.
5. Joyce, C. J., 2024. Review of Roy van Wijk, *Athens and Boiotia: interstate relations in the archaic and classical periods* (Cambridge: Cambridge University Press, 2024). *Bryn Mawr Classical Review*, [Online]. Available at: https://bmcr.brynmawr.edu/2024/2024.08.31/.
6. Homer, *The Iliad* 4.408, *The Odyssey* 11.263 and many other references.
7. Hesiod, *Works and Days* 156–165.
8. Plutarch, *Life of Martellus* 21.2.
9. Herodotus, *The Histories* 6.108.
10. The Plataeans, meanwhile, were the only non-Athenians present at the victory over the Persians in the Battle of Marathon, primarily due to their strife with the Thebans.
11. Pausanias, *Description of Greece* 9.6.2.
12. *Hellenica Oxyrhynchia* 16.3.
13. *Ibid.* 16.4.
14. Beck, H., 1997. "Thebes, the Boiotian League, and the Rise of Federalism in Fourth Century Greece." In: Bernardini, P. A. (ed.) *Presenza e funzione della città di Tebe nella cultura greca*. Pisa, Roma: Istituti editoriali e poligrafici internazionali, p. 335
15. *Ibid.*, p. 344.
16. *Ibid.*
17. Diodorus Siculus, *The Library of History* 11.81.3.
18. Hunt, P., 2007. Review of Mogens Herman Hansen, *The shotgun method: the demography of the ancient Greek city-state culture* (Columbia: University of Missouri Press, 2006). *Bryn Mawr Classical Review*, [Online]. Available at: https://bmcr.brynmawr.edu/2007/2007.04.58/#_ftnref2; Bintliff, J. and Snodgrass, A., 1985. "The Boiotia Survey, a Preliminary Report: The first four years." *Journal of Field Archaeology*, 12, pp. 123–61.

Chapter 2

1. Xenophon, *Hellenica* 2.23.
2. Xenophon, *Agesilaus* 1.1.
3. Plutarch, *Life of Agesilaus* 6.4.
4. *Ibid.* 6.5–6.
5. Hamilton, C. D., 1991. *Agesilaus and the Failure of Spartan Hegemony.* Ithaca, NY: Cornell University Press, p. 95.
6. Xenophon, *Hellenica* 3.5.1.
7. *Ibid.* 4.8.12–16.
8. *Ibid.* 5.1.28.
9. *Ibid.* 5.1.31.
10. *Ibid.* 5.1.34.
11. *Ibid.* 5.1.31.
12. *Ibid.* 5.1.33.

Chapter 3

1. Plutarch, *Comparison of Lycurgus and Numa* 1.5.
2. Plato, *The Laws* 6.776.
3. Thucydides, *History of the Peloponnesian War* 4.80.3.
4. *Ibid.* 5.34.
5. Xenophon, *Hellenica* 6.5.28.
6. Plutarch, *Sayings of Spartan Women* 2.5.
7. Aristotle, *Politics* 2.1270.
8. Herodotus, *The Histories* 7.234.2. This number is given by the exiled Spartan king Demaratus and may include non-citizens in addition to Spartiates.
9. Herodotus, *The Histories* 9.28.2.
10. Xenophon, *Hellenica* 3.4.20–24.
11. Herodotus, *The Histories* 9.10.
12. Figueira, T. J., 2003. "The Demography of the Spartan Helots." In: N. Luraghi and S. E. Alcock (eds) *Helots and Their Masters in Laconia and Messenia: Histories, Ideologies, Structures.* Hellenic Studies Series 4. Washington, DC: Center for Hellenic Studies, pp. 165–213.
13. See note 18 below. Figueira, 'Population Patterns', p. 212. This is the adjusted number for Pylos.
14. Figueira, 'Population Patterns', p. 212. This is the adjusted number for Mantinea. Kagan (2003) gives 9,000 as the total size of the army, roughly similar to Figueira. (Kagan, D., 2003. *The Peloponnesian War.* New York: Viking Press.)
15. Figueira, 'Population Patterns', p. 212.
16. *Ibid.*
17. All figures taken from the primary source texts and analysed by Thomas J. Figueira in Figueira, T. J., 1986. 'Population Patterns in Late Archaic and Classical Sparta', *Transactions of the American Philological Association*, vol. 116, pp. 165–213.
18. Cartledge, P., 2004. *The Spartans: The World of the Warrior-Heroes of Ancient Greece.* New York: Vintage Books, p. 222.
19. Xenophon, *Hellenica* 5.2.1.
20. *Ibid.* 5.2.2.
21. *Ibid.* 5.2.5.

22. Plutarch, *Life of Pelopidas* 4.4.
23. Xenophon, *Hellenica* 5.2.7.
24. *Ibid.* 5.1.31.
25. Xenophon, *Hellenica* 5.1.24.
26. Plutarch, *Life of Pelopidas* 5.1.
27. Diodorus Siculus gives a more negative version of the conquest of Thebes. He argues that Sparta planned to conquer Thebes because of their growth of power. (*Library of History* 15.20.1). Xenophon may have massaged this event to appease his Spartan masters, but Plutarch – writing approximately within a century or so of Diodorus Siculus – gives a similar version to Xenophon in his lives of Agesilaus and Pelopidas.
28. Xenophon, *Hellenica* 5.1.28.
29. *Ibid.* 5.2.30.
30. *Ibid.* 5.2.34.
31. Plutarch, *Life of Agesilaus* 23.3.
32. Xenophon, *Hellenica* 5.2.32.

Chapter 4

1. Plutarch, *Life of Pelopidas* 4.3.
2. Cornelius Nepos, *The Lives of Eminent Commanders* 16.1
3. Plutarch, *Life of Pelopidas* 2.5.
4. *Ibid.* 3.1.
5. *Ibid.* 3.4.
6. *Ibid.* 3.3.
7. *Ibid.* 3.4.
8. *Ibid.* 3.3
9. Cornelius Nepos, *The Lives of Eminent Commanders* 15.2.2.
10. *Ibid.* 15.2.4.
11. *Ibid.* 15.3.1–2.
12. *Ibid.* 15.4.1–4.
13. *Ibid.* 15.5.1.
14. Cornelius Nepos, *The Lives of Eminent Commanders* 15.5.3–4.
15. Plutarch, *Life of Pelopidas* 7.3.
16. *Ibid.*
17. Athenian Inscription Online, *IG II² 34*. Translated by Lambert, S. and Rhodes, P.J. [Online]. Available at: https://www.atticinscriptions.com/inscription/AIO/802.
18. Kallet-Marx, R. M., 1985. 'Athens, Thebes, and the Foundation of the Second Athenian League.' *Classical Antiquity*, 4(2), p. 127.

Chapter 5

1. Xenophon, *Hellenica* 5.3.27.
2. *Ibid.* 5.4.1.
3. Hamilton, *Agesilaus and the Failure of Spartan Hegemony* p. 153.
4. Plutarch, *Life of Pelopidas* 8.1.
5. Plutarch, *De Genio Socratis* 2.1.
6. *Ibid.* 3.1.
7. *Ibid.*
8. Plutarch, *Life of Pelopidas* 9.4.

   9. Plutarch, *De Genio Socratis* 4.1.
10. Plutarch, *Life of Pelopidas* 10.4.
11. Plutarch, *De Genio Socratis* 27.1.
12. *Ibid.*
13. *Ibid.*
14. Plutarch, *Life of Pelopidas* 12.2.
15. Xenophon, *Hellenica* 5.4.11.

Chapter 6
   1. Plutarch, *Life of Pelopidas* 14.1.
   2. Diodorus claims it was Cleombrotus who encouraged the attack on the Piraeus.
   3. Xenophon, *Hellenica* 5.4.21.
   4. Plutarch, *Life of Pelopidas* 14.2.
   5. Xenophon, *Hellenica* 5.4.23.
   6. Plutarch, *Life of Agesilaus* 24.6.
   7. Xenophon, *Hellenica* 5.4.32.
   8. *Ibid.* 5.4.23.
   9. Plutarch, *Life of Pelopidas* 13.4.
10. *Ibid.* 18.2.
11. Plato, *The Symposium* 178d–179b.
12. Cartledge, *Thebes: The Forgotten City of Ancient Greece* p. 191.
13. Xenophon, *Constitution of the Lacedaemonians* 2.12. Translation my own.
14. Plutarch, *Life of Pelopidas* 18.2.
15. Demosthenes, *Against the Law of the Leptines* 20.78.
16. Diodorus Siculus, *The Library of History* 15.31.4.
17. Cornelius Nepos, *Live of Eminent Commanders* 20.1.
18. Plutarch, *Life of Pelopidas* 19.4.
19. Plutarch, *Life of Agesilaus* 26.3.
20. Plutarch, *Life of Pelopidas* 15.2.
21. *IG II² 43*. Translated by Lambert, S. and Rhodes, P.J. In: Kirchner, J. (ed.), 1913–1940. *Inscriptiones Graecae. Vol. II et III. Inscriptiones Atticae Euclidis anno posteriores. Editio altera.* Reimer (1913-1916), De Gruyter – Berlin. [Online]. Available at: https://www. atticinscriptions.com/inscription/IGII2/43.
22. Xenophon, *Ways and Means* 1.1.
23. Athenian Inscription Online, *IG II² 43*.

Chapter 7
   1. Strabo, *The Geography* 9.2.23.
   2. Xenophon, *Hellenica* 5.4.51.
   3. *Ibid.* 5.4.58.
   4. *Ibid.* 5.4.60.
   5. Plutarch, *Life of Dion* 5.6.
   6. Plutarch, *Life of Phocion* 6.1.
   7. Diodorus Siculus, *The Library of History* 15.34.6.
   8. Polyaenus, *Strategems* 3.11.11
   9. Diodorus Siculus, *The Library of History* 15.34.6.
10. Plutarch, *Life of Phocion* 6.2.

11. Polyaenus, *Strategems* 3.11.11.
12. Isocrates, *Antidosis* 15.116–17.
13. Statius, *Thebaid* 2.32.
14. Strabo, *The Geography* 8.6.20.
15. Xenophon, *Hellenica* 5.4.65.
16. Polyaenus, *Strategems* 3.10.6.
17. Polyaenus, *Strategems* 3.10.1.
18. Xenophon, *Hellenica* 5.4.66.

Chapter 8
 1. Homer, *The Iliad* 9.381.
 2. Pausanias, *Description of Greece* 9.38.
 3. Strabo, *The Geography* 9.2.40.
 4. Diodorus Siculus, *The Library of History* 15.37.1.
 5. Plutarch, *Life of Pelopidas* 17.1.
 6. Dahm, M., 2021. *Leuctra 371 BC: The Destruction of Spartan Dominance*. Oxford: Osprey Publishing, p. 17.
 7. Plutarch, *Life of Pelopidas* 17.4.
 8. Plutarch, *Life of Agesilaus* 27.3.
 9. Plutarch, *Life of Pelopidas* 17.6.
10. Xenophon likely includes a brief reference to Tegyra in *Hellenica* 6.4.10 when discussing the poor performance of Spartan cavalry in comparison to the more experienced Theban cavalry and their experiences with the Orchomenians.
11. Diodorus Siculus, *The Library of History* 15.37.2.
12. Isocrates, 1980. *Plataicus* 30. In: Norlin, G. (ed.) *Isocrates with an English Translation*. Cambridge, MA: Harvard University Press; London: William Heinemann Ltd. Translation my own.
13. The exact dating of the Peace of 374 is difficult to pinpoint. G. L. Cawkwell in 'Notes on the Peace of 375/4' (1963) proposes 375 and C. D. Hamilton (1991, p.190) agrees. More importantly, the narrative in this book bundles the more detailed descriptions from Xenophon 6.3.1–20 with Plutarch's *Life of Agesilaus* 28 and Diodorus 15.38. There was likely a second peace conference in 371, also in Sparta, that discussed the same terms and yielded the same outcomes. It is difficult to parse out the differences between each conference, especially given Xenophon's steadfast omission of Epaminondas. In this study, I have combined the two peace conferences into one and dated it to 374, as the act of determining which content belonged to which conference is beyond my skills. While I believe there is adequate evidence for the treatment of these as one conference, my primary objective is narrative clarity. I respectfully defer to wiser historians on the precise chronology of the Peace of 375/4 and its relationship with the Peace of 371.
14. Plutarch, *Life of Agesilaus* 27.4.
15. Plutarch, *De Genio Socrates* 3.1.
16. Xenophon, *Hellenica* 6.3.15.
17. Plutarch, *Life of Agesilaus* 27.4.
18. *Ibid.* 28.1–3.
19. Xenophon, *Hellenica* 6.3.18.
20. Diodorus Siculus, *The Library of History* 15.38.4.
21. *Ibid.* 15.40.1.

22. Xenophon, *Hellenica* 6.2.14.
23. Xenophon, *Hellenica* 6.2.19.
24. Strassler, R. B., 2009. *The Landmark Xenophon's Hellenica*. New York: Anchor Books; 2010 (pb) p. 372.
25. Diodorus Siculus, *The Library of History* 15.47.7.
26. Significant overlap between the Peace Conferences of 375/4 and 371 complicates the chronology of multiple details, including the dialogue of Epaminondas and Agesilaus, which may belong to 371 rather than the earlier conference. See preceding note.
27. Diodorus Siculus, *The Library of History* 15.33.3.

Chapter 9

1. Aristotle, *Rhetoric* 1.12.31.
2. Xenophon, *Hellenica* 6.1.6.
3. Hamilton, *Agesilaus and the Failure of Spartan Hegemony* p. 188.
4. Xenophon, *Hellenica* 6.1.9.
5. Xenophon, Plutarch, Diodorus Siculus, and Pausanias give differing ranges of the Spartan army's size. They are united, however, in stating that the number of Spartiates was substantially low.
6. Figueira, 'Population Patterns', p. 212.
7. Xenophon, *Hellenica* 6.4.3.
8. Diodorus Siculus, *The Library of History* 15.50.5.
9. Plutarch, *Life of Pelopidas* 20.1.
10. Plutarch, *Life of Martellus* 21.2.
11. Plutarch, *Life of Pelopidas* 20.2.
12. In his *Description of Greece* 9.13.6–7, Pausanias names them as Malgis and Xenocrates voting with Epaminondas, and Damocleidas, Damophilus and Simangelus voting against. The tiebreaker was the late arrival of Brachyllides. Neither he nor Plutarch list Pelopidas as a boeotarch.
13. Plutarch, *Life of Pelopidas* 20.4.
14. I propose the smaller valley with the centre of 38°15'56"N 23°09'37"E. This is conjecture, but fits the criteria and general location.
15. Diodorus Siculus, *The Library of History* 15.52.4. Here, Epaminondas, is quoting Homer, *The Iliad* 12.243.
16. Cicero, *De Divinatione* 34.74.
17. Diodorus Siculus, *The Library of History* 15.53.4.
18. Cicero, *De Divinatione* 34.74.
19. *Ibid.* 34.75.
20. *Ibid.*
21. Xenophon, *Hellenica* 6.4.5.

Chapter 10

1. For example, Diodorus claims Jason of Pherae and his Thessalians arrived *before* the battle while Xenophon has them arriving after the battle.
2. Xenophon, *Hellenica* 4.6.8.
3. Pausanias, *Description of Greece* 9.13.8.
4. Xenophon, *Hellenica* 6.4.9.
5. *Ibid.* 6.4.12.

6. *Ibid.* 6.4.11.
7. Diodorus Siculus, *The Library of History* 15.55.1.
8. Hamilton, *Agesilaus and the Failure of Spartan Hegemony* p. 210.
9. Plutarch, *Life of Pelopidas* 23.2.
10. Diodorus Siculus, *The Library of History* 15.55.3.
11. Plutarch, *Life of Pelopidas* 23.2.
12. Diodorus Siculus, *The Library of History* 15.55.5.
13. *Ibid.*
14. Pausanias, *Description of Greece* 9.13.9.
15. Xenophon, *Hellenica* 6.4.13.
16. Plutarch, *Life of Pelopidas* 23.4.
17. Athenaeus, *Deipnosophists* 13.83.

Chapter 11
1. Pausanias, *Description of Greece* 9.13.11.
2. Plutarch, *Life of Agesilaus* 30.1.
3. Polyaenus, *Stratagems* 3.1.13.
4. Cicero, *De Officiis*, 1.61.
5. Cornelius Nepos, *The Lives of Eminent Commanders* 15.10.4.
6. Xenophon, *Hellenica* 6.4.20.
7. Plutarch, *Life of Agesilaus* 31.1.
8. Plutarch, *Life of Pelopidas* 31.3.
9. *Ibid.*, 32.8.
10. Plutarch, *Life of Agesilaus* 34.1.
11. Plutarch, *Life of Pelopidas* 26.5.
12. *Ibid.*, 30.7.
13. *Ibid.*, 32.1.
14. *Ibid.*, 33.1.
15. Xenophon, *Hellenica* 7.5.1.
16. *Ibid.*, 7.5.8.
17. *Ibid.*, 7.5.19.
18. *Ibid.*, 7.5.23.
19. Diodorus Siculus, *The Library of History* 15.86.2–3.
20. Cornelius Nepos, *The Lives of Eminent Commanders* 15.9.3.
21. Diodorus Siculus, *The Library of History* 15.88.3–4.

Conclusions
1. Plutarch, *Life of Pelopidas* 18.5.
2. Cornelius Nepos, *The Lives of Eminent Commanders* 15.10.2.

Bibliography

Primary Sources

Aristotle, 1891. *The Constitution of Athens.* Translated by Kenyon, Sir F. G. London: G. Bell.

Aristotle, 1932. *Politics.* Translated by Rackham, H. London: William Heinemann.

Aristotle, 1926. *Rhetoric.* Translated by Freese, J. H. Loeb Classical Library. Cambridge, MA: Harvard University Press.

Athenaeus, 1854. *The Deipnosophists.* Translated by Yonge, C. D. London: Henry G. Bohn.

Athenian Inscription Online, *IG II² 34.* Translated by Lambert, S. and Rhodes, P.J. [Online]. Available at: https://www.atticinscriptions.com/inscription/AIO/802.

Cicero, 1923. *De Divinatione.* Translated by Falconer, W. A. Loeb Classical Library. Cambridge: Harvard University Press.

Cicero, 1913. *De Officiis.* Translated by Miller, W. Vol. XXI. Cambridge, MA: Harvard University Press.

Cornelius Nepos, 1853. 'Lives of Eminent Commanders.' In: Watson, J. S. (trans.) *Justin, Cornelius Nepos, and Eutropius: Literally Translated, with Notes and a General Index.* London: Henry G. Bohn.

Demosthenes, 1926. *Against Leptines.* Translated by Vince, C. A. and Vince, J. H. Cambridge, MA: Harvard University Press; London: William Heinemann Ltd.

Diodorus Siculus, 1954. *The Library of History: Volume VI: Books 14–15.19.* Translated by Oldfather, C. H. Cambridge: Harvard University Press.

Diogenes Laertius, 1925. *Lives of Eminent Philosophers.* Translated by Hicks, R. D. Cambridge: Harvard University Press.

Hellenica Oxyrhynchia, 1988. Translated by McKechnie, P. Available at: https://topostext.org/work.php?work_id=89.

Herodotus, 1910. *The History of Herodotus.* Translated by Rawlinson, G. Oxford: Oxford University Press.

Hesiod, 1914. *Hesiod, the Homeric Hymns and Homerica.* Translated by H. G. Evelyn-White. Cambridge, MA: Harvard University Press.

Isocrates, 1980. *Isocrates with an English Translation.* Translated by Norlin, G. Cambridge, MA: Harvard University Press; London: William Heinemann Ltd. *Plataicus* 30.

Isocrates, 1980. *Antidosis.* In *Isocrates with an English Translation.* Translated by Norlin, G. Cambridge, MA: Harvard University Press; London: William Heinemann Ltd.

Pausanias, 1918. *Description of Greece.* Translated by Jones, W. H. S. and Ormerod, H. A. Cambridge: Harvard University Press and London: William Heinemann Ltd.

Plato, 1875. *The Laws.* Translated by Jowett, B. Oxford: Oxford University Press.

Plato, 1888. *The Republic.* Translated by Jowett, B. Oxford: Oxford University Press.

Plato, 1892. *The Symposium.* In: Jowett, B. (trans.) *The Dialogues of Plato.* Oxford: Oxford University Press.

Pliny the Elder, 1855. *Natural History*. Translated by Riley, H. T. and Bostock, J. Available at: https://topostext.org/work/148.

Plutarch, 1914. 'Comparison of Lycurgus and Numa.' In: Perrin, B. (trans.) *Parallel Lives*. Cambridge: Harvard University Press.

Plutarch, 1914. 'Life of Agesilaus.' In: Perrin, B. (trans.) *Parallel Lives*. Cambridge: Harvard University Press.

Plutarch, 1914. 'Life of Artaxerxes.' In: Perrin, B. (trans.) *Parallel Lives*. Cambridge: Harvard University Press.

Plutarch, 1914. 'Life of Dion.' In: Perrin, B. (trans.) *Parallel Lives*. Cambridge: Harvard University Press.

Plutarch, 1914. 'Life of Lysander.' In: Perrin, B. (trans.) *Parallel Lives*. Cambridge: Harvard University Press.

Plutarch, 1914. 'Life of Lycurgus.' In: Perrin, B. (trans.) *Parallel Lives*. Cambridge: Harvard University Press.

Plutarch, 1914. 'Life of Martellus.' In: Perrin, B. (trans.) *Parallel Lives*. Cambridge: Harvard University Press.

Plutarch, 1914. 'Life of Pelopidas.' In: Perrin, B. (trans.) *Parallel Lives*. Cambridge: Harvard University Press.

Plutarch, 1914. 'Life of Phocion.' In: Perrin, B. (trans.) *Parallel Lives*. Cambridge: Harvard University Press.

Plutarch, 1931. 'Sayings of the Spartans.' In: Babbitt, F. C. (trans.) *Moralia, Vol. III*. Cambridge: Harvard University Press.

Plutarch, 1931. 'Sayings of Spartan Women.' In: Babbitt, F. C. (trans.) *Moralia, Vol. III*. Cambridge: Harvard University Press.

Polyaenus, 1793. *Polyaenus's Stratagems of War*. Translated by Shepherd, R. London: George Nicol.

Ps-Plutarch, 1936. *Love Stories*. Translated by Fowler, H. N. Chicago: University of Chicago Press.

Statius, 1928. *The Thebaid*. Translated by Mozley, J. H. Loeb Classical Library. Available at: https://topostext.org/work/149.

Strabo, 1917–1932. *The Geography*. Translated by Jones, H. L. Loeb Classical Library. Cambridge: Harvard University Press.

Thucydides, 1874. *The History of the Peloponnesian War*. Translated by Crawley, R. Cambridge: Harvard University Press.

Xenophon, 1894. *Agesilaus*. Translated by Dakyns, H. G. London and New York: Macmillan and Co.

Xenophon, 1891. *Anabasis*. Translated by Dakyns, H. G. London and New York: Macmillan and Co.

Xenophon, 1925. *Constitution of the Lacedaemonians*. Translated by Marchant, E.C. In: *Scripta Minora*. Cambridge: Harvard University Press. Available at: https://topostext.org/work/798.

Xenophon, 1891. *Hellenica*. Translated by Dakyns, H. G. London and New York: Macmillan and Co.

Xenophon, 1897. *Ways and Means*. Translated by Dakyns, H.G. London and New York: Macmillan and Co.

Secondary Sources

Asmanti, L. (2015). *Conon the Athenian: Warfare and Politics in the Aegean, 414–386 B.C.* Stuttgart: Franz Steiner Verlag.

Beck, H. (1997). 'Thebes, the Boiotian League, and the Rise of Federalism in Fourth Century Greece.' In: Bernardini, P. A. (ed.) *Presenza e funzione della città di Tebe nella cultura greca : atti del convegno internazionale, Urbino, 7–9 luglio 1997.* Pisa, Rome: Istituti editoriali e poligrafici internazionali, pp. 331–44.

Bintliff, J. and Snodgrass, A. (1985). 'The Boiotia Survey, a Preliminary Report: The first four years'. *Journal of Field Archaeology*, 12, pp. 123–61.

Bresson, A. (2010). "Knidos: topography for a battle." In: R. van Bremen & J. Carbon (eds) *Hellenistic Karia*. Pessac: Ausonius Editions, pp. 435–51.

Cartledge, P. (2004). *The Spartans: The World of the Warrior-Heroes of Ancient Greece*. New York: Vintage Books.

Cartledge, P. (2020). *Thebes: The Forgotten City of Ancient Greece*. London: Picador.

Cawkwell, G. L. (1963). 'Notes on the Peace of 375/4.' *Historia: Zeitschrift für Alte Geschichte*, 12(1), pp. 84–95.

Cole, M. (2021). *The Bronze Lie: Shattering the Myth of Spartan Warrior Supremacy*. Oxford: Osprey Publishing.

Chambers, J. T. (1978). 'On Messenian and Laconian Helots in the Fifth Century B.C.' *The Historian*, 40(2), pp. 271–285.

Dahm, M. (2021). *Leuctra 371 BC: The Destruction of Spartan Dominance*. Oxford: Osprey Publishing.

Doran, T. (2011). *Demographic Fluctuation and Institutional Response in Sparta*. PhD dissertation, University of California at Berkeley.

Doran, T. (2018). *Spartan Oliganthropia*. Leiden: Brill.

Figueira, T. J. (2003). "The Demography of the Spartan Helots." In: Luraghi, N. and Alcock, S. E. (eds) *Helots and Their Masters in Laconia and Messenia: Histories, Ideologies, Structures*. Washington, DC: Center for Hellenic Studies, pp. 165–213.

Figuera, T. J. (1986). 'Population Patterns in Late Archaic and Classical Sparta.' *Transactions of the American Philological Association (1974-)*, 116, pp. 165–213.

Fornis, C. and Suárez, D. P. (2008). 'De la guerra del Peloponeso a la Paz del Rey (I): Prosopografía política ateniense.' *Rivista storica dell'antichità*, 38, pp. 45–88.

Forrest, W. G. (1968). *A History of Sparta, 950–192 B.C.* New York: W. W. Norton & Co.

Hamilton, C. D. (1991). *Agesilaus and the Failure of Spartan Hegemony*. Ithaca, NY: Cornell University Press.

Hamilton, C. D. (1979). *Sparta's Bitter Victories: Politics and Diplomacy in the Corinthian War*. Ithaca, NY: Cornell University Press.

Hornblower, S. (2011). *The Greek World 479–323 BC*. London: Routledge.

Hunt, P. (2007). Review of Mogens Herman Hansen, *The shotgun method: the demography of the ancient Greek city-state culture*. Columbia: University of Missouri Press. *Bryn Mawr Classical Review*, [Online]. Available at: https://bmcr.brynmawr.edu/2007/2007.04.58/#_ftnref2.

Joyce, C. J. (2024). Review of Roy van Wijk, *Athens and Boiotia: interstate relations in the archaic and classical periods*. Cambridge: Cambridge University Press. *Bryn Mawr Classical Review*, [Online]. Available at: https://bmcr.brynmawr.edu/2024/2024.08.31/.

Kagan, D. (2003). *The Peloponnesian War*. New York: Viking Press.

Kallet-Marx, R. M. (1985). 'Athens, Thebes, and the Foundation of the Second Athenian League.' *Classical Antiquity*, 4(2), pp. 127–51.

Kirchner, J. (ed.) (1913–1940). *Inscriptiones Graecae. Vol. II et III. Inscriptiones Atticae Euclidis anno posteriores. Editio altera.* Reimer (1913-1916), De Gruyter – Berlin. IG II2 43. Translated by Lambert, S. and Rhodes, P.J. [Online]. Available at: https://www.atticinscriptions.com/inscription/IGII2/43.

Lazenby, J. F. (2012). *The Spartan Army.* Barnsley: Pen & Sword Military.

Lendon, J. E. (2005). *Soldiers and Ghosts: A History of Battle in Classical Antiquity.* New Haven: Yale University Press.

Pascual, J. (2016). 'Conon, the Persian Fleet and a Second Naval Campaign in 393 BC.' *Historia: Zeitschrift für Alte Geschichte,* 65(1), pp. 14–30.

Pascual, J. (2006). "Poleis and Confederacy in Boiotia in the early Fourth century BC." In: *Coins, Cults, History and Inscriptions VII: Studies in Honor of John M. Fossey III.* The Ancient World, 36, pp. 22–45.

Rahe, P. A. (2016). *The Spartan Regime: Its Character, Origins, and Grand Strategy.* New Haven, CT: Yale University Press.

Ray, F. E. (2012). *Greek and Macedonian Land Battles of the 4th Century B.C.* Jefferson, NC: McFarland & Co.

Romm, J. (2021). *The Sacred Band: Three Hundred Theban Lovers Fighting to Save Greek Freedom.* New York: Scribner.

Schmidt, K. (1999). 'The Peace of Antalcidas and the Idea of the koine eirene: a Panhellenic Peace Movement.' *Revue internationale des droits de l'antiquité,* 46, pp. 81–98.

Strassler, R. D. (2009). *The Landmark Xenophon's Hellenika.* New York: Anchor Books.

Index